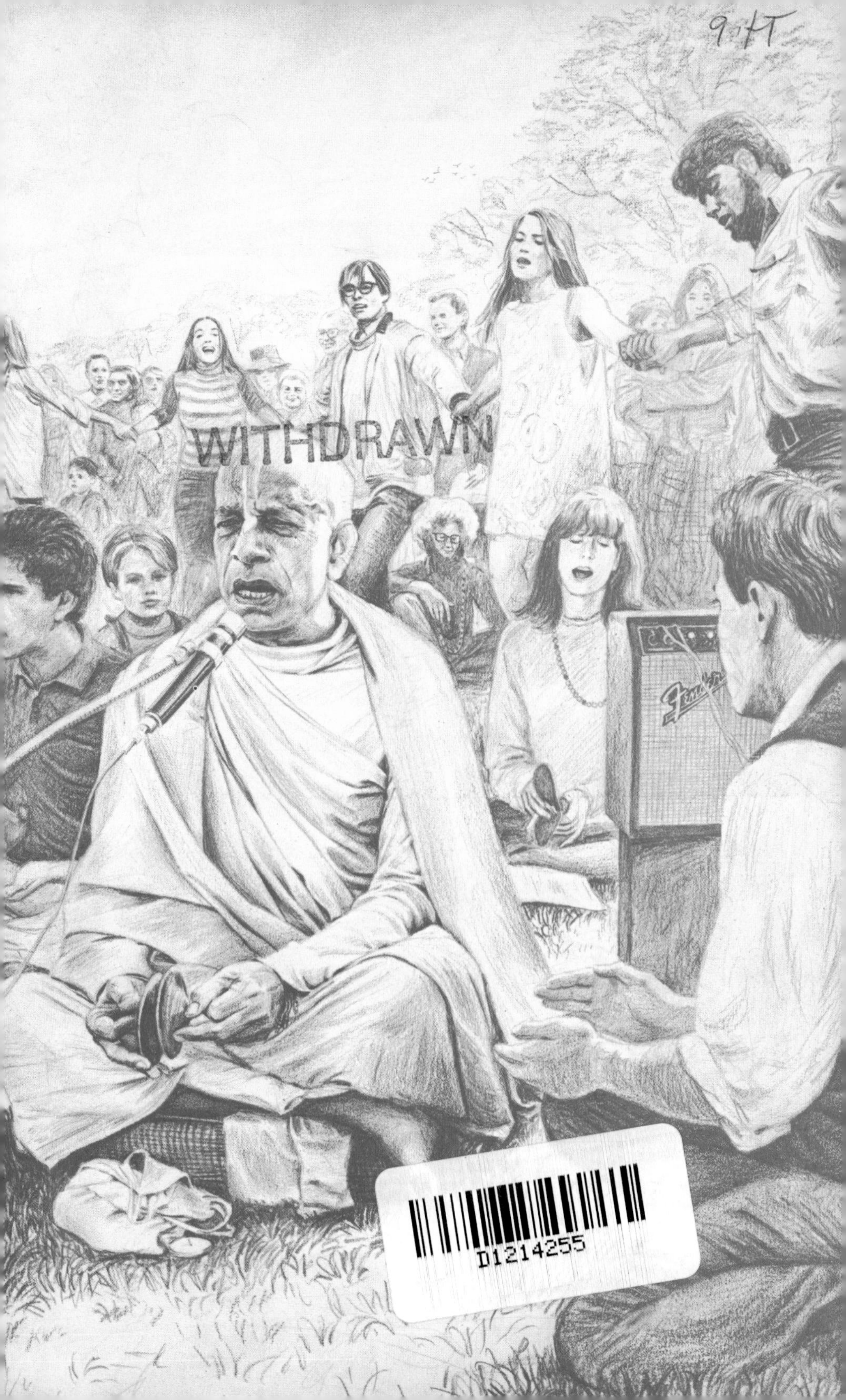

BL 1175 .B445 G67 v.3
Gosvami
Srila Prabhupada-lilamrta.

Śrīla Prabhupāda-līlāmṛta, Volume 3

ONLY HE COULD LEAD THEM

tvaṁ naḥ sandarśito dhātrā
dustaraṁ nistitīrṣatām
kaliṁ sattva-haraṁ puṁsāṁ
karṇa-dhāra ivārṇavam

We think that we have met Your Goodness by the will of providence, just so that we may accept you as captain of the ship for those who desire to cross the difficult ocean of Kali, which deteriorates all the good qualities of a human being.

—*Śrīmad-Bhāgavatam*

Śrīla Prabhupāda-līlāmṛta, Volume 3

ONLY HE COULD LEAD THEM

San Francisco/India
1967

A Biography of
His Divine Grace

A. C. Bhaktivedanta Swami Prabhupāda

Founder-Ācārya of the International Society for Krishna Consciousness

Satsvarūpa dāsa Goswami

THE BHAKTIVEDANTA BOOK TRUST
Los Angeles · London · Paris · Bombay · Sydney

Readers interested in the subject matter of this book
are invited by the Bhaktivedanta Book Trust
to correspond with the Secretary:

Bhaktivedanta Book Trust
3764 Watseka Avenue
Los Angeles, California 90034

First Printing, 1981: 10,000 copies

Printed in the United States of America

Library of Congress Cataloging in Publication Data

Gosvāmī, Satsvarūpa Dāsa, 1939–
Srila Prabhupada-lilamrta.

"Books by ....A. C. Bhaktivedanta Swami Prabhupada"
v. 3, p.
Includes index.
CONTENTS —v. 3. San Francisco; India
1967: only he could lead them.
1. Bhaktivedanta Swami, A. C., 1896–1977. 2. Gurus
—Biography. 3. International Society for Krishna
Consciousness—Biography. I. Title.
BL1175.B445G67 294.5'61'0924 [B] 80-5071
ISBN 0-89213-110-1 (v. 3)

Contents

Foreword

In the course of doing research for my book on the Hare Kṛṣṇa movement and afterwards—during the late sixties and seventies—I had the good fortune, on several occasions, to meet and speak with A. C. Bhaktivedanta Swami Prabhupāda. I feel honored, therefore, to write the Foreword to this volume.

This work by Satsvarūpa dāsa Goswami is an eloquent tribute to the memory of a man who played a central role in American religious history during the countercultural sixties and seventies. It will provide a mine of information to scholars and to anyone else interested in the movement Prabhupāda brought to America from India, and in the counterculture itself, the social milieu in which the movement took root and flourished in its early years.

In this volume we encounter one of the most important periods in Śrīla Prabhupāda's life, as he courageously establishes and develops his movement in San Francisco's Haight-Ashbury district, the counterculture capital of the West Coast. That he, an elderly foreigner with a thick Bengali accent and a relative stranger to Western (what to speak of countercultural) ways could minister so effectively to the hippies of the Haight-Ashbury—where sexual promiscuity and drug abuse were blended into a "do-your-own-thing" ethic and where bowing to any sort of authority was rejected on principle—gives some indication of his extraordinary ability and fortitude. The author presents a number of brief case histories of some of Śrīla Prabhupāda's early followers, personal accounts that illuminate the struggle of many youths to find meaning and an alternative way of life within a counterculture lacking cohesion and direction. Unable to identify with the religious institutions of the establishment, these young people found truth in the message of Śrīla Prabhupāda and experiential validation of that truth in the chanting of the *mahā-mantra*, the divine names of Kṛṣṇa. In reading these accounts, the reader will be struck with Śrīla Prabhupāda's personal qualities—his strength of purpose, his genuine humility, and his deep spirituality—by which he gently led his erring disciples from hedonism to Kṛṣṇa. He was a practical man. He knew that not all who attended his sessions would become converts. But he believed that even a little contact with Kṛṣṇa consciousness would bring them tangible spiritual benefit.

In this volume we have, in effect, a fascinating close-up study of the process of religious conversion, about which psychologists and sociologists are so intrigued. We witness how Śrīla Prabhupāda's disciples gradually changed their ways, accepting moral and spiritual discipline under his compassionate guidance, and we learn of backsliders whose conversions were insufficient to keep them from giving in to sensual temptations. For some of his followers, those with doubts and inner struggles, conversion was a slow or vascillating process. This compelling story reveals much of the process and degrees of conversion. The incidents themselves clearly contradict the loosely made claims of some uninformed critics that the Hare Kṛṣṇa movement employs some kind of occult "mind-control." These examples make it sufficiently clear that conversion to Kṛṣṇa consciousness is a process that engages the full range of intellectual, emotional, and volitional faculties.

Although never compromising his lofty principles, Śrīla Prabhupāda mobilized existing resources of the contemporary subculture to make the Vaiṣṇava faith better known. Without endorsing the drug abuse of the hippies to whom he was ministering, he dared to have set up and then appear at a "Mantra-Rock Dance" featuring such attractions as Janis Joplin and the Grateful Dead. What a contrast! Amid the intermingling of incense and marijuana smoke and pulsating strobe lights illuminating depictions of Kṛṣṇa's life, Śrīla Prabhupāda delivered his timeless message of Kṛṣṇa consciousness. Then, with the aid of poet Allen Ginsberg, he soon had the entire crowd dancing and swaying like grain in the wind as they chanted the *mahā-mantra:* Hare Kṛṣṇa, Hare Kṛṣṇa, Kṛṣṇa Kṛṣṇa, Hare Hare/ Hare Rāma, Hare Rāma, Rāma Rāma, Hare Hare.

This is also the story of Śrīla Prabhupāda's sacrificial life. He brought his message to America at an advanced age when most elderly gentlemen in India are content to retire in comfort in the bosom of their families. As might be expected, the accumulative strain of traveling, lecturing, and sleeping little while spending his early morning hours translating and commenting on religious texts he was preparing for publication brought illness. His weak health led him to return to India and to his Vedic doctors, in whom he showed considerably more faith than in Western medicine. Still, he was not content to remain in India, and this volume closes with his return to America and to his anxiously waiting disciples.

Perhaps more than anything else, this volume reveals those extraordinary personal attributes of Śrīla Prabhupāda that elicited such deep reverence and affection from his disciples. Besides being a man of deep moral strength, humility, and holiness, he was genuinely renounced. Unlike many modern *gurus*, he was content to live as his disciples did. Even when his health failed and he returned to the blazing heat of Delhi for his recovery, he sought nothing better than a poorly furnished room, without air-conditioning, in a Hindu temple where he had resided before coming to America. Śrīla Prabhupāda's life, as it is revealed here, is the epitome of his ideal, an ideal that he set forth for others to follow. In an age of pervasive hypocrisy and cynicism, it is this kind of rare model that we need.

Dr. J. Stillson Judah
Professor Emeritus, History of Religions
Graduate Theological Union and Pacific
School of Religion
Berkeley, California

Preface

After the disappearance of His Divine Grace A. C. Bhaktivedanta Swami Prabhupāda from this mortal world on November 14, 1977, many of his disciples saw a need for an authorized biography of Śrīla Prabhupāda. The responsibility of commissioning such a work rested with the Governing Body Commission of the International Society for Krishna Consciousness. At their annual meeting in 1978, the GBC resolved that a biography of Śrīla Prabhupāda should be written and that I would be the author.

According to the Vaiṣṇava tradition, if one aspires to write transcendental literature, he must first take permission from his spiritual master and Kṛṣṇa. A good example of this is Kṛṣṇadāsa Kavirāja Gosvāmī, the author of Lord Caitanya Mahāprabhu's authorized biography, *Śrī Caitanya-caritāmṛta.* As Kṛṣṇadāsa Kavirāja has explained:

> In Vṛndāvana there were also many other great devotees, all of whom desired to hear the last pastimes of Lord Caitanya.
>
> By their mercy, all these devotees ordered me to write of the last pastimes of Śrī Caitanya Mahāprabhu. Because of their order only, although I am shameless, I have attempted to write this *Caitanya-caritāmṛta.*
>
> Having received the order of the Vaiṣṇavas, but being anxious within my heart, I went back to the temple of Madana-mohana in Vṛndāvana to ask His permission also.

This transcendental process is further described by His Divine Grace Śrīla Prabhupāda in his commentary on the *Caitanya-caritāmṛta* as follows:

> To write about the transcendental pastimes of the Supreme Personality of Godhead is not an ordinary endeavor. Unless one is empowered by the higher authorities or advanced devotees, one cannot write transcendental

> literature, for all such literature must be above suspicion, or in other words, it must have none of the defects of conditioned souls, namely mistakes, illusions, cheating, and imperfect sense perception. The words of Kṛṣṇa and the disciplic succession that carries the orders of Kṛṣṇa are actually authoritative.... One must first become a pure devotee following the strict regulative principles and chanting sixteen rounds daily, and when one thinks he is actually on the Vaiṣṇava platform, he must then take permission from the spiritual master, and that permission must also be confirmed by Kṛṣṇa from within his heart.

So to say the *Śrīla Prabhupāda-līlāmṛta* is an authorized biography does not mean that it is a flattering portrait commissioned by an official body, but that it is an authorized literature presented by one who is serving the order of Kṛṣṇa and *guru* through the disciplic succession. As such, *Śrīla Prabhupāda-līlāmṛta* is not written from the mundane or speculative viewpoint, nor can ordinary biographers comprehend the significance and meaning of the life of a pure devotee of God. Were such persons to objectively study the life of Śrīla Prabhupāda, the esoteric meanings would evade them. Were they to charitably try to praise Śrīla Prabhupāda, they would not know how. But because *Śrīla Prabhupāda-līlāmṛta* is authorized through the transcendental process, it can transparently present the careful reader with a true picture of Śrīla Prabhupāda.

Another important aspect of the authenticity of *Śrīla Prabhupāda-līlāmṛta* is the vast amount of carefully researched information that I am able to focus into each volume. The leading devotees of the Kṛṣṇa consciousness movement, in addition to giving me permission to render this work, have also invited the world community of ISKCON devotees to help me in gathering detailed information about the life and person of Śrīla Prabhupāda. The Bhaktivedanta Book Trust, Prabhupāda's publishing house, has given me his collection of letters, totaling over seven thousand; and scores of Prabhupāda's disciples have granted interviews and submitted diaries and memoirs of their association with Śrīla Prabhupāda. Aside from his disciples, we have interviewed many persons in various walks of life who met Śrīla Prabhupāda over the years. The result is that we have a rich, composite view of Śrīla Prabhupāda, drawn from many persons who knew him in many different situations and stages of his life. The Acknowledgments section in this book lists the persons who are cooperating to bring about *Śrīla Prabhupāda-līlāmṛta.*

Despite the authorized nature of this book and despite the support of my many well-wishers, I must confess that in attempting to describe the glories of our spiritual master, His Divine Grace A. C. Bhaktivedanta Swami Prabhupāda, I am like a small bird trying to empty the ocean by carrying drops of water to the land. The picture I have given of Śrīla Prabhupāda is only a glimpse into his unlimited mercy, and that glimpse has only been possible by the grace of *guru* and Kṛṣṇa.

Satsvarūpa dāsa Goswami

Acknowledgments

Maṇḍaleśvara dāsa continues to be my editor and good friend in this ongoing work.

The members of our staff at the Gītā-nāgarī farm community were Baladeva Vidyābhūṣaṇa dāsa, who conducted many interviews and gathered information for this volume, Ācārya-devī dāsī, typist, and Gaura-pūrṇimā dāsa, who arranged the material for me in an organized form. Sureśvara dāsa, Kṛṣṇa-sneha dāsa, and Vimala-devī dāsī also assisted me at Gītā-nāgarī in various capacities. Jayādvaita Swami read and corrected the final manuscript.

Rājendranātha dāsa, Bhaktivedanta Book Trust production manager, supervised this volume's production. The BBT press staff of Kuśakratha dāsa, Śrīkānta dāsa, Dhṛṣṭaketu dāsa, Siṁheśvara dāsa, Bṛhad-mṛdaṅga dāsa, Kīrtana-rasa dāsa, Balāi-devī dāsī, Sītā-devī dāsī, Kṣamā-devī dāsī, Rukmiṇī-devī dāsī, Mamatā-devī dāsī, Subhadrā-devī dāsī, and others did the designing, composing, proofreading, indexing, and layout. Vidyānanda dāsa, Nitya-tṛptā-devī dāsī, Ekanātha dāsa, and Parama-rūpa dāsa, who are compiling an archives of Śrīla Prabhupāda, supplied materials for this volume.

The memoirs of Hayagrīva dāsa, Mukunda dāsa, Yamunā-devī dāsī, Līlāvatī-devī dāsī, Upendra dāsa, etc., provided the substance for the San Francisco chapters. Interviews with Acyutānanda Swami were the main source of information for the India period.

Introduction

This third volume of the ongoing biography of His Divine Grace A. C. Bhaktivedanta Swami Prabhupāda covers the events of Śrīla Prabhupāda's life during 1967.

Volume 1, *A Lifetime in Preparation*, tells of Śrīla Prabhupāda's first sixty-nine years, all of them in India. From his earliest boyhood, in Calcutta, he learned from his Vaiṣṇava father to worship Kṛṣṇa. And when, as a young husband and a follower of Gandhi, he met his spiritual master, Śrīla Bhaktisiddhānta Sarasvatī, the devotional practices of childhood took on a new significance. At their first meeting, Śrīla Bhaktisiddhānta Sarasvatī advised Śrīla Prabhupāda to spread the message of Kṛṣṇa consciousness to the world. And Prabhupāda was so impressed that he wanted to take up the mission.

Although responsibilities to family and business kept Śrīla Prabhupāda from fully taking up the work of actively spreading Kṛṣṇa consciousness, he gradually molded his life according to his spiritual master's order. During World War II and the years of India's struggle for independence, Śrīla Prabhupāda wrote, printed, and distributed a spiritual journal, *Back to Godhead*, in which he applied spiritual solutions to the world's crises. Retiring in his fifties from family and business, Prabhupāda dedicated himself to writing and to starting a worldwide organization, the League of Devotees, in Jhansi, India. Whereas formerly business and family had impeded his spiritual vocation, now he struggled against poverty and obscurity.

In 1956 he moved to Vṛndāvana, the place most sacred to Lord Kṛṣṇa. Three years later, at the age of sixty-three, he accepted the renounced order, *sannyāsa*, and began translating the Sanskrit *Śrīmad-Bhāgavatam* and planning how to go to America. After publishing three volumes of *Śrīmad-Bhāgavatam*, in 1965 he obtained free passage on a steamship to America.

Volume 2, *Planting the Seed*, begins with Śrīla Prabhupāda's two-month voyage to America. Surviving two heart attacks, he arrived in New York with no money and no specific plan. Although by 1965 America had already seen many Indian *swamis*, Prabhupāda was the first pure Vaiṣṇava in America. He held the first *kīrtanas* (congregational chanting of Hare Kṛṣṇa)—in a Bowery loft, in a Lower East Side storefront, and in Washington Square Park, Greenwich Village. His chanting in Tompkins Square Park drew interest from the news media. *The New York Times* ran an article with the headline "Swami's Flock Chants in Park to Find Ecstasy."

The "flock" consisted of boys and girls who had rejected America's materialism and, although looking for something more, had found themselves in the 1960s counterculture of protests, marijuana, and LSD. Prabhupāda gave these young people their first spiritual food (*prasādam*) and accepted them as his disciples. He was their spiritual father, their *guru*, living with them and carefully nurturing their first months of spiritual life. Then, six months after beginning his International Society for Krishna Consciousness, he suddenly left to start a second center, in San Francisco.

The first half of *Only He Could Lead Them* tells of Śrīla Prabhupāda's bringing Kṛṣṇa consciousness to a place even more strange than New York's Lower East Side—to wide-open, wild-Western Haight-Ashbury, where hundreds of thousands of hippies had congregated for a "Summer of Love" and where the Swami and the chanting of Hare Kṛṣṇa were warmly welcomed and celebrated.

The title of Volume 3 stresses that only Śrīla Prabhupāda could continue the movement he had begun. His disciples in New York and San Francisco were following *him*, drawn by his purity, gravity, charm, tolerance, and humor, and they were hearing from *him*. *He* had started the Kṛṣṇa consciousness movement, and *he* was maintaining it. Now that he had set a pattern, he could confidently repeat it in one city after another—but only by personally going to each place. Certainly Kṛṣṇa consciousness could not be spread by a swami of the nondevotional schools of impersonal or physical *yoga*. And even among the Vaiṣṇava followers of Lord Caitanya, Śrīla Prabhupāda was the only one willing to come preach in America. The field was all his.

"Only He Could Lead Them" has another meaning. Only Śrīla Prabhupāda could determine and demonstrate how to transplant Kṛṣṇa consciousness into an alien culture like that of America. His spiritual master had not given him such details, nor did the scriptures say what to do in a culture where women demanded equality with men, where chemical intoxication was the norm, and where even spiritually inclined people were too restless to chant on beads the traditional sixty-four rounds of the Hare Kṛṣṇa *mantra.* Prabhupāda had to become the *ācārya* (one who teaches by example) for establishing Kṛṣṇa consciousness in the West. And he had to make many unprecedented decisions. When confronting couples who lived as boyfriend and girl friend, Śrīla Prabhupāda asked them to become his married disciples. He agreed to go to a psychedelic dance hall and chant Hare Kṛṣṇa with the Grateful Dead, the Jefferson Airplane, and other rock groups. And he adjusted the daily quota for chanting to a minimum of sixteen rounds instead of sixty-four.

Just when Śrīla Prabhupāda's disciples in New York and San Francisco were succeeding—growing more affectionate, dependent, and willing to assist him in spreading Kṛṣṇa consciousness—suddenly he was stricken with a heart attack. Although this attack was similar to the two he had suffered during his sea journey to America, this time he almost lost his mortal life. He became partially paralyzed, and his disciples took him to a hospital.

More than ever, Śrīla Prabhupāda and his followers saw that the Kṛṣṇa consciousness movement depended solely on him. Were his heart to stop beating, the spiritual lives of his disciples and the momentum of his movement would also stop. In San Francsico and New York, Śrīla Prabhupāda's followers prayed all night to Lord Kṛṣṇa, "Our master has not finished his work. Please protect him." And they realized that they had more love for their Swamiji and more faith in him than they had ever imagined. They needed him to lead them.

After the initial crisis passed, Prabhupāda tried recuperating at a beach house near San Francisco. But with the sun staying behind the clouds and his health not improving, he decided to go back to Vṛndāvana, India—perhaps, he said, to die. When some disciples asked if it would be possible for another Vaiṣṇava *swami* to come in Prabhupāda's place, Prabhupāda answered by speaking of his own spiritual master: "He was no ordinary spiritual master. He saved me." Prabhupāda explained that if another *guru* were to present even one thing differently, the disciples would become confused. No, the *guru* was not replaceable. Only he could lead them.

Śrīla Prabhupāda, accompanied by a few disciples, returned to Vṛndāvana. But almost as soon as he arrived he was intent upon returning to America. "Vṛndāvana is an inspiration only," he wrote to his American disciples. "But our real field work is all over the world."

In India Prabhupāda tried to arrange to print his books and visited some of his Godbrothers. In Calcutta he returned to the Rādhā-Govinda temple he had visited daily as a child. Seeing the temple in poor repair and the worship neglected impressed upon him even more that devotion to Kṛṣṇa was dying in India. In America, however, it had only begun to bloom.

After spending six months in India and receiving many letters from his disciples entreating that he come back to America, Śrīla Prabhupāda returned to the West to continue, on a larger scale than ever, the work he had begun: transplanting Kṛṣṇa consciousness in the West.

Śrīla Prabhupāda-līlāmṛta will be completed in several more volumes. According to scripture, the word *līlā* (as in *līlāmṛta*) means "pastime," and it specifically refers to activities that are causeless and cannot be checked. In other words, the pastimes of God or His pure devotee are transcendental. Although the activities of Śrīla Prabhupāda may appear ordinary, they have an internal meaning. But even in the ordinary sense, *Only He Could Lead Them* is the story of sincere love, heartbreak at separation, and reunion. It is a historical document of how God lives in the world in the form of His representative, the pure devotee. And it is also a real and human story of Śrīla Prabhupāda and his American disciples. Continuing the theme of the earlier volumes, *Only He Could Lead Them* shows the forceful determination of a saint who lived only to carry out the order of his spiritual master.

SDG

CHAPTER ONE

"Swami Invites the Hippies"

January 16, 1967

As the United Airlines jet descended on the San Francisco Bay area, Śrīla Prabhupāda turned to his disciple Raṇacora and said, "The buildings look like matchboxes. Just imagine how it looks from Kṛṣṇa's viewpoint."

Śrīla Prabhupāda was seventy-one years old, and this had been his first air trip. Raṇacora, nineteen and dressed in a suit and tie, was supposed to be Śrīla Prabhupāda's secretary. He was a new disciple but had raised some money and had asked to fly to San Francisco with Prabhupāda.

During the trip Śrīla Prabhupāda had spoken little. He had been chanting: "Hare Kṛṣṇa, Hare Kṛṣṇa, Kṛṣṇa Kṛṣṇa, Hare Hare/ Hare Rāma, Hare Rāma, Rāma Rāma, Hare Hare." His right hand in his cloth bead bag, he had been fingering one bead after another as he chanted silently to himself. When the plane had first risen over New York City, he had looked out the window at the buildings growing smaller and smaller. Then the plane had entered the clouds, which to Prabhupāda had appeared like an ocean in the sky. He had been bothered by pressure blocking his ears and had mentioned it; otherwise he hadn't said much, but had only chanted Kṛṣṇa's names over and over. Now, as the plane began its descent, he continued to chant, his voice slightly audible—"Kṛṣṇa, Kṛṣṇa, Kṛṣṇa . . ."—and he looked out the window at the vista of thousands of matchbox houses and streets stretching in charted patterns in every direction.

When the announcement for United Airlines Flight 21 from New York came over the public-address system, the group of about fifty hippies gathered closer together in anticipation. For a moment they appeared almost apprehensive, unsure of what to expect or what the Swami would be like.

Roger Segal: *We were quite an assorted lot, even for the San Francisco airport. Mukunda was wearing a Merlin the Magician robe with paisley squares all around, Sam was wearing a Moroccan sheep robe with a hood—he even smelled like a sheep—and I was wearing a sort of blue homemade Japanese samurai robe with small white dots. Long strings of beads were everywhere. Buckskins, boots, army fatigues, people wearing small, round sunglasses—the whole phantasmagoria of San Francisco at its height.*

Only a few people in the crowd knew Swamiji: Mukunda and his wife, Jānakī; Ravīndra-svarūpa; Rāya Rāma—all from New York. And Allen Ginsberg was there. (A few days before, Allen had been one of the leaders of the Human Be-In in Golden Gate Park, where over two hundred thousand had come together—"A Gathering of the Tribes . . . for a joyful pow-wow and Peace Dance.") Today Allen was on hand to greet Swami Bhaktivedanta, whom he had met and chanted with several months before on New York's Lower East Side.

Swamiji would be pleased, Mukunda reminded everyone, if they were all chanting Hare Kṛṣṇa when he came through the gate. They were already familiar with the Hare Kṛṣṇa *mantra.* They had heard about the Swami's chanting in the park in New York or they had seen the article about Swamiji and the chanting in the local underground paper, *The Oracle.* Earlier today they had gathered in Golden Gate Park—most of them responding to a flyer Mukunda had distributed—and had chanted there for more than an hour before coming to the airport in a caravan of cars. Now many of them—also in response to Mukunda's flyer—stood with incense and flowers in their hands.

As the disembarking passengers entered the terminal gate and walked up the ramp, they looked in amazement at the reception party of flower-bearing chanters. The chanters, however, gazed past these ordinary, tired-looking travelers, searching for that special person who was supposed to be on the plane. Suddenly, strolling toward them was the Swami, golden-complexioned, dressed in bright saffron robes.

Prabhupāda had heard the chanting even before he had entered the terminal, and he had begun to smile. He was happy and surprised. Glancing over the faces, he recognized only a few. Yet here were fifty people receiving him and chanting Hare Kṛṣṇa without his having said a word!

Mukunda: *We just had a look at Swamiji, and then we bowed down—myself, my wife, and the friends I had brought, Sam and Marjorie. And then all of the young men and women there followed suit and all bowed down to Swamiji, just feeling very confident that it was the right and proper thing to do.*

The crowd of hippies had formed a line on either side of a narrow passage through which Swamiji would walk. As he passed among his new admirers, dozens of hands stretched out to offer him flowers and incense. He smiled, collecting the offerings in his hands while Raṇacora looked on. Allen Ginsberg stepped forward with a large bouquet of flowers, and Śrīla Prabhupāda graciously accepted it. Then Prabhupāda began offering the gifts back to all who reached out to receive them. He proceeded through the terminal, the crowd of young people walking beside him, chanting.

At the baggage claim Śrīla Prabhupāda waited for a moment, his eyes taking in everyone around him. Lifting his open palms, he beckoned everyone to chant louder, and the group burst into renewed chanting, with Prabhupāda standing in their midst, softly clapping his hands and singing Hare Kṛṣṇa. Gracefully, he then raised his arms above his head and began to dance, stepping and swaying from side to side.

To the mixed chagrin, amusement, and irresistible joy of the airport workers and passengers, the reception party stayed with Prabhupāda until he got his luggage. Then they escorted him outside into the sunlight and into a waiting car, a black 1949 Cadillac Fleetwood. Prabhupāda got into the back seat with Mukunda and Allen Ginsberg. Until the moment the car pulled away from the curb, Śrīla Prabhupāda, still smiling, continued handing flowers to all those who had come to welcome him as he brought Kṛṣṇa consciousness west.

The Cadillac belonged to Harvey Cohen, who almost a year before had allowed Prabhupāda to stay in his Bowery loft. Harvey was driving, but because of his chauffeur's hat (picked up at a Salvation Army store) and his black suit and his beard, Prabhupāda didn't recognize him.

"Where is Harvey?" Prabhupāda asked.

"He's driving," Mukunda said.

"Oh, is that you? I didn't recognize you."

Harvey smiled. "Welcome to San Francisco, Swamiji."

Śrīla Prabhupāda was happy to be in another big Western city on behalf of his spiritual master, Bhaktisiddhānta Sarasvatī, and Lord Caitanya. The further west one goes, Lord Caitanya had said, the more materialistic the people. Yet, Lord Caitanya had also said that Kṛṣṇa consciousness should spread all over the world. Prabhupāda's Godbrothers had often wondered about Lord Caitanya's statement that one day the name of Kṛṣṇa would be sung in every town and village. Perhaps that verse should be taken symbolically, they said; otherwise, what could it mean—Kṛṣṇa in every town? But Śrīla Prabhupāda had deep faith in that statement by Lord Caitanya and in the instruction of his spiritual master. Here he was in the far-Western city of San Francisco, and already people were chanting. They had enthusiastically received him with flowers and *kīrtana.* And all over the world there were other cities much like this one.

The temple Mukunda and his friends had obtained was on Frederick Street in the Haight-Ashbury district. Like the temple at 26 Second Avenue in New York, it was a small storefront with a display window facing the street. A sign over the window read, SRI SRI RADHA KRISHNA TEMPLE. Mukunda and his friends had also rented a three-room apartment for Swamiji on the third floor of the adjoining building. It was a small, bare, run-down apartment facing the street.

Followed by several carloads of devotees and curious seekers, Śrīla Prabhupāda arrived at 518 Frederick Street and entered the storefront, which was decorated only by a few madras cloths on the wall. Taking his seat on a cushion, he led a *kīrtana* and then spoke, inviting everyone to take up Kṛṣṇa consciousness. After his lecture he left the storefront and walked next door and up the two flights of stairs to his apartment. As he entered his apartment, number 32, he was followed not only by his devotees and admirers but also by reporters from San Francisco's main newspapers: the *Chronicle* and the *Examiner.* While some devotees cooked his lunch and Raṇacora unpacked his suitcase, Swamiji talked with the reporters, who sat on the floor, taking notes on their pads.

Reporter: "Downstairs, you said you were inviting everyone to Kṛṣṇa consciousness. Does that include the Haight-Ashbury Bohemians and beatniks?"

Prabhupāda: "Yes, everyone, including you or anybody else, be he or she what is called an 'acidhead' or a hippie or something else. But once he is accepted for training, he becomes something else from what he had been before."

Reporter: "What does one have to do to become a member of your movement?"

Prabhupāda: "There are four prerequisites. I do not allow my students to keep girl friends. I prohibit all kinds of intoxicants, including coffee, tea, and cigarettes. I prohibit meat-eating. And I prohibit my students from taking part in gambling."

Reporter: "Do these shall-not commandments extend to the use of LSD, marijuana, and other narcotics?"

Prabhupāda: "I consider LSD to be an intoxicant. I do not allow any one of my students to use that or any intoxicant. I train my students to rise early in the morning, to take a bath early in the day, and to attend prayer meetings three times a day. Our sect is one of austerity. It is the science of God."

Although Prabhupāda had found that reporters generally did not report his philosophy, he took the opportunity to preach Kṛṣṇa consciousness. Even if the reporters didn't want to delve into the philosophy, his followers did. "The big mistake of modern civilization," Śrīla Prabhupāda continued, "is to encroach upon others' property as though it were one's own. This creates an unnatural disturbance. God is the ultimate proprietor of everything in the universe. When people know that God is the ultimate proprietor, the best friend of all living entities, and the object of all offerings and sacrifices—then there will be peace."

The reporters asked him about his background, and he told briefly about his coming from India and beginning in New York.

After the reporters left, Prabhupāda continued speaking to the young people in his room. Mukunda, who had allowed his hair and beard to grow but who wore around his neck the strand of large red beads Swamiji had given him at initiation, introduced some of his friends and explained that they were all living together and that they wanted to help Swamiji present Kṛṣṇa consciousness to the young people of San Francisco. Mukunda's wife, Jānakī, asked Swamiji about his plane ride. He said it had been pleasant except for some pressure in his ears. "The houses looked like matchboxes," he said, and with his thumb and forefinger he indicated the size of a matchbox.

He leaned back against the wall and took off the garlands he had received that day, until only a beaded necklace—a common, inexpensive item with a small bell on it—remained hanging around his neck. Prabhupāda held it, inspected the workmanship, and toyed with it. "This is special," he said, looking up, "because it was made with devotion." He continued to pay attention to the necklace, as if receiving it had been one of the most important events of the day.

When his lunch arrived, he distributed some to everyone, and then Raṇacora efficiently though tactlessly asked everyone to leave and give the Swami a little time to eat and rest.

Outside the apartment and in the storefront below, the talk was of Swamiji. No one had been disappointed. Everything Mukunda had been telling them about him was true. They particularly enjoyed how he had talked about seeing everything from Kṛṣṇa's viewpoint.

That night on television Swamiji's arrival was covered on the eleven o'clock news, and the next day it appeared in the newspapers. The *Examiner's* story was on page two—"Swami Invites the Hippies"—along with a photo of the temple, filled with followers, and some shots of Swamiji, who looked very grave. Prabhupāda had Mukunda read the article aloud.

"The lanky 'Master of the Faith,' " Mukunda read, "attired in a flowing ankle-long robe and sitting cross-legged on a big mattress—"

Swamiji interrupted, "What is this word *lanky*?"

Mukunda explained that it meant tall and slender. "I don't know why they said that," he added. "Maybe it's because you sit so straight and tall, so they think that you are very tall." The article went on to describe many of the airport greeters as being "of the long-haired, bearded and sandaled set."

San Francisco's largest paper, the *Chronicle*, also ran an article: "Swami in Hippie-Land—Holy Man Opens S.F. Temple." The article began, "A holy man from India, described by his friend and beat poet Allen Ginsberg as one of the more conservative leaders of his faith, launched a kind of evangelistic effort yesterday in the heart of San Francisco's hippie haven."

Śrīla Prabhupāda objected to being called conservative. He was indignant: "Conservative? How is that?"

"In respect to sex and drugs," Mukunda suggested.

"Of course, we are conservative in that sense," Prabhupāda said. "That simply means we are following *śāstra*. We cannot depart from *Bhagavad-gītā*. But conservative we are not. Caitanya Mahāprabhu was so strict that He would not even look on a woman, but we are accepting everyone into this movement, regardless of sex, caste, position, or whatever. Everyone is invited to come chant Hare Kṛṣṇa. This is Caitanya Mahāprabhu's munificence, His liberality. No, we are not conservative."

* * *

Śrīla Prabhupāda rose from bed and turned on the light. It was one A.M. Although the alarm had not sounded and no one had come to wake him, he had risen on his own. The apartment was cold and quiet. Wrapping his *cādar* around his shoulders, he sat quietly at his makeshift desk (a trunk filled with manuscripts) and in deep concentration chanted the Hare Kṛṣṇa *mantra* on his beads.

After an hour of chanting, Śrīla Prabhupāda turned to his writing. Although two years had passed since he had published a book (the third and final volume of the First Canto of *Śrīmad-Bhāgavatam*), he had daily been working, sometimes on his translation and commentary of the Second Canto but mostly on *Bhagavad-gītā*. In the 1940s in India he had written an entire *Bhagavad-gītā* translation and commentary, but his only copy had mysteriously disappeared. Then in 1965, after a few months in America, he had begun again, starting with the Introduction, which he had composed in his room on Seventy-second Street in New York. Now thousands of manuscript pages filled his trunk, completing his *Bhagavad-gītā*. If his New York disciple Hayagrīva, formerly an English professor, could edit it, and if some of the other disciples could get it published, that would be an important achievement.

But publishing books in America seemed difficult—more difficult than in India. Even though in India he had been alone, he had managed to publish three volumes in three years. Here in America he had many followers; but many followers meant increased responsibilities. And none of his followers as yet seemed seriously inclined to take up typing, editing, and dealing with American businessmen. Yet despite the dim prospects for publishing his *Bhagavad-gītā*, Śrīla Prabhupāda had begun translating another book, *Caitanya-caritāmṛta*, the principal Vaiṣṇava scripture on the life and teachings of Lord Caitanya.

Putting on his reading glasses, Prabhupāda opened his books and turned on the dictating machine. He studied the Bengali and Sanskrit texts, then picked up the microphone, flicked the switch to *record*, flashing on a small red light, and began speaking: "While the Lord was going, chanting and dancing, . . ." (he spoke no more than a phrase at a time, flicking the switch, pausing, and then dictating again) "thousands of people were following Him, . . . and some of them were laughing, some were dancing, . . . and some singing. . . . Some of them were falling on the ground offering obeisances to the Lord." Speaking and pausing, clicking the switch on and off, he would sit straight, sometimes gently rocking and nodding his head as he urged forward his words. Or he would bend low over his books, carefully studying them through his reading glasses.

An hour passed, and Prabhupāda worked on. The building was dark except for Prabhupāda's lamp and quiet except for the sound of his voice and the click and hum of the dictating machine. He wore a faded peach turtleneck jersey beneath his gray wool *cādar*, and since he had just risen from bed, his saffron *dhotī* was wrinkled. Without having washed his face or gone to the bathroom, he sat absorbed in his work. At least for these few rare hours, the street and the Rādhā-Kṛṣṇa temple were quiet.

This situation—with the night dark, the surroundings quiet, and him at his transcendental literary work—was not much different from his early-morning hours in his room at the Rādhā-Dāmodara temple in Vṛndāvana, India. There, of course, he had had no dictating machine, but he had worked during the same hours and from the same text, *Caitanya-caritāmṛta.* Once he had begun a verse-by-verse translation with commentary, and another time he had written essays on the text. Now, having just arrived in this corner of the world, so remote from the scenes of Lord Caitanya's pastimes, he was beginning the first chapter of a new English version of *Caitanya-caritāmṛta.* He called it *Teachings of Lord Caitanya.*

He was following what had become a vital routine in his life: rising early and writing the *paramparā* message of Kṛṣṇa consciousness. Putting aside all other considerations, disregarding present circumstances, he would merge into the timeless message of transcendental knowledge. This was his most important service to Bhaktisiddhānta Sarasvatī. The thought of producing more books and distributing them widely inspired him to rise every night and translate.

Prabhupāda worked until dawn. Then he stopped and prepared himself to go down to the temple for the morning meeting.

* * *

Though some of the New York disciples had objected, Śrīla Prabhupāda was still scheduled for the Mantra-Rock Dance at the Avalon Ballroom. It wasn't proper, they had said, for the devotees out in San Francisco to ask their spiritual master to go to such a place. It would mean amplified guitars, pounding drums, wild light shows, and hundreds of drugged hippies. How could his pure message be heard in such a place?

But in San Francisco Mukunda and others had been working on the Mantra-Rock Dance for months. It would draw thousands of young people, and the San Francisco Rādhā-Kṛṣṇa Temple stood to make thousands of dollars. So although among his New York disciples Śrīla Prabhupāda had expressed uncertainty, he now said nothing to deter the enthusiasm of his San Francisco followers.

Sam Speerstra, Mukunda's friend and one of the Mantra-Rock organizers, explained the idea to Hayagrīva, who had just arrived from New York: "There's a whole new school of San Francisco music opening up. The Grateful Dead have already cut their first record. Their offer to do this dance is a great publicity boost just when we need it."

"But Swamiji says that even Ravi Shankar is *māyā*," Hayagrīva said.

"Oh, it's all been arranged," Sam assured him. "All the bands will be onstage, and Allen Ginsberg will introduce Swamiji to San Francisco. Swamiji will talk and then chant Hare Kṛṣṇa, with the bands joining in. Then he leaves. There should be around four thousand people there."

Śrīla Prabhupāda knew he would not compromise himself; he would go, chant, and then leave. The important thing was to spread the chanting of Hare Kṛṣṇa. If thousands of young people gathering to hear rock music could be engaged in hearing and chanting the names of God, then what was the harm? As a preacher, Prabhupāda was prepared to go anywhere to spread Kṛṣṇa consciousness. Since chanting Hare Kṛṣṇa was absolute, one who heard or chanted the names of Kṛṣṇa—anyone, anywhere, in any condition—could be saved from falling to the lower species in the next life. These young hippies wanted something spiritual, but they had no direction. They were confused, accepting hallucinations as spiritual visions. But they were seeking genuine spiritual life, just like many of the young people on the Lower East Side. Prabhupāda decided he would go; his disciples wanted him to, and he was their servant and the servant of Lord Caitanya.

Mukunda, Sam, and Harvey Cohen had already met with rock entrepreneur Chet Helms, who had agreed that they could use his Avalon Ballroom and that, if they could get the bands to come, everything above the cost for the groups, the security, and a few other basics would go as profit for the San Francisco Rādhā-Kṛṣṇa Temple. Mukunda and Sam had then gone calling on the music groups, most of whom lived in the Bay area, and one after another the exciting new San Francisco rock bands—the Grateful Dead, Moby Grape, Big Brother and the Holding Company, Jefferson Airplane, Quicksilver Messenger Service—had agreed to appear with Swami Bhaktivedanta for the minimum wage of $250 per group. And Allen Ginsberg had agreed. The lineup was complete.

In San Francisco every rock concert had an art poster, many of them designed by the psychedelic artist called Mouse. One thing about Mouse's posters was that it was difficult to tell where the letters left off and the background began. He used dissonant colors that made his posters seem to flash on and off. Borrowing from this tradition, Harvey Cohen had created a unique poster—KRISHNA CONSCIOUSNESS COMES WEST—using red and blue concentric circles and a candid photo of Swamiji smiling in Tompkins Square Park. The devotees put the posters up all over town.

Hayagrīva and Mukunda went to discuss the program for the Mantra-Rock Dance with Allen Ginsberg. Allen was already well known as an advocate of the Hare Kṛṣṇa *mantra;* in fact, acquaintances would often greet him with "Hare Kṛṣṇa!" when he walked on Haight Street. And he was known to visit and recommend that others visit the Rādhā-Kṛṣṇa Temple. Hayagrīva, whose full beard and long hair rivaled Allen's, was concerned about the melody Allen would use when he chanted with Swamiji. "I think the melody you use," Hayagrīva said, "is too difficult for good chanting."

"Maybe," Allen admitted, "but that's the melody I first heard in India. A wonderful lady saint was chanting it. I'm quite accustomed to it, and it's the only one I can sing convincingly."

With only a few days remaining before the Mantra-Rock Dance, Allen came to an early-morning *kīrtana* at the temple and later joined Śrīla Prabhupāda upstairs in his room. A few devotees were sitting with Prabhupāda eating Indian sweets when Allen came to the door. He and Prabhupāda smiled and exchanged greetings, and Prabhupāda offered him a sweet, remarking that Mr. Ginsberg was up very early.

"Yes," Allen replied, "the phone hasn't stopped ringing since I arrived in San Francisco."

"That is what happens when one becomes famous," said Prabhupāda. "That was the tragedy of Mahatma Gandhi also. Wherever he went, thousands of people would crowd about him, chanting, 'Mahatma Gandhi *ki jaya*! Mahatma Gandhi *ki jaya*!' The gentleman could not sleep."

"Well, at least it got me up for *kīrtana* this morning," said Allen.

"Yes, that is good."

The conversation turned to the upcoming program at the Avalon Ballroom. "Don't you think there's a possibility of chanting a tune that would be more appealing to Western ears?" Allen asked.

"Any tune will do," said Prabhupāda. "Melody is not important. What is important is that you will chant Hare Kṛṣṇa. It can be in the tune of your own country. That doesn't matter."

Prabhupāda and Allen also talked about the meaning of the word *hippie*, and Allen mentioned something about taking LSD. Prabhupāda replied that LSD created dependence and was not necessary for a person in Kṛṣṇa consciousness. "Kṛṣṇa consciousness resolves everything," Prabhupāda said. "Nothing else is needed."

At the Mantra-Rock Dance there would be a multimedia light show by the biggest names in the art, Ben Van Meter and Roger Hillyard. Ben and Roger were expert at using simultaneous strobe lights, films, and slide shows to fill an auditorium with optical effects reminiscent of LSD visions. Mukunda had given them many slides of Kṛṣṇa to use during the *kīrtana*. One evening, Ben and Roger came to see Swamiji in his apartment.

Roger Hillyard: *He was great. I was really impressed. It wasn't the way he looked, the way he acted, or the way he dressed, but it was his total being. Swamiji was very serene and very humorous, and at the same time obviously very wise and in tune, enlightened. He had the ability to relate to a lot of different kinds of people. I was thinking, "Some of this must be really strange for this person—to come to the United States and end up in the middle of Haight-Ashbury with a storefront for an* āśrama *and a lot of very strange people around." And yet he was totally right there, right there with everybody.*

On the night of the Mantra-Rock Dance, while the stage crew set up equipment and tested the sound system and Ben and Roger organized their light show upstairs, Mukunda and others collected tickets at the door. People lined up all the way down the street and around the block, waiting for tickets at $2.50 apiece. Attendance would be good, a capacity crowd, and most of the local luminaries were coming. LSD pioneer Timothy Leary arrived and was given a special seat onstage. Swami Kriyananda came, carrying a tamboura. A man wearing a top hat and a suit with a silk sash that said SAN FRANCISCO arrived, claiming to be the mayor. At the door, Mukunda stopped a respectably dressed young man who didn't have a ticket. But then someone tapped Mukunda on the shoulder: "Let him in. It's all right. He's Owsley." Mukunda apologized and submitted, allowing Augustus Owsley Stanley II, folk hero and famous synthesizer of LSD, to enter without a ticket.

Almost everyone who came wore bright or unusual costumes: tribal robes, Mexican ponchos, Indian *kurtās,* "God's-eyes," feathers, and beads. Some hippies brought their own flutes, lutes, gourds, drums, rattles, horns, and guitars. The Hell's Angels, dirty-haired, wearing jeans, boots, and denim jackets and accompanied by their women, made their entrance, carrying chains, smoking cigarettes, and displaying their regalia of German helmets, emblazoned emblems, and so on—everything but their motorcycles, which they had parked outside.

The devotees began a warm-up *kīrtana* onstage, dancing the way Swamiji had shown them. Incense poured from the stage and from the corners of the large ballroom. And although most in the audience were high on drugs, the atmosphere was calm; they had come seeking a spiritual experience. As the chanting began, very melodiously, some of the musicians took part by playing their instruments. The light show began: strobe lights flashed, colored balls bounced back and forth to the beat of the music, large blobs of pulsing color splurted across the floor, walls, and ceiling.

A little after eight o'clock, Moby Grape took the stage. With heavy electric guitars, electric bass, and two drummers, they launched into their first number. The large speakers shook the ballroom with their vibrations, and a roar of approval rose from the audience.

Around nine-thirty, Prabhupāda left his Frederick Street apartment and got into the back seat of Harvey's Cadillac. He was dressed in his usual saffron robes, and around his neck he wore a garland of gardenias, whose sweet aroma filled the car. On the way to the Avalon he talked about the need to open more centers.

At ten o'clock Prabhupāda walked up the stairs of the Avalon, followed by Kīrtanānanda and Raṇacora. As he entered the ballroom, devotees blew conchshells, someone began a drum roll, and the crowd parted down the center, all the way from the entrance to the stage, opening a path for him to walk. With his head held high, Prabhupāda seemed to float by as he walked through the strange milieu, making his way across the ballroom floor to the stage.

Suddenly the light show changed. Pictures of Kṛṣṇa and His pastimes flashed onto the wall: Kṛṣṇa and Arjuna riding together on Arjuna's chariot, Kṛṣṇa eating butter, Kṛṣṇa subduing the whirlwind demon, Kṛṣṇa playing the flute. As Prabhupāda walked through the crowd, everyone stood, applauding and cheering. He climbed the stairs and seated himself softly on a waiting cushion. The crowd quieted.

Looking over at Allen Ginsberg, Prabhupāda said, "You can speak something about the *mantra.*"

Allen began to tell of his understanding and experience with the Hare Kṛṣṇa *mantra.* He told how Swamiji had opened a storefront on Second Avenue and had chanted Hare Kṛṣṇa in Tompkins Square Park. And he invited everyone to the Frederick Street temple. "I especially recommend the early-morning *kīrtanas,*" he said, "for those who, coming down from LSD, want to stabilize their consciousness on reentry."

Prabhupāda spoke, giving a brief history of the *mantra.* Then he looked over at Allen again: "You may chant."

Allen began playing his harmonium and chanting into the microphone, singing the tune he had brought from India. Gradually more and more people in the audience caught on and began chanting. As the *kīrtana* continued and the audience got increasingly enthusiastic, musicians from the various bands came onstage to join in. Raṇacora, a fair drummer, began playing Moby Grape's drums. Some of the bass and other guitar players joined in as the devotees and a large group of hippies mounted the stage. The multicolored oil slicks pulsed, and the balls bounced back and forth to the beat of the *mantra,* now projected onto the wall: Hare Krishna, Hare Krishna, Krishna Krishna, Hare Hare/ Hare Rama, Hare Rama, Rama Rama, Hare Hare. As the chanting spread throughout the hall, some of the hippies got to their feet, held hands, and danced.

Allen Ginsberg: *We sang Hare Kṛṣṇa all evening. It was absolutely great—an open thing. It was the height of the Haight-Ashbury spiritual enthusiasm. It was the first time that there had been a music scene in San Francisco where everybody could be part of it and participate. Everybody could sing and dance rather than listen to other people sing and dance.*

Jānakī: *People didn't know what they were chanting for. But to see that many people chanting—even though most of them were intoxicated—made Swamiji very happy. He loved to see the people chanting.*

Hayagrīva: *Standing in front of the bands, I could hardly hear. But above all, I could make out the chanting of Hare Kṛṣṇa, building steadily. On the wall behind, a slide projected a huge picture of Kṛṣṇa in a golden helmet with a peacock feather, a flute in His hand.*

Then Śrīla Prabhupāda stood up, lifted his arms, and began to dance. He gestured for everyone to join him, and those who were still seated stood up and began dancing and chanting and swaying back and forth, following Prabhupāda's gentle dance.

Roger Segal: *The ballroom appeared as if it was a human field of wheat blowing in the wind. It produced a calm feeling in contrast to the Avalon Ballroom atmosphere of gyrating energies. The chanting of Hare Kṛṣṇa continued for over an hour, and finally everyone was jumping and yelling, even crying and shouting.*

Someone placed a microphone before Śrīla Prabhupāda, and his voice resounded strongly over the powerful sound system. The tempo quickened. Śrīla Prabhupāda was perspiring profusely. Kīrtanānanda insisted that the *kīrtana* stop. Swamiji was too old for this, he said; it might be harmful. But the chanting continued, faster and faster, until the words of the *mantra* finally became indistinguishable amidst the amplified music and the chorus of thousands of voices.

Then suddenly it ended. And all that could be heard was the loud hum of the amplifiers and Śrīla Prabhupāda's voice, ringing out, offering obeisances to his spiritual master: "Oṁ Viṣṇupāda Paramahaṁsa Parivrājakācārya Aṣṭottara-śata Śrī Śrīmad Bhaktisiddhānta Sarasvatī Goswami Mahārāja *ki jaya*! . . . All glories to the assembled devotees!"

Śrīla Prabhupāda made his way offstage, through the heavy smoke and crowds, and down the front stairs, with Kīrtanānanda and Raṇacora close behind him. Allen announced the next rock group.

As Swamiji left the ballroom and the appreciative crowd behind, he commented, "This is no place for a *brahmacārī*."

The next morning the temple was crowded with young people who had seen Swamiji at the Avalon. Most of them had stayed up all night. Śrīla Prabhupāda, having followed his usual morning schedule, came down at seven, held *kīrtana*, and delivered the morning lecture.

Later that morning, while riding to the beach with Kīrtanānanda and Hayagrīva, Swamiji asked how many people had attended last night's *kīrtana*. When they told him, he asked how much money they had made, and they said they weren't sure but it was approximately fifteen hundred dollars.

Half-audibly he chanted in the back seat of the car, looking out the window as quiet and unassuming as a child, with no indication that the night before he had been cheered and applauded by thousands of hippies, who had stood back and made a grand aisle for him to walk in triumph across the strobe-lit floor amid the thunder of the electric basses and pounding drums of the Avalon Ballroom. For all the fanfare of the night before, he remained untouched, the same as ever in personal demeanor: he was aloof, innocent, and humble, while at the same time appearing very grave and ancient. As Kīrtanānanda and Hayagrīva were aware, Swamiji was not of this world. They knew that he, unlike them, was always thinking of Kṛṣṇa.

They walked with him along the boardwalk, near the ocean, with its cool breezes and cresting waves. Kīrtanānanda spread the *cādar* over Prabhupāda's shoulders. "In Bengali there is one nice verse," Prabhupāda remarked, breaking his silence. "I remember. 'Oh, what is that voice across the sea calling, calling: *Come here, come here. . . .*' " Speaking little, he walked the boardwalk with his two friends, frequently looking out at the sea and sky. As he walked he softly sang a *mantra* that Kīrtanānanda and Hayagrīva had never heard before: "*Govinda jaya jaya, gopāla jaya jaya, rādhā-ramaṇa hari, govinda jaya jaya.*" He sang slowly, in a deep voice, as they walked along the boardwalk. He looked out at the Pacific Ocean: "Because it is great, it is tranquil."

"The ocean seems to be eternal," Hayagrīva ventured.

"No," Prabhupāda replied. "Nothing in the material world is eternal."

* * *

In New York, since there were so few women present at the temple, people had inquired whether it were possible for a woman to join the Kṛṣṇa consciousness movement. But in San Francisco that question never arose. Most of the men who came to learn from Swamiji came with their girl friends. To Prabhupāda these boys and girls, eager for chanting and hearing about Kṛṣṇa, were like sparks of faith to be fanned into steady, blazing fires of devotional life. There was no question of his asking the newcomers to give up their girl friends or boyfriends, and yet he uncompromisingly preached, "no illicit sex." The dilemma, however, seemed to have an obvious solution: marry the couples in Kṛṣṇa consciousness.

Because traditionally a *sannyāsī* would never arrange or perform marriages, by Indian standards someone might criticize Prabhupāda for allowing *any* mingling of the sexes. But Prabhupāda gave priority to spreading Kṛṣṇa consciousness. What Indian, however critical, had ever tried to transplant the essence of India's spiritual culture into the Western culture? Prabhupāda saw that to change the American social system and completely separate the men from the women would not be possible. But to compromise his standard of no illicit sex was also not possible. Therefore, Kṛṣṇa conscious married life, the *gṛhastha-āśrama*, would be the best arrangement for many of his new aspiring disciples. In

Kṛṣṇa consciousness husband and wife could live together and help one another in spiritual progress. It was an authorized arrangement for allowing a man and woman to associate. If as spiritual master he found it necessary to perform marriages himself, he would do it. But first these young couples would have to become attracted to Kṛṣṇa consciousness.

Joan Campanella had grown up in a wealthy suburb of Portland, Oregon, where her father was a corporate tax attorney. She and her sister had had their own sports cars and their own boats for sailing on Lake Oswego. Disgusted by the sorority life at the University of Oregon, Joan had dropped out during her first term and enrolled at Reed College, where she had studied ceramics, weaving, and calligraphy. In 1963, she had moved to San Francisco and become the co-owner of a ceramics shop. Although she had then had many friends among fashionable shopkeepers, folksingers, and dancers, she had remained aloof and introspective.

It was through her sister Jan that Joan had first met Śrīla Prabhupāda. Jan had gone with her boyfriend Michael Grant to live in New York City, where Michael had worked as a music arranger. In 1965 they had met Swamiji while he was living alone on the Bowery, and they had become his initiated disciples (Mukunda and Jānakī). Swamiji had asked them to get married, and they had invited Joan to the wedding. As a wedding guest for one day, Joan had then briefly entered Swamiji's transcendental world at 26 Second Avenue, and he had kept her busy all day making dough and filling *kacaurī* pastries for the wedding feast. Joan had worked in one room, and Swamiji had worked in the kitchen, although he had repeatedly come in and guided her in making the *kacaurīs* properly, telling her not to touch her clothes or body while cooking and instructing her not to smoke cigarettes, because the food was to be offered to Lord Kṛṣṇa and therefore had to be prepared purely. Joan had been convinced by this brief association that Swamiji was a great spiritual teacher, but she had returned to San Francisco without pursuing Kṛṣṇa consciousness further.

A few months later, Mukunda and Jānakī had driven to the West Coast with plans of going soon to India but had changed their plans when Mukunda had received a letter from Swamiji asking him to try to start a

Kṛṣṇa conscious temple in California. Mukunda had talked about Swamiji to Joan and other friends, and he had found that a lot of young people were interested. Joan had then accompanied Mukunda, Jānakī, and a boy named Roger Segal to the mountains in Oregon, where they had visited their mutual friends Sam and Marjorie, who had been living in a forest lookout tower.

Mukunda had explained what he had known of Kṛṣṇa consciousness, and the six of them had begun chanting Hare Kṛṣṇa together. They had been especially interested in Swamiji's teachings about elevating consciousness without drugs. Mukunda had talked excitedly about Swamiji's having asked him to start a temple in California, and soon he and his wife, Jānakī; Sam and his girl friend Marjorie; and Roger and Joan; now intimate friends, had moved to an apartment in San Francisco to find a storefront and set the stage for Swamiji.

After Swamiji's arrival, Joan had begun attending the temple *kīrtanas.* She felt drawn to Swamiji and the chanting, and she especially liked the informal visiting hours. Swamiji would sit in his rocking chair with his hand in his bead bag, chanting the holy names, and Joan would sit fascinated, watching his fingers moving within the bag.

One day during Swamiji's visiting hours, while Swamiji was sitting in his rocking chair and Joan and others were sitting at his feet, Jānakī's cat crept in through the hallway door and began slowly coming down the hallway. The cat came closer and closer and slowly meandered right in front of Swamiji's feet. It sat down, looking up intently at Swamiji, and began to meow. None of the devotees knew what to expect. Swamiji began gently stroking the back of the cat with his foot, saying, "Hare Kṛṣṇa, Hare Kṛṣṇa. Are you feeding him *prasādam* milk?"

Joan: *I was touched by Swamiji's activities and his kindness—even to cats—and I longed for more association with him.*

Joan came to understand that serving Swamiji was a serious matter. But she didn't want to jump into initiation until she was one-hundred-percent sure about it. Sometimes she would cry in ecstasy, and sometimes she would fall asleep during Swamiji's lecture. So she remained hesitant and skeptical, wondering, "How can I actually apply Swamiji's teachings to my life?"

One evening Swamiji asked her, "When are you going to be initiated?" Joan said that she didn't know but that she relished reading his books and chanting Hare Kṛṣṇa. She said that because she was attracted to the mountains and to elevated spiritual consciousness, she wanted to travel to Tibet.

Swamiji, sitting in his rocking chair, looked down at Joan as she sat at his feet. She felt he was looking right through her. "I can take you to a higher place than Tibet," he said. "Just see."

Joan suddenly felt that Swamiji knew everything about her, and she understood, "Oh, I have to see through his eyes what Kṛṣṇa consciousness is." He was promising that he would take her to some very elevated realm, but *she would have to see it.* It was then that Joan decided to become Swamiji's disciple.

When she told her boyfriend Roger, he was astounded. He and Joan had been coming to the *kīrtanas* and lectures together, but he still had doubts. Maybe it would be good for him and Joan to get married but not initiated. Joan, however, was more determined. She explained to Roger that Swamiji hadn't come just to perform marriages; you had to get initiated first.

Roger Segal had grown up in New York. He was following a *haṭha-yoga guru,* had experimented with psychedelic chemicals, and had traveled in the Deep South as a civil rights activist, taking part in freedom marches with the blacks. Large-bodied, sociable, and outgoing, he had lots of friends in San Francisco. At the airport, in a merry mood with the Haight-Ashbury crowd, he had seen Swamiji for the first time and been especially struck by Swamiji's regal bearing and absence of self-consciousness. The concept of reincarnation had always intrigued him, but after attending some of Swamiji's lectures and hearing him explain transmigration of the soul, he felt he had found someone who definitely knew the answer to any question about life after death.

One night, after attending the program at the temple, Roger returned to his apartment and sat down on the fire escape to meditate on what Swamiji had said. The world is false, he had said. "But it feels real to me," Roger thought. "If I pinch my arm, I feel pain. So how is that illusion? This fire escape is real; otherwise I would be falling in space. This space is real, isn't it?"

Roger decided he didn't understand what Swamiji meant by *illusion.* "If I try to walk through the wall," he thought, "would that be real or not? Maybe the wall's reality is just in my mind." To test the illusion he went inside his apartment, concentrated his mind, and walked against the wall—smack. He sat down again and thought, "What does Swamiji mean when he says that the world is illusion?" He decided he should ask at the next meeting.

He did. And Śrīla Prabhupāda told him that actually the world is real, because it was created by God, the supreme reality. But it is unreal in the sense that everything material is temporary. When a person takes the temporary world to be permanent and all in all, he is in illusion. Only the spiritual world, Swamiji explained, is eternal and therefore real.

Roger was satisfied by Swamiji's answer. But he had other difficulties: he thought Swamiji too conservative. When Swamiji said that people's dogs must be kept outside the temple, Roger didn't like it. Many visitors brought pet dogs with them to the temple, and now there was a hitching post in front of the building just to accommodate the pets on leashes. But Swamiji wouldn't allow any pets inside. "This philosophy is for humans," he said. "A cat or dog cannot understand it, although if he hears the chanting of Hare Kṛṣṇa he can receive a higher birth in the future."

Roger also had other points of contention with what he considered Swamiji's conservative philosophy. Swamiji repeatedly spoke against uncontrolled habits like smoking, but Roger couldn't imagine giving up such things. And the instructions about restricting sex life especially bothered him. Yet despite his not following very strictly, Roger felt himself developing a love for Swamiji and Kṛṣṇa. He sensed that Swamiji had much to teach him and that Swamiji was doing it in a certain way and a certain order. Roger knew that Swamiji saw him as a baby in spiritual life who had to be spoonfed; he knew he had to become submissive and accept whatever Swamiji gave him.

Sam Speerstra, tall and slender with curly reddish-gold hair, was athletic (he had trained as an Olympic skier) yet artistic (he was a writer and wood sculptor). He had graduated from Reed College in Oregon and gone on as a Fulbright scholar to a small college in Switzerland, where he had obtained an M.A. in philosophy. He was popular—as Mukunda saw him, "the epitome of the rugged individualist."

When Mukunda had visited Sam at his mountain lookout tower and told him about Swamiji and Kṛṣṇa consciousness, Sam had been intrigued by the new ideas. Sam's life had nearly reached a dead end, but he had seen hope in what Mukunda and Jānakī had been saying about Swamiji. After spending only a few days with Mukunda, Sam had been eager to help him establish a temple of Kṛṣṇa consciousness in San Francisco.

Sam was the one who knew the local rock stars and had persuaded them to appear at the Avalon with Swami Bhaktivedanta, whom he had never met. Sam had seen Swamiji for the first time when Swamiji had arrived at the San Francisco airport; and Sam had later insisted that he had seen a flash of light come from Swamiji's body.

At first Sam had been afraid to say anything, nor had he known *what* to say—Prabhupāda was completely new to him and seemed so elevated. But the day after the program at the Avalon, when Mukunda told Prabhupāda that Sam had arranged the dance, Prabhupāda sent for him to find out how much money they had made. Sitting across from Prabhupāda, who sat behind his small desk, Sam informed him that they had made about fifteen hundred dollars profit. "Well then," Śrīla Prabhupāda said, "you will be the treasurer." Then Śrīla Prabhupāda asked him, "What is your idea of God?"

"God is one," Sam replied.

Prabhupāda asked, "What is the purpose of worshiping God?"

Sam replied, "To become one with God."

"No," Prabhupāda said. "You cannot become one with God. God and you are always two different individuals. But you can become one in *interest* with Him." And then he told Sam about Kṛṣṇa. After they talked, Prabhupāda said, "You can come up every day, and I will teach you how to do books." So Sam began meeting with Prabhupāda for half an hour a day to learn bookkeeping.

Sam: *I had never been very good at keeping books, and I really didn't want to do it. But it was a good excuse to come and see Swamiji every day. He would chew me out when I would spend too much money or when I couldn't balance the books properly. I really loved the idea that he was so practical that he knew bookkeeping. He became so much more of a friend from the beginning, rather than some idealized person from another sphere of life. I took almost all my practical questions to him. I learned to answer things for myself based on the way Swamiji always answered day-to-day problems. And the first thing he made me do was to get married to my girl friend.*

Mukunda and his wife, Jānakī, whose apartment was just down the hall from Śrīla Prabhupāda's, were the only couple Śrīla Prabhupāda had already initiated and married. Mukunda, who often wore his strand of large red *japa* beads in two loose loops around his neck, had grown long hair and a short, thick black beard since coming to San Francisco. He had entered the "summer of love" spirit of Haight-Ashbury and was acquainted with many of the popular figures. Although occasionally earning money as a musician, he spent most of his time promoting Prabhupāda's mission, especially by meeting people to arrange gala programs like the one at the Avalon. He was a leader in bringing people to assist Prabhupāda, yet he had no permanent sense of commitment. He was helping because it was fun. Having little desire to be different from his many San Francisco friends, he did not strictly follow Prabhupāda's principles for regulated spiritual life.

In his exchanges with Śrīla Prabhupāda, Mukunda liked to assume a posture of fraternal camaraderie, rather than one of menial servitude, and Śrīla Prabhupāda reciprocated. Sometimes, however, Prabhupāda would assert himself as the teacher. Once when Prabhupāda walked into Mukunda's apartment, he noticed a poster on the wall showing a matador with a cape and sword going after a bull. "This is a horrible picture!" Śrīla Prabhupāda exclaimed, his face showing displeasure. Mukunda looked at the poster, realizing for the first time what it meant. "Yes, it is horrible," he said, and tore it off the wall.

Śrīla Prabhupāda was eager to have someone play the *mṛdaṅga* properly during the *kīrtanas*, and Mukunda, a musician, was a likely candidate.

Mukunda: *The day the drum came I asked Swamiji if I could learn, and he said yes. I asked him when, and he said, "When do you want?" "Now?" I asked. He said, "Yes." I was a little surprised to get such a quick appointment. But I brought the drum to his room, and he began to show me the basic beat. First there was* gee ta ta, gee ta ta, gee ta ta. *And then one slightly more complicated beat,* gee ta ta, gee ta ta, gee ta ta geeeee ta.

As I began to play the beat, I kept speeding it up, and he kept telling me to slow down. He spent a lot of time just showing me how to strike the heads of the drum. Then I finally began to get it a little. But he had to keep admonishing me to slow down and pronounce the syllables as I hit the drum—gee ta ta. *The syllables, he said, and the drum should sound the same. I should make it sound like that and always pronounce them.*

I was determined and played very slowly for a long, long time. I was concentrating with great intensity. Then suddenly I was aware of Swamiji standing motionless beside me. I didn't know how long he was going to stand there without saying anything, and I became a little uncomfortable. But I continued playing. When I got up the courage to look up and see his face, to my surprise he was moving his head back and forth in an affirming way with his eyes closed. He seemed to be enjoying the lesson. This came as a complete surprise to me. Although I had taken music lessons before and had spent many years taking piano lessons, I can never remember an instance when the teacher seemed to actually enjoy my playing. I felt very wonderful to see that here was a teacher who was so perfect, who enjoyed what he was teaching so much, not because it was his personal teaching or his personal method, but because he was witnessing Kṛṣṇa's energy pass through him to a conditioned soul like myself. And he was getting great pleasure out of it. I had a deeper realization that Swamiji was a real teacher, although I had no idea what a spiritual master really was.

To Mukunda's wife, Jānakī, Kṛṣṇa consciousness meant dealing in a personal way with Swamiji. As long as he was around she was all right. She enjoyed asking him questions, serving him, and learning from him how to cook. She didn't care much for studying the philosophy of Kṛṣṇa consciousness, but she quickly developed an intense attraction for him.

Jānakī: *There were a group of us sitting around in Swamiji's apartment, and I asked him if he had any children. He looked at me as if I had said something strange, and he said, "You are not my child?" I said,*

"Well, yes." And he said, "Are not all these my children?" And his answer was so quick that I never doubted that he seriously meant what he said.

For several hours each morning Prabhupāda showed Jānakī, Joan, and others how to cook. One day in the kitchen he noticed a kind of berry he had never tasted, and he asked Jānakī what they were. She told him strawberries. He immediately popped one into his mouth, saying, "That's very tasty." And he proceeded to eat another and another, exclaiming, "Very tasty!"

One time Jānakī was making whipped cream when Prabhupāda came into the kitchen and asked, "What's that?"

She replied, "It's whipped cream."

"What is whipped cream?" he asked.

"It's cream," she replied, "but when you beat it, it fluffs up into a more solid form."

Although always adamant about kitchen rules (one of the most important being that no one could eat in the kitchen), Śrīla Prabhupāda immediately dipped his finger into the whipped cream and tasted it. "This is yogurt," he said.

In a lighthearted, reprimanding way that was her pleasure, Jānakī replied, "No, Swamiji, it's whipped cream."

Śrīla Prabhupada corrected her, "No, it is yogurt." And again he put his finger into it and tasted it, saying, "Oh, it tastes very nice."

"Swamiji!" Jānakī accused him. "You're eating in the kitchen!" Śrīla Prabhupāda merely smiled and shook his head back and forth, saying, "That is all right."

Jānakī: *One time I told him, "Swamiji, I had the most exciting dream. We were all on a planet of our very own, and everybody from earth had come there. They had all become pure devotees, and they were all chanting. You were sitting on a very special chair high off the ground, and the whole earth was clapping and chanting Hare Kṛṣṇa." Swamiji smiled and said, "Oh, that's such a lovely dream."*

Bonnie McDonald, age nineteen, and her boyfriend Gary McElroy, twenty, had both come to San Francisco from Austin, where they had been living together as students at the University of Texas. Bonnie was a slight, fair blonde with a sweet southern drawl. She was born and raised in southeast Texas in a Baptist family. In high school she had become agnostic, but later, while traveling in Europe and studying the religious art there and the architecture of the great cathedrals, she had concluded that these great artists couldn't have been completely wrong.

Gary, the son of a U.S. Air Force officer, had been raised in Germany, Okinawa, and other places around the world before his family had settled in Texas. His dark hair and bushy brows gave him a scowling look, except when he smiled. He was one of the first students at the University of Texas to wear long hair and experiment with psychedelic drugs. While taking LSD together, he and Bonnie had become obsessed with the idea of going on a spiritual search, and without notifying their parents or school they had driven to the West Coast "in search of someone who could teach us about spiritual life."

They had spent a few frustrating months searching through spiritual books and amongst spiritual groups in Haight-Ashbury. They had become vegetarians. Gary had started teaching himself to play electric guitar while Bonnie had gone to Golden Gate Park every day to perform a self-styled *haṭha-yoga* meditation. But gradually they had become disillusioned and had felt themselves becoming degraded from drugs.

When the disciple is ready, the *guru* will appear, they had read; and they had waited eagerly for the day when their *guru* would come. Although Bonnie had spent most of her time in the parks of San Francisco, one day she had been looking through a tableful of magazines in a Haight-Ashbury head shop when she had found a copy of *Back to Godhead*, the mimeographed journal produced by Śrīla Prabhupāda's disciples in New York. She had been particularly attracted to Hayagrīva's article about Swamiji. The descriptions of Swamiji's smile, his bright eyes, his pointy-toed shoes, and the things he said had given her a feeling that this might be the *guru* she had been looking for. And when she had learned that this same Swamiji had opened an *āśrama* in Haight-Ashbury, she had immediately started searching through the neighborhood until she had found the temple on Frederick Street.

Before Bonnie and Gary met Swamiji they had both been troubled. Gary was in anxiety about the threat of being drafted into the Army, and both of them were disillusioned because they had not found the truth they had come to San Francisco to find. So on meeting Śrīla Prabhupāda in his room they began to explain their situation.

Bonnie: *He was sitting in a rocking chair in his little apartment, and he looked at us like we were crazy—because we were—and said, "You come to my classes. Simply come to my classes every morning and every evening, and everything will be all right." That sounded to us like an unbelievable panacea, but because we were so bewildered, we agreed to it.*

I told him I had traveled all over Europe, and he said, "Oh, you have traveled so much." And I said to him, "Yes, I have traveled so much, I have done so many things, but none of it ever made me happy." He was pleased with that statement. He said, "Yes, that is the problem."

We began going to his morning lectures. For us it was a long distance to get there at seven in the morning, but we did it every morning with the conviction that this was what he had said to do and we were going to do it. Then one day he asked us, "What do you do?" When we said that formerly we had been art students at college, he told us to paint pictures of Kṛṣṇa. Shortly after that, we asked to be initiated.

Joan and Roger were soon initiated, receiving the names Yamunā and Guru dāsa. And the very next day they were married. At their wedding ceremony, Swamiji presided, wearing a bulky garland of leaves and rhododendron flowers. He sat on a cushion on the temple floor, surrounded by his followers and paraphernalia for the sacrificial fire. Before him was the small mound of earth where he would later build the fire. He explained the meaning of Kṛṣṇa conscious marriage and how husband and wife should assist one another and serve Kṛṣṇa, keeping Him in the center. Swamiji had commented that he did not like the Western women's dress, and at his request, Yamunā was dressed in a *sārī.*

Although Swamiji had called for ghee (clarified butter) as one of the sacrificial ingredients, the devotees, thinking ghee too costly, had substituted melted margarine. He had called for firewood also, and the devotees had supplied him the bits of a broken orange crate. Now, with Yamunā and Guru dāsa seated before him on the opposite side of the mound of earth, he picked up a small piece of the splintered orange crated, dipped it into what was supposed to be ghee, and held it in the candle flame to begin the fire. The splinter flamed, sputtered, and went out. He picked up another splinter and moistened it in the melted margarine, but when he touched it to the flame it made the same *svit-svit* sound and sputtered out. After trying unsuccessfully four or five times, Swamiji looked up and said, "This marriage will have a very slow start." Yamunā began to cry.

Bonnie and Gary were initiated just two weeks after they had met Swamiji. Bonnie's initiated name was Govinda dāsī, and Gary's was Gaurasundara. Although still dressed in blue jeans, even at their initiation, and not professing to know much of what was going on, they had confidence in Swamiji. They knew that their minds were still hazy from drugs, but they took their initiation seriously and became strict followers. Gaurasundara threw out whatever marijuana he had, and he and Govinda dāsī began eating only food they had offered to Lord Kṛṣṇa. Two weeks after their initiation, Swamiji conducted their marriage ceremony.

On the evening of the wedding Govinda dāsī's father came from Texas, even though he objected to Kṛṣṇa consciousness as radically un-American. Walking up to Śrīla Prabhupāda's seat in the temple, Govinda dāsī's father asked, "Why do ya have to change my daughter's name? Why does she have to have an Indian name?"

Prabhupāda looked at him and then, with a mischievous gleam, looked at Mr. Patel, an Indian guest standing nearby with his family. "You don't like Indians?" he asked.

Everyone who heard Swamiji laughed—except for Govinda dāsī's father, who replied, "Well, yeah, they're all right. But why does Bonnie have to have a different name?"

"Because she has asked me to give her one," Śrīla Prabhupāda replied. "If you love her, you will like what she likes. Your daughter is happy. Why do you object?" The discussion ended there, and Govinda dāsī's father remained civil. Later he enjoyed taking *prasādam* with his daughter and son-in-law.

Govinda dāsī: *Gaurasundara and I set about reading the three volumes of Swamiji's* Śrīmad-Bhāgavatam. *And at the same time Swamiji had told me to paint a large canvas of Rādhā and Kṛṣṇa and a cow. So every day for the whole day I would paint, and Gaurasundara would read out loud from the* Śrīmad-Bhāgavatam—*one volume after another. We did this continuously for two months. During this time Swamiji also asked me to do a portrait of him standing before a background painting of Lord Caitanya dancing. Swamiji wanted it so that Lord Caitanya's foot would be touching his head. I tried. It was a pretty horrible painting, and yet he was happy with it.*

Prabhupāda's thoughtful followers felt that some of the candidates for initiation did not intend to fulfill the exclusive lifelong commitment a disciple owes to his *guru.* "Swamiji," they would say, "some of these people come only for their initiation. We have never seen them before, and we never see them again." Śrīla Prabhupāda replied that that was the risk he had to take. One day in a lecture in the temple, he explained that although the reactions for a disciple's past sins are removed at initiation, the spiritual master remains responsible until the disciple is delivered from the material world. Therefore, he said, Lord Caitanya warned that a *guru* should not accept many disciples.

One night in the temple during the question-and-answer session, a big, bearded fellow raised his hand and asked Prabhupāda, "Can I become initiated?"

The brash public request annoyed some of Prabhupāda's followers, but Prabhupāda was serene. "Yes," he replied. "But first you must answer two questions. Who is Kṛṣṇa?"

The boy thought for a moment and said, "Kṛṣṇa is God."

"Yes," Prabhupāda replied. "And who are you?"

Again the boy thought for a few moments and then replied, "I am the servant of God."

"Very good," Prabhupāda said. "Yes, you can be initiated tomorrow."

Śrīla Prabhupāda knew that it would be difficult for his Western disciples to stick to Kṛṣṇa consciousness and attain the goal of pure devotional service. All their lives they had had the worst of training, and despite their nominal Christianity and philosophical searching, most of them knew nothing of the science of God. They did not even know that illicit sex and meat-eating were wrong, although when he told them they accepted what he said. And they freely chanted Hare Kṛṣṇa. So how could he refuse them?

Of course, whether they would be able to persevere in Kṛṣṇa conscious-

Śrīla Prabhupāda in the San Francisco Rādhā-Kṛṣṇa temple, early 1967.

A few days prior to the Mantra-Rock Dance: Allen Ginsberg visiting Śrīla Prabhupāda in his room.

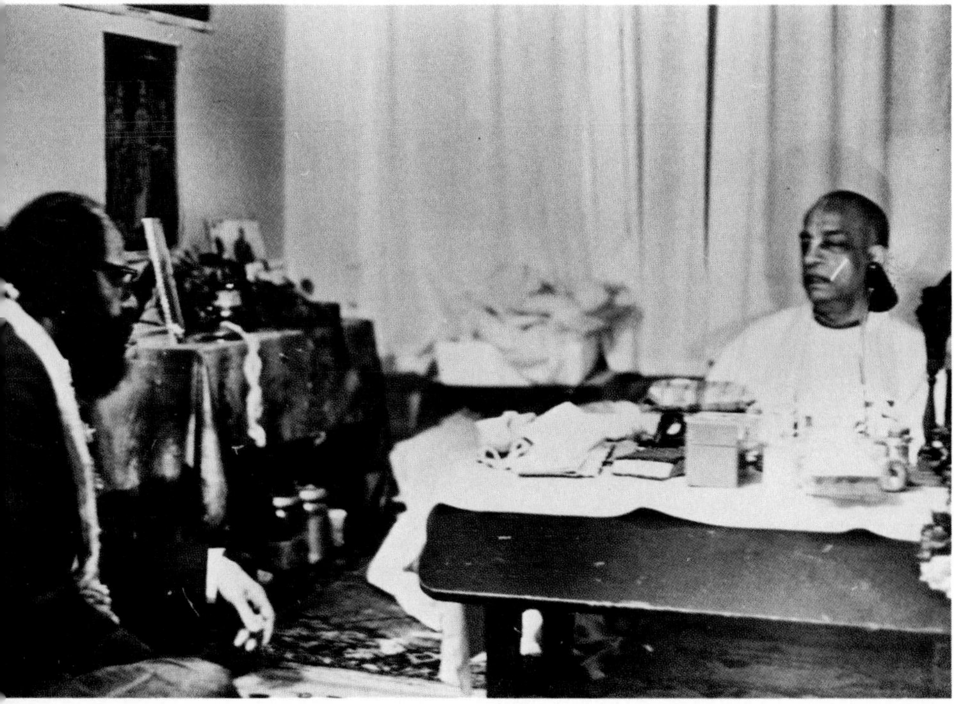

This poster advertised Śrīla Prabhupāda's appearance at the Mantra-Rock Dance.

Śrīla Prabhupāda at his desk applying *tilaka* (*below*), taking *prasādam* (*above right*), and reading (*below right*).

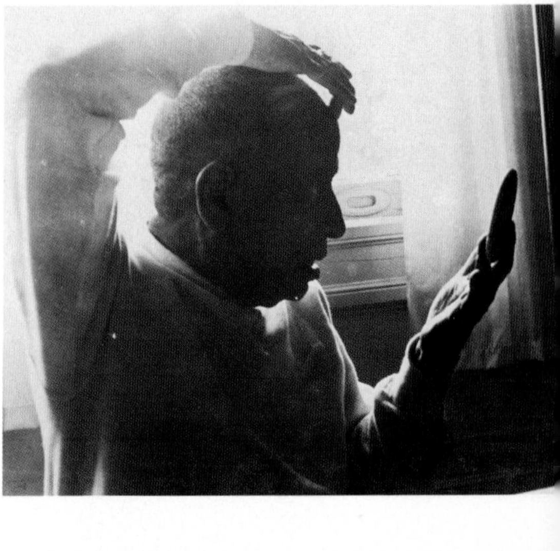

Śrīla Prabhupāda at his desk working.

Śrīla Prabhupāda entering the Rādhā-Kṛṣṇa temple at 513 Frederick Street.

A *kīrtana* in the Rādhā-Kṛṣṇa temple storefront.

Śrīla Prabhupāda leading *kīrtana* in the temple (*above right and right*).

In the early morning Śrīla Prabhupāda would walk with some of his disciples near Golden Gate Park's Stowe Lake.

Śrīla Prabhupāda chants in Golden Gate Park.

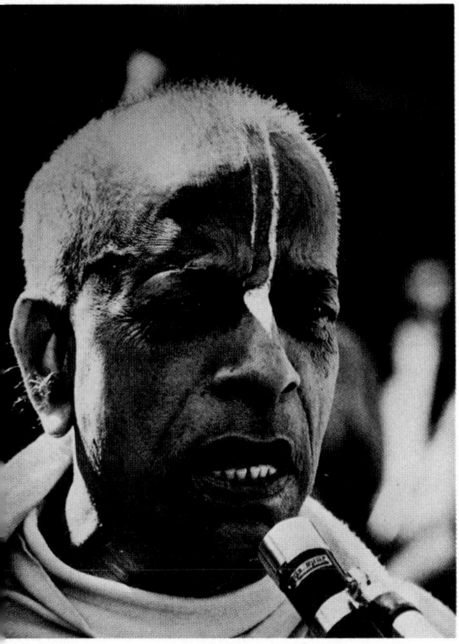

Vibro Champ
Amp
Fender

SLOW

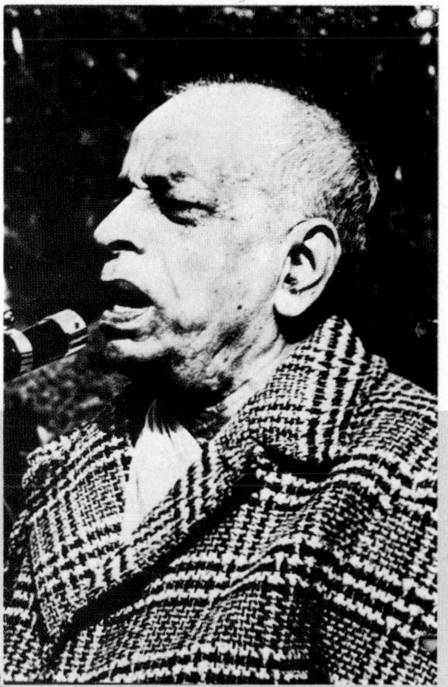

anting in Golden Gate Park (*continued*).

Śrīla Prabhupāda before the sea wall on a San Francisco beach.

In March of 1967 Śrīla Prabhupāda accompanied some of his San Francisco disciples to the beach for *kīrtana*.

Śrīla Prabhupāda leaving his apartment en route to New York, April 9, 1967.

Śrīla Prabhupāda and some of his New York disciples performing *kīrtana* at the Cosmic Love-In at the Village East Theater.

Śrīla Prabhupāda's house at Stinson Beach (*left*). Stinson Beach (*below*).

Śrīla Prabhupāda with some of his San Francisco disciples, in 1968.

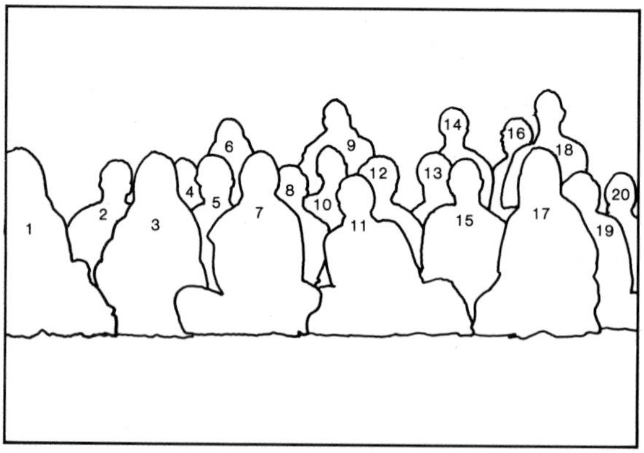

(1) Karuṇāmayī dāsī, (2) Jayānanda dāsa, (3) Yamunā dāsī, (4) Cidānanda dāsa, (5) Jīvānanda dāsa, (6) Govinda dāsī, (7) Harṣarāṇī dāsī, (8) Murāri dāsa, (9) Śrīla Prabhupāda, (10) Uddhava dāsa, (11) Līlāvatī dāsī, (12) Śyāmasundara dāsa, (13) Kārttikeya dāsa, (14) Gaurasundara dāsa, (15) Upendra dāsa, (16) Subala dāsa, (17) Mālatī dāsī, (18) Kṛṣṇa dāsa, (19) Gargamuni dāsa, (20) Śāradīyā dāsī.

Śrīla Prabhupāda leaving the San Francisco temple en route to India, July 22, 1967.

The deities of Jagannātha, Subhadrā, and Balarāma riding on their cart (a flatbed truck) during the first Ratha-yātrā festival in America, July 9, 1967.

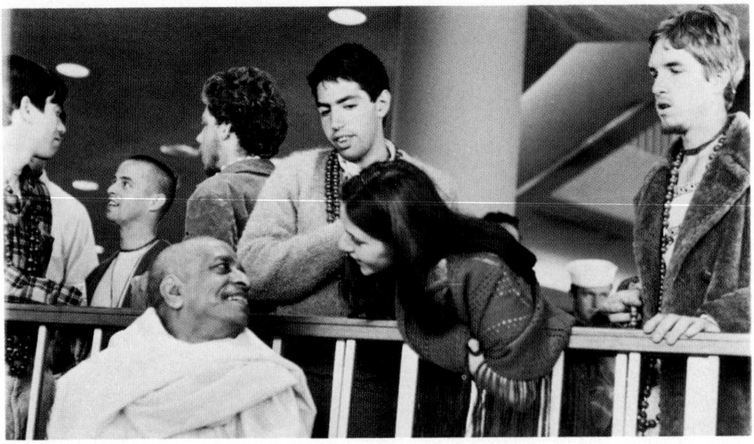

At the San Francisco airport, Jānakī steals Śrīla Prabhupāda's ticket.

Śrīla Prabhupāda's quarters at the Chippiwada Rādhā-Kṛṣṇa temple in Delhi.

Śrīla Prabhupāda and some of his disciples, just before Śrīla Prabhupāda and Kīrtanānanda depart for India, July 23, 1967.

AIR-INDIA

Śrīla Prabhupāda's quarters at the Rādhā-Dāmodara temple, Vṛndāvana, India.

Śrīla Prabhupāda at the home of his sister in Calcutta. Sitting to Śrīla Prabhupāda's right is Acyutānanda; Rāmānuja is sitting on his left. Prabhupāda's sister, Bhavatarini, is seated on the floor.

Śrīla Prabhupāda performing *kīrtana* with Acyutānanda, Rāmānuja, and members of the Mullik family in the courtyard of the Rādhā-Govinda temple, Calcutta (*far left and left*).

Śrīla Prabhupāda viewing Rādhā-Govinda, the Mullik family's Deities in Calcutta.

ness despite the ever-present attractions of *māyā* would be seen in time. Some would fall—that was the human tendency. But some would not. At least those who sincerely followed his instructions to chant Hare Kṛṣṇa and avoid sinful activities would be successful. He gave the example that a person could say that today's fresh food, if not properly used, would spoil in a few days. But if it is fresh now, to say that in the future it will be misused and therefore spoil is only a surmise. Yes, in the future anyone could fall down. But Prabhupāda took it as his responsibility to engage his disciples *now*. And he was giving them the methods which if followed would protect them from ever falling down.

Aside from Vedic standards, even by the standard of Swamiji's New York disciples the devotees in San Francisco were not very strict. Some continued going to the doughnut shop, eating food without offering it to Kṛṣṇa, and eating forbidden things like chocolate and commercial ice cream. Some even indulged in after-*kīrtana* cigarette breaks right outside the temple door. Some got initiated without knowing precisely what they had agreed to practice.

Kīrtanānanda: *The mood in San Francisco was a lot more relaxed. The devotees liked to go to the corner and have their coffee and doughnuts. But Prabhupāda loved the way so many people were coming. And he loved the program at the Avalon Ballroom. But there were two sides: those who strictly followed the rules and regulations and emphasized purity and then those who were not so concerned about strictness but who wanted to spread Kṛṣṇa consciousness as widely as possible. Swamiji was so great that he embraced both groups.*

Michael Wright, twenty-one, had recently gotten out of the Marine Corps, and Nancy Grindle, eighteen, was fresh out of high school. They had met in college in Los Angeles. Feeling frustrated and in need of something tangible to which to dedicate their lives, they had come to San Francisco to join the hippies. But they soon realized that they and the Haight-Ashbury hippies, whom they found dirty, aimless, unproductive, and lost in their search for identity, had little in common. So Nancy took a job as a secretary for the telephone company, and Michael found work as a lineman for the electric company. Then they heard about the Swami in Haight-Ashbury and decided to visit the temple.

It was an evening *kīrtana*, and the irrepressible hippies were twirling, twisting, and wiggling. Michael and Nancy took a seat on the floor off to one side, impressed more by the presence of the Swami than by the *kīrtana*. After the *kīrtana* Prabhupāda lectured, but they found his accent heavy. They wanted to understand—they had an innate feeling that he was saying something valuable—and yet the secrets seemed locked behind a thick accent and within a book written in another language. They decided to come back in the morning and try again.

At the morning program they found a smaller group: a dozen devotees with beads for chanting draped around their necks, a few street people. The *kīrtana* seemed sweeter and more mellow, and Michael and Nancy chanted and danced along with the devotees. Then Prabhupāda spoke, and this time they caught a few of his ideas. They stayed for breakfast and became friends with Mukunda and Jānakī, Sam and Marjorie (now Śyāmasundara and Mālatī), Yamunā and Guru dāsa, and Govinda dāsī and Gaurasundara. They liked the devotees and promised to come again that evening. Soon they were regularly attending the morning and evening programs, and Nancy, along with the other women, was attending Prabhupāda's weekend cooking classes.

Michael was open to Prabhupāda's ideas, but he had difficulty accepting the necessity of surrendering to a spiritual authority. His tendency was to reject authorities. But the more he thought about it, the more he saw that Prabhupāda was right—he had to accept an authority. He reasoned, "Every time I stop at a red light, I'm accepting an authority." And finally he concluded that to progress in spiritual understanding he would have to accept a spiritual authority. Yet because he didn't want to accept it, he was in a dilemma. Finally, after hearing Prabhupāda's lectures for two weeks, Michael decided to surrender to Prabhupāda's authority and try to become Kṛṣṇa conscious.

Michael: *Nancy and I decided to get married and become Swamiji's disciples and members of his Society. We told some of the devotees, "We would like to see Swamiji." They said, "Yes, just go up. He's on the third floor." We were a little surprised that there were no formalities required, and when we got to the door his servant Raṇacora let us in. We went in with our shoes on, so Raṇacora had to ask us to take them off.*

I didn't know exactly what to say to Swamiji—I was depending on my future wife to make the initial opening—but then I finally said, "We came because we would like to become members of your Kṛṣṇa conscious Society." *He said this was very nice. Then I said that actually the main reason we were there was that we wanted to be married. We knew that he performed marriage ceremonies and that it was part of the Society's requirements that couples had to be duly married before they could live together. Swamiji asked me if I liked the philosophy and if I had a job. My answer to both questions was yes. He explained that first of all we would have to be initiated, and then we could be married the next month.*

At their initiation Michael received the name Dayānanda, and Nancy received the name Nandarāṇī. Soon Prabhupāda performed their marriage.

Nandarāṇī: *We knew it would be a very big wedding. In Haight-Ashbury, whenever Swamiji would perform a wedding hundreds of people would come, and the temple would be filled. My parents were coming, and Dayānanda's parents were also coming.*

Swamiji said that it was proper that I cook. He said I should come to his apartment on the morning of the wedding and he would help me cook something for the wedding feast. So that morning I put on my best jeans and my best sweatshirt and my boots, and I went off to Swamiji's apartment. When I got upstairs I walked in with my boots on. Swamiji was sitting there in his rocking chair. He smiled at me and said, "Oh, you have come to cook." I said, "Yes." He sat there and looked at me—one of those long silent stares. He said, "First take off the boots."

After I took off my boots and my old leather jacket, Swamiji got up and went into the kitchen. He got a very large pot that had been burned so thick on the bottom that practically there was no metal visible. He handed it to me and said, "We want to boil milk in this pot. It has to be washed."

There wasn't a sink in Swamiji's kitchen, only a teeny round basin. So I went into the bathroom, put the pot in the bathtub, and rinsed it out. I assumed Swamiji didn't want the black off the bottom, because it was burned on. So I brought it back to him, and he said, "Oh, that is very clean, but just take off this little black on the bottom here."

I said okay and got a knife and crawled into the bathtub and started scrubbing the black off. I worked and worked and worked, and I scrubbed and scrubbed. I had cleanser up to my elbows, and I made a mess everywhere. I had gotten about half the black off—the rest seemed to be more or less an integral part of the bottom—so I took the pot back to Swamiji and said, "This is the best I can do. All of this is burned on." He said, "Yes, yes, you've done a wonderful job. Now just take off this black that's left."

So I went back into the bathtub and scrubbed and scrubbed and scrubbed. It was almost midday when I came out of the bathtub with all the black scrubbed off the bottom of that pot. He was so happy when I brought the pot in. It was sparkling. A big smile came on his face, and he said, "Oh, this is perfect." I was exhausted.

Then Swamiji welcomed me into his kitchen and taught me how to make rasagullās. *We boiled the milk, curdled it, and then I sat down and began rolling the curd into balls on a tray. As I rolled the balls I would put them in a little row along the tray. And every single ball had to be exactly the same size. Swamiji would take his thumb and first and second fingers and shoot the balls out of the row when they weren't the right size. And I would have to remake them until they were the right size. This went on until I had a full tray of balls all the same size.*

Then Swamiji showed me how to boil the balls of curd in sugar water. Mālatī, Jānakī, and I were cooking in the kitchen, and Swamiji was singing.

At one point, Swamiji stopped singing and asked me, "Do you know what your name means?" I couldn't even remember what my name was. He had told me at initiation, but because none of us used our devotee names, I couldn't remember what mine was. I said, "No, Swamiji, what does my name mean?" He said, "It means you are the mother of Kṛṣṇa." And he laughed loudly and went back to stirring the rasagullās. *I couldn't understand who Kṛṣṇa was, who in the world His mother would be, or how I was in any way related to her. But I was satisfied that Swamiji felt that I was somebody worth being.*

I finished cooking that afternoon about four o'clock, and then I went home to get dressed for the wedding. Although I had never worn anything but old dresses and jeans, Swamiji had suggested to the other ladies that they find a way to put me into a sārī *for the wedding. So we bought a piece of silk to use for a* sārī. *I went to Mālatī's house. She was going to try to help me put it on. I couldn't keep it on, so she had to sew it on me. Then they decorated me with flowers and took me to Swamiji and showed him. He was very happy. He said, "This is the way our women should always look. No more jeans and dresses. They should always wear* sārīs."

Actually, I looked a fright—I kept stumbling, and they had had to sew the cloth on me—but Swamiji thought it was wonderful. The cloth was all one color, so Swamiji said, "Next time you should buy cloth that has a little border on the bottom, so it's two colors. I like two colors better."

When we went downstairs to the wedding, Swamiji met my relatives. He spoke to them very politely. My mother cried a lot during the ceremony. I was very satisfied that she had been blessed by meeting Swamiji.

Steve Bohlert, age twenty, born and raised in New York and now living the hippie life in San Francisco, had read in *The Oracle* about Swami Bhaktivedanta's coming to San Francisco. The idea of meeting an Indian swami had interested him, and responding to a notice he had seen posted on Haight Street, he had gone along with Carolyn Gold, the woman he was living with, to the airport to meet Swami Bhaktivedanta. He and Carolyn had both gotten a blissful lift by chanting Hare Kṛṣṇa and seeing Prabhupāda, and they began regularly attending the lectures and *kīrtanas* at the temple. Steve decided he wanted to become like the Swami, so he and Carolyn went together to see Prabhupāda and request initiation. Speaking privately with Prabhupāda in his room, they discussed obedience to the spiritual master and becoming vegetarian. When Prabhupāda told them that they should either stop living together or get married, they said they would like to get married. An initiation date was set.

Prabhupāda asked Steve to shave his long hair and beard. "Why do you want me to shave my head?" Steve protested. "Kṛṣṇa had long hair, Rāma had long hair, Lord Caitanya had long hair, and Christ had long hair. Why should I shave my head?"

Prabhupāda smiled and replied, "Because now you are following me." There was a print on the wall of Sūradāsa, a Vaiṣṇava. "You should shave your head like that," Prabhupāda said, pointing to Sūradāsa.

"I don't think I'm ready to do that yet," Steve said.

"All right, you are still a young man. There is still time. But at least you should shave your face clean and cut your hair like a man."

On the morning of the initiation, Steve shaved off his beard and cut his hair around his ears so that it was short in front—but long in the back.

"How's this?" he asked.

"You should cut the back also," Prabhupāda replied. Steve agreed.

To Steve Prabhupāda gave the name Subala and to Carolyn the name Kṛṣṇā-devī. A few days later he performed their wedding.

Since each ceremony was another occasion for *kīrtana* and *prasādam* distribution, onlookers became attracted. And as the spiritual names and married couples increased with each ceremony, Prabhupāda's spiritual family grew. The harmonious atmosphere was like that of a small, loving family, and Prabhupāda dealt with his disciples intimately, without the formalities of an institution or hierarchy.

Disciples would approach him for various reasons, entering the little apartment to be alone with him as he sat on a mat before his makeshift desk in the morning sunlight. With men like Mukunda, Guru dāsa, and Śyāmasundara, Swamiji was a friend. With Jānakī and Govinda dāsī he was sometimes ready to be chided, almost like their naughty son, or he would be their grandfatherly teacher of cooking, the enforcer of the rules of kitchen cleanliness. And to all of them he was the unfathomable pure devotee of Lord Kṛṣṇa who knew the conclusions of all the Vedic scriptures and who knew beyond all doubts the truth of transmigration. He could answer all questions. He could lead them beyond material life, beyond Haight-Ashbury hippiedom and into the spiritual world with Kṛṣṇa.

* * *

It was seven P.M. Śrīla Prabhupāda entered the temple dressed in a saffron *dhotī*, an old turtleneck jersey under a cardigan sweater, and a *cādar* around his shoulders. Walking to the dais in the rear of the room, he took his seat. The dais, a cushion atop a redwood plank two feet off the floor, was supported between two redwood columns. In front of the dais stood a cloth-covered lectern with a bucket of cut flowers on either side. Covering the wall behind the dais was a typical Indian madras, with Haridāsa's crude painting of Lord Caitanya in *kīrtana* hanging against it.

Śrīla Prabhupāda picked up his *karatālas*, wrapped the cloth straps around his forefingers, and looked out at his young followers sitting cross-legged on the burgundy rug. The men were bearded, and almost everyone wore long hair, beads, exotic clothing, and trinkets. The bulbs hanging from the ceiling diffused their light through Japanese paper lanterns, and Navaho "God's-eye" symbols dangled from strings. Prabhupāda began the ringing one-two-*three* rhythm, and Śyāmasundara began pumping the harmonium. Although the harmonium was a simple instrument—a miniature piano keyboard to be played with the right hand and a bellows to be pumped with the left hand—no one in the Frederick Street storefront knew how to play it, so it became simply "the drone." Another important *kīrtana* instrument, the two-headed *mṛdaṅga* from India, was meant for intricate rhythmic accompaniments, but even Mukunda could play it only very simply, matching the one-two-*three* of Prabhupāda's *karatālas.*

There were other instruments on hand: a kettledrum (the pride of the temple), Hayagrīva's old cornet, a few conchshells, and a horn Hayagrīva had made by shellacking a piece of kelp he had found on the beach. Some guests had brought their own flutes, pipes, and bongos. But for now they let their instruments remain still and clapped to Prabhupāda's rhythm as he sang the evening prayers.

Prabhupāda's Sanskrit hymn praised the Vaiṣṇava spiritual masters; for each great devotee in the disciplic succession, he sang a specific prayer. First he chanted the poetic description of the transcendental qualities of Śrīla Bhaktisiddhānta Sarasvatī, then Gaurakiśora dāsa Bābājī, Bhaktivinoda Ṭhākura—one after another. One prayer described Śrīla Bhaktisiddhānta as "the deliverer of the fallen souls," and another praised Gaurakiśora dāsa Bābājī as "renunciation personified, always merged in the feeling of separation and intense love for Kṛṣṇa." Śrīla Prabhupāda sang of Lord Caitanya, the golden-complexioned Supreme Personality of Godhead who distributed pure love of Kṛṣṇa. And he sang of Lord Kṛṣṇa, the ocean of mercy, the friend of the distressed, the source of creation. As Prabhupāda became absorbed in the *bhajana,* his body trembled with ecstatic emotion. The group on the floor sat swaying from side to side, watching him, his eyes closed in meditation, his delicate, practiced fingers expertly playing the cymbals. They heard the heartfelt minor moods and tones of his voice, unlike anything they had heard before.

Then he began the familiar *mantra* they had come to hear—Hare Kṛṣṇa, Hare Kṛṣṇa, Kṛṣṇa Kṛṣṇa, Hare Hare—and immediately they joined him. The horns and drums sounded, and soon all the other instrument players joined in. Gradually, a few at a time, members of the audience rose to their feet and began to dance. Prabhupāda's followers stood and began stepping from side to side as he had shown them, sometimes raising their hands in the air. Others moved as they pleased. Occasionally opening his eyes and glancing around, Prabhupāda sat firmly, chanting, though his head and body were trembling.

After twenty minutes many of the young dancers were leaping, jumping, and perspiring, as Prabhupāda continued to sing, leading the dancers by the beat of his *karatālas.* His eyes were closed, yet he controlled the entire wild congregation, playing his *karatālas* loudly. The chanting and dancing continued, and Prabhupāda approved.

The *kīrtana* of these hippies was different from the chanting of Indian *brāhmaṇas,* but Prabhupāda didn't mind—his standard was devotion. In his Rādhā-Kṛṣṇa temple, whatever *he* accepted, Kṛṣṇa accepted; this was his offering to Kṛṣṇa through his spiritual master, Bhaktisiddhānta Sarasvatī. Prabhupāda was absolutely confident. Even if his young devotees didn't know how to play the harmonium keyboard or the *mṛdaṅga,* even if they didn't know that congregational *kīrtana* should be done not in constant unison (as they were doing) but responsively, and even if they didn't know how to honor the *guru*—still, because they were chanting and dancing, he encouraged them and nodded to them: "Yes."

Wild elements were there, of course—people whose minds and intentions were far away in some chemically induced fantasy—yet the mood was dominated by Śrīla Prabhupāda's followers, who danced with arms upraised and watched their leader carefully. Although in many ways they were still like hippies, they were Swamiji's disciples, and they wanted to please him and follow his instructions; they wanted to attain Kṛṣṇa consciousness. For all the varied punctuation of horns and timpani, the *kīrtana* remained sweet; Hayagrīva even played his cornet in tune, and only during every other *mantra.*

Śrīla Prabhupāda knew that some aspects of the *kīrtana* were wrong or below standard, but he accepted the offering—and not awkwardly, but lovingly. He simply wanted these American boys and girls to chant. That they dressed irregularly, jumped too savagely, or had the wrong philosophy did not overconcern him. These boys and girls were chanting Hare

Kṛṣṇa; so at least for the present, they were pure. The hippies knew that, too. And they loved it.

Just as in Jānakī's dream, Śrīla Prabhupāda's pleasure was to see the whole world engaged in *kīrtana.* Somehow or other, he would say, people should be engaged in Kṛṣṇa consciousness. And this was the instruction of Lord Caitanya's chief follower, Rūpa Gosvāmī, who had written, *tasmāt kenāpy upāyena manaḥ kṛṣṇe niveśayet. . . :* "Somehow or other, fix the mind on Kṛṣṇa; the rules and regulations can come later."

Inherent in this attitude of Śrīla Prabhupāda's and Śrīla Rūpa Gosvāmī's was a strong conviction about the purifying force of the holy name; if engaged in chanting Hare Kṛṣṇa, even the most fallen person could gradually become a saintly devotee. Śrīla Prabhupāda would often quote a verse from *Śrīmad-Bhāgavatam* affirming that persons addicted to sinful acts could be purified by taking shelter of the devotees of the Lord. He knew that every Haight-Ashbury hippie was eligible to receive the mercy of the holy name, and he saw it as his duty to his spiritual master to distribute the gift of Kṛṣṇa consciousness freely, rejecting no one. Yet while living amongst these *mlecchas,* he required a certain standard of behavior, and he was adamant about preserving the purity of his Kṛṣṇa consciousness Society.

For example, if he were going to distribute free food to the public, it could not be ordinary food but must be *prasādam,* food offered to Kṛṣṇa. Feeding hungry people was futile unless they were given *prasādam* and the chance of liberation from birth and death. And although in the *kīrtanas* he allowed openness and free expression and welcomed the wildest participation, the transcendental sound of the holy name had to dominate. He never allowed the *kīrtana* to degenerate into mere beating on drums or chanting of any old words, nor could anyone in the group become so crazy that others wouldn't be able to hear or take part in congregational chanting.

In his attempts to "somehow or other" get these young people chanting Hare Kṛṣṇa, Prabhupāda instinctively knew what to allow and what not to allow. He was the master, and his new disciples followed him when he permitted an egoistic, sensual dancer to jump around the temple or a drugged madman to argue with him in a question-and-answer period. When a person was too disruptive, Prabhupāda was not afraid to stop him. But stopping was rare. The main thing was giving.

The *kīrtana* lasted more than an hour, as the chanters joined hands and danced around the room and incense poured out the front door.

* * *

The morning and evening *kīrtanas* had already made the Rādhā-Kṛṣṇa temple popular in Haight-Ashbury, but when the devotees began serving a daily free lunch, the temple became an integral part of the community. Prabhupāda told his disciples simply to cook and distribute *prasādam*—that would be their only activity during the day. In the morning they would cook, and at noon they would feed everyone who came—sometimes 150 to 200 hippies from the streets of Haight-Ashbury.

Before the morning *kīrtana*, the girls would put oatmeal on the stove, and by breakfast there would be a roomful of hippies, most of whom had been up all night. The cereal and fruit was for some the first solid food in days.

But the main program was the lunch. Mālatī would go out and shop, getting donations whenever possible, for whole-wheat flour, garbanzo flour, split peas, rice, and whatever vegetables were cheap or free: potatoes, carrots, turnips, rutabagas, beets. Then every day the cooks would prepare spiced mashed potatoes, buttered *capātīs*, split-pea *dāl*, and a vegetable dish—for two hundred people. The lunch program was possible because many merchants were willing to donate to the recognized cause of feeding hippies.

Harṣarāṇī: *The lunch program attracted a lot of the Hippie Hill crowd, who obviously wanted food. They were really hungry. And there were other people who would come also, people who were working with the temple but weren't initiated. The record player would be playing the Swamiji's record. It was a nice, family atmosphere.*

Haridāsa: *It was taken outside too, outside the front. But the main food was served inside. It was amazing. The people would just all huddle together, and we would really line them wall to wall. A lot of them would simply eat and leave. Other stores along Haight-Ashbury were selling everything from beads to rock records, but our store was different, because we weren't selling anything—we were giving it away.*

And we were welcoming everybody. We were providing a kind of refuge from the tumult and madness of the scene. So it was in that sense a hospital, and I think a lot of people were helped and maybe even saved. I don't mean only their souls—I mean their minds and bodies were saved, because of what was going on in the streets that they just simply couldn't handle. I'm talking about overdoses of drugs, people who were plain lost and needed comforting and who sort of wandered or staggered into the temple.

Some of them stayed and became devotees, and some just took prasādam *and left. Daily we had unusual incidents, and Swamiji witnessed it and took part in it. The lunch program was his idea.*

Mukunda: *The Salvation Army came in one day for lunch. They just unloaded a whole truckload of people on us—about thirty or forty.*

Larry Shippen: *Some of the community of loose people cynically took advantage of the free food. They didn't appreciate the Swami, because they said he was, in his own way, an orthodox minister and they were much more interested in being unorthodox. It was a fairly cynical thing.*

Those who were more interested and had questions—the spiritual seekers—would visit Swamiji in his room. Many of them would come in complete anxiety over the war in Vietnam or whatever was going on—trouble with the law, bad experiences on drugs, a falling out with school or family.

There was much public concern about the huge influx of youth into San Francisco, a situation that was creating an almost uncontrollable social problem. Police and social welfare workers were worried about health problems and poor living conditions, especially in Haight-Ashbury. Some middle-class people feared a complete hippie takeover. The local authorities welcomed the service offered by Swami Bhaktivedanta's temple, and when civic leaders in Haight-Ashbury talked of forming a council to deal with the crisis, they requested Swami Bhaktivedanta to take part. He agreed, but lost interest after the first meeting. No one seemed seriously interested in hearing his solution.

Master Subramuniya: *A lot of responsible citizens in San Francisco were very happy that Swami Bhaktivedanta was working amongst the young people. The young people at that time were searching and needed somebody of a very high caliber who would take an interest in them and who would say, "You should do this, and you should not do that." The consensus was that no one could tell the young people what to do, because they were completely out of hand with drugs and so forth. But Swamiji told them what to do, and they did it. And everyone was appreciative, especially the young people.*

Harṣarāṇī: *Just from a medical standpoint, doctors didn't know what to do with people on LSD. The police and the free clinics in the area couldn't handle the overload of people taking LSD. The police saw Swamiji as a certain refuge.*

Michael Bowen: *Bhaktivedanta had an amazing ability through devotion to get people off drugs, especially speed, heroin, burn-out LSD cases—all of that.*

Haridāsa: *The police used to come with their paddy wagons through the park in the early hours of the morning and pick up runaway teenagers sleeping in the park. The police would round them up and try to send them back home. The hippies needed all the help they could get, and they knew it. And the Rādhā-Kṛṣṇa temple was certainly a kind of spiritual haven. Kids sensed it. They were running, living on the streets, no place where they could go, where they could rest, where people weren't going to hurt them. A lot of kids would literally fall into the temple. I think it saved a lot of lives; there might have been a lot more casualties if it hadn't been for Hare Kṛṣṇa. It was like opening a temple in a battlefield. It was the hardest place to do it, but it was the place where it was most needed. Although the Swami had no precedents for dealing with any of this, he applied the chanting with miraculous results. The chanting was wonderful. It worked.*

Śrīla Prabhupāda knew that only Kṛṣṇa consciousness could help. Others had their remedies, but Prabhupāda considered them mere patchwork. He knew that ignorantly identifying the self with the body was the real cause of suffering. How could someone help himself, what to speak of others, if he didn't know who he was, if he didn't know that the body was only a covering of the real self, the spirit soul, which could be happy only in his original nature as an eternal servant of Kṛṣṇa?

Understanding that Lord Kṛṣṇa considered anyone who approached Him a virtuous person and that even a little devotional service would never be lost and could save a person at the time of death, Śrīla Prabhupāda had opened his door to everyone, even the most abject runaway. But for a lost soul to fully receive the balm of Kṛṣṇa consciousness, he would first have to stay awhile and chant, inquire, listen, and follow.

As Allen Ginsberg had advised five thousand hippies at the Avalon, the early-morning *kīrtana* at the temple provided a vital community service for those who were coming down from LSD and wanted "to stabilize their consciousness on reentry." Allen himself sometimes dropped by in the morning with acquaintances with whom he had stayed up all night.

Allen Ginsberg: *At six-thirty in the morning we went over to Swami Bhaktivedanta's space station for some chanting and a little Kṛṣṇa consciousness. There were about thirty or forty people there, all chanting Hare Kṛṣṇa to this new tune they've made up, just for mornings. One kid got a little freaked out by the scene at first, but then he relaxed, and afterwards he told me, "You know, at first I thought: What* is *this? But then suddenly I realized I was just not grooving with where I was. I wasn't being where I was."*

On occasion, the "reentries" would come flying in out of control for crash landings in the middle of the night. One morning at two A.M. the boys sleeping in the storefront were awakened by a pounding at the door, screaming, and police lights. When they opened the door, a young hippie with wild red hair and beard plunged in, crying, "Oh, Kṛṣṇa, Kṛṣṇa! Oh, help me! Oh, don't let them get me. Oh, for God's sake, help!"

A policeman stuck his head in the door and smiled. "We decided to bring him by here," he said, "because we thought maybe you guys could help him."

"I'm not comfortable in this body!" the boy screamed as the policeman shut the door. The boy began chanting furiously and turned white, sweating profusely in terror. Swamiji's boys spent the rest of the early morning consoling him and chanting with him until the Swami came down for *kīrtana* and class.

The devotees often sent distressed young people to Swamiji with their problems. And they allowed almost anyone to see Swamiji and take up his valuable time. While walking around San Francisco, Ravīndra-svarūpa once met a man who claimed to have seen people from Mars in his tent when he had been stationed in Vietnam. The man, who had just been discharged from an army hospital, said that the Martians had talked to him. Ravīndra-svarūpa told him about Swamiji's book *Easy Journey to Other Planets*, which verified the idea of life on other planets, and he suggested that the Swami could probably tell him more about the people from Mars. So the man visited the Swami up in his apartment. "Yes," Swamiji answered, "there are Martians."

Gradually, Prabhupāda's followers became more considerate of their spiritual master and began protecting him from persons they thought might be undesirable. One such undesirable was Rabbit, perhaps the dirtiest hippie in Haight-Ashbury. Rabbit's hair was always disheveled, dirty, and even filled with lice. His clothes were ragged and filthy, and his dirt-caked body stank. He wanted to meet Prabhupāda, but the devotees refused, not wanting to defile Prabhupāda's room with Rabbit's nasty, stinking presence. One night after the lecture, however, Rabbit waited outside the temple door. As Prabhupāda approached, Rabbit asked, "May I come up and see you?" Prabhupāda agreed.

As for challengers, almost every night someone would come to argue with Prabhupāda. One man came regularly with prepared arguments from a philosophy book, from which he would read aloud. Prabhupāda would defeat him, and the man would go home, prepare another argument, and come back again with his book. One night, after the man had presented his challenge, Prabhupāda simply looked at him without bothering to reply. Prabhupāda's neglect was another defeat for the man, who got up and left.

Israel, like Rabbit, was another well-known Haight-Ashbury character. He had a long ponytail and often played the trumpet during *kīrtana.* After one of Prabhupāda's evening lectures, Israel challenged, "This chanting may be nice, but what will it do for the world? What will it do for humanity?"

Prabhupāda replied, "Are you not in the world? If you like it, why will others not like it? So you chant loudly."

A mustached man standing at the back of the room asked, "Are you Allen Ginsberg's *guru*?" Many of the devotees knew that the question was loaded and that to answer either yes or no would be difficult.

Śrīla Prabhupāda replied, "I am nobody's *guru.* I am everybody's servant." To the devotees, the whole exchange became transcendental due to Swamiji's reply. Swamiji had not simply given a clever response; he had answered out of a deep, natural humility.

One morning a couple attended the lecture, a woman carrying a child and a man wearing a backpack. During the question-and-answer period the man asked, "What about my mind?" Prabhupāda gave him philosophical replies, but the man kept repeating, "What about my mind? What about my mind?"

With a pleading, compassionate look, Prabhupāda said, "I have no other medicine. Please chant this Hare Kṛṣṇa. I have no other explanation. I have no other answer."

But the man kept talking about his mind. Finally, one of the women devotees interrupted and said, "Just do what he says. Just try it." And Prabhupāda picked up his *karatālas* and began *kīrtana.*

One evening a boy burst into a lecture exclaiming that a riot was gathering on Haight Street. The Swami should come immediately, address the crowd, and calm everyone down. Mukunda explained that it wasn't necessary for Swamiji to go; others could help. The boy just stared at Prabhupāda as if giving an ultimatum: unless Swamiji came immediately, there would be a riot, and Swamiji would be to blame. Prabhupāda spoke as if preparing to do what the boy wanted: "Yes, I am prepared." But nobody went, and there was no riot.

Usually during the *kīrtana* at least one dancer would carry on in a narcissistic, egoistic way, occasionally becoming lewd to the point where Prabhupāda would ask the person to stop. One evening, before Śrīla Prabhupāda had come down from his apartment, a girl in a miniskirt began writhing and gyrating in the temple during *kīrtana.* When one of the devotees went upstairs and told Prabhupāda, he replied, "That's all right. Let her use her energy for Kṛṣṇa. I'm coming soon, and I will see for myself." When Prabhupāda arrived and started another *kīrtana,* the girl, who was very skinny, again began to wriggle and gyrate. Prabhupāda opened his eyes and saw her; he frowned and glanced at some of his disciples, indicating his displeasure. Taking the girl aside, one of the women escorted her out. A few minutes later the girl returned, wearing slacks and dancing in a more reserved style.

Prabhupāda was sitting on his dais, lecturing to a full house, when a fat girl who had been sitting on the window seat suddenly stood up and began hollering at him. "Are you just going to sit there?" she yelled.

"What are you going to do now? Come on! Aren't you going to say something? What are you going to do? *Who are* you?" Her action was so sudden and her speech so violent that no one in the temple responded. Unangered, Prabhupāda sat very quietly. He appeared hurt. Only the devotees sitting closest to him heard him say softly, as if to himself, "It is the darkest of darkness."

Another night while Prabhupāda was lecturing, a boy came up and sat on the dais beside him. The boy faced out toward the audience and interrupted Prabhupāda: "I would like to say something now."

Prabhupāda politely said, "Wait until after the class. Then we have questions."

The boy waited for a few minutes, still sitting on the dais, and Prabhupāda continued to lecture. But again the boy interrupted: "I got something to say. I want to say what I have to say now." The devotees in the audience looked up, astonished, thinking that Swamiji would handle the matter and not wanting to cause a disturbance. None of them did anything; they simply sat while the boy began talking incoherently.

Then Prabhupāda picked up his *karatālas:* "All right, let us have *kīrtana.*" The boy sat in the same place throughout the *kīrtana,* looking crazily, sometimes menacingly, at Prabhupāda. After half an hour the *kīrtana* stopped.

Prabhupāda cut an apple into small pieces, as was his custom. He then placed the paring knife and a piece of apple in his right hand and held his hand out to the boy. The boy looked at Prabhupada, then down at the apple and knife. The room became silent. Prabhupāda sat motionless, smiling slightly at the boy. After a long, tense moment, the boy reached out. A sigh rose from the audience as the boy chose the piece of apple from Prabhupāda's open hand.

Haridāsa: *I used to watch how Swamiji would handle things. It wasn't easy. To me, that was a real test of his powers and understanding—how to handle these people, not to alienate or antagonize or stir them up to create more trouble. He would turn their energy so that before they knew it they were calm, like when you pat a baby and it stops crying. Swamiji had a way of doing that with words, with the intonation of his voice, with his patience to let them carry on for a certain period of time, let them work it out, act it out even. I guess he realized that the devotees just couldn't say, "Listen, when you come to the temple you can't behave this way." It was a delicate situation there.*

Often someone would say, "I am God." They would get an insight or hallucination from their drugs. They would try to steal the spotlight. They wanted to be heard, and you could feel an anger against the Swami from people like that. Sometimes they would speak inspired and poetic for a while, but they couldn't sustain it, and their speech would become gibberish. And the Swami was not one to simply pacify people. He wasn't going to coddle them. He would say, "What do you mean? If you are God, then you have to be all-knowing. You have to have the attributes of God. Are you omniscient and omnipotent?" He would then name all the characteristics that one would have to have to be an avatāra, *to be God. He would rationally prove the person wrong. He had superior knowledge, and he would rationally explain to them, "If you are God, can you do this? Do you have this power?"*

Sometimes people would take it as a challenge and would try to have a verbal battle with the Swami. The audience's attention would then swing to the disturbing individual, the person who was grabbing the spotlight. Sometimes it was very difficult. I used to sit there and wonder, "How is he going to handle this guy? This one is really a problem." But Swamiji was hard to defeat. Even if he couldn't convince the person, he convinced the other people in the crowd so that the energy of the room would change and would tend to quiet the person. Swamiji would win the audience by showing them that this person didn't know what he was talking about. And the person would feel the vibrations of the room change, that the audience was no longer listening or believing his spiel, and so the person would shut up.

So Swamiji would remove the audience rather than the person. He would do it without crushing the person. He would do it by superior intelligence, but also with a lot of compassion. When I saw him do these things, then I realized he was a great teacher and a great human being. He had the sensitivity not to injure a person physically or emotionally, so that when the person sat down and shut up, he wouldn't be doing it in defeat or anger—he wouldn't be hurt. He would just be outwitted by the Swami.

Even while translating in the privacy of his room, Śrīla Prabhupāda was interrupted by disturbances. Once police cars and ambulances—sirens screaming, lights flashing—converged beneath his window after the Hell's Angels had started a fight in the Diggers' store, in the next building.

On another occasion, about one-thirty A.M., while Prabhupāda was dictating *Teachings of Lord Caitanya*, a girl repeatedly knocked and called at Prabhupāda's door. At first he ignored the interruption. Since his arrival in San Francisco, he had completed many pages for this important book. Lord Caitanya's discussions with Rūpa Gosvāmī and Sanātana Gosvāmī, Rāmānanda Rāya, and others explored many Kṛṣṇa conscious topics mentioned only briefly in *Bhagavad-gītā*. In the West almost no one knew about these teachings of Lord Caitanya, and now Śrīla Prabhupāda intended to compile these teachings in one volume, providing the most complete presentation of *bhakti-yoga* ever introduced in English. Such a book would give great substance to the Kṛṣṇa consciousness movement. But now his solitary concentration was being interrupted by a knocking at his door and a woman's voice calling.

Getting up from his desk, Prabhupāda went to the front room but did not open the door: "Who is there?"

A young woman answered, "I want to speak to you."

"Come back later in the morning," Prabhupāda told her.

He knew that in San Francisco, just as in New York, he would not always be able to write peacefully. Preaching in America meant having to tolerate just this—a crazy call in the middle of the night, tearing one away from ecstatic concentration on the pastimes of Lord Caitanya. The lost souls of Haight-Ashbury—with their illusions of knowledge, their cries for help, their arrogant challenges—pulled his attention away from his mission of translating and commenting on the scriptures. Now, alone in his apartment, speaking through the locked door, Prabhupāda told his intruder that he had work to do and that she should go away. He promised he would see her later that day.

He was ready to speak with the hippies all day, but the early morning hours were the special time for his literary work. Preaching face to face to the conditioned souls was important; he had come here to preach. But he had picked these early hours to speak intimately to the whole world through his books—without disturbance.

The girl, however, continued pounding and calling, until Prabhupāda finally opened the door. There, standing in the hallway, he saw a teenage hippie with a glassy stare and deranged appearance. He asked her what she wanted. She remained tensely silent. "Speak," he told her. She stepped into his room. He saw her helpless—a victim in the ocean of *māyā*—and he asked her repeatedly what she wanted. Finally, the girl stared at him with widened eyes and exclaimed, *"Looook! Maha ula!"*

Prabhupāda decided to awaken Mukunda, who lived down the hall. He stepped barefoot into the hallway. The girl followed, shutting the self-locking door behind her. Now he was locked out of his apartment. She continued to stare at him defiantly, in the bare, unfriendly surroundings of a corridor of locked doors at one in the morning.

This was why the *bābājīs* of Vṛndāvana stayed in their little cottages chanting the holy name: to avoid being bothered by ungodly people. (The *bābājīs,* of course, never even dreamed of these bizarre intrusions from the psychedelic San Francisco night.)

At Mukunda's door Prabhupāda began pounding and calling loudly, "Mukunda! Mukunda!" Mukunda awoke and opened the door, astonished to see his spiritual master standing barefoot in the hallway, a wild-eyed young girl standing a few feet behind. Yet Prabhupāda remained grave and aloof. "This girl came to my door," he began. He explained briefly what had happened and what should now be done. He did not appear angry or harassed by the girl, and he indicated that Mukunda should deal kindly with her.

Mukunda remembered when Prabhupāda had been driven out of his New York Bowery loft by his roommate David Allen, who had gone mad on LSD. Then also, Prabhupāda had remained coolheaded though caught by a dangerous and awkward circumstance. Mukunda went downstairs and awoke Hayagrīva, who had a key to Prabhupāda's apartment. Śrīla Prabhupāda then returned to his room and to his dictation of *Teachings of Lord Caitanya.*

Mukunda saw the girl down to the street and admonished her not to bother an elderly gentleman like the Swami at such an hour. Staring at Mukunda, she said, "You're not ready," and walked away.

At seven o'clock, when Prabhupāda came down to the temple for the morning class, the girl was sitting in the audience in a calmer state of mind. She apologized. Later in the day, Prabhupāda repeated the story in good humor, recounting how he had several times asked the girl to speak. He opened his eyes wide, imitating her expression, and said, "Look! *Maha ula*!" and laughed.

* * *

"We shall go for a walk at six-thirty," Śrīla Prabhupāda said one morning. "You can drive me to the park."

Several devotees accompanied him to Golden Gate Park's Stowe Lake. They knew the park well and led Śrīla Prabhupāda on a scenic walk around the lake, over a bridge, through forest-enclosed paths, and across a small rivulet, hoping to please him with nature's beauty.

As he walked, striding quickly, he would point to a tree or stop to examine a flower. "What is this tree?" he would ask. "What is this flower?" although his disciples were usually at a loss to answer. "When Caitanya Mahāprabhu passed through the forest of Vṛndāvana," he said, "all the plants, trees, and creepers were delighted to see Him and rejoiced in His presence. The plant life there is like that in the spiritual sky—fully conscious."

"And these trees, Swamiji—how conscious are they?"

"Oh, the spirit soul is there," Prabhupāda said, "but the consciousness has been arrested temporarily. Perception is more limited."

Whatever Prabhupāda saw he saw through the eyes of scripture, and his comments on the most ordinary things were full of transcendental instruction. As he walked, he reflected aloud, "Those who want to see God must first have the qualifications to see God. They must be purified. Just like the cloud is now covering the sun. They say, 'Oh, the sun is not out,' but the sun is there. Only our eyes are covered."

Like tour guides the boys led Prabhupāda to the more picturesque areas. They came upon swans gliding on the lake. "*Śrīmad-Bhāgavatam*," Prabhupāda said, "compares devotees to swans, and literature about Lord Kṛṣṇa to beautiful, clear lakes." The nondevotees, he said, were like crows attracted by the rubbish of mundane topics. Walking over a gravel path, he stopped and drew their attention: "Look at the pebbles. As many pebbles there are, there are that many universes. And in each universe there are innumerable living entities."

The devotees delighted in bringing Swamiji to a rhododendron glen, its big bushes completely covered with white and pink flowers. And they felt privileged to see Kṛṣṇa through Swamiji's eyes.

The next morning, when Prabhupāda again wanted to go to the park, more devotees accompanied him; they had heard from the others how Swamiji had displayed a different mood while walking. Again the boys were ready to lead him along new trails around the lake; but without announcing a change in plans, he walked up and down the macadam road beside the lake.

Prabhupāda and his followers came upon a flock of sleeping ducks. Awakened by the sound of people walking on the path, the ducks began quacking, moving their wings, and walking away. When a few devotees hurried ahead to shoo the ducks from Prabhupāda's path, the ducks began making sounds of grouching and grumbling. "Move, you ducks," one devotee said. "You're disturbing Swamiji." Prabhupāda said quietly, "As we are thinking they are disturbing us, they are thinking we are disturbing them."

Prabhupāda stopped beneath a large tree and pointed to some bird droppings on the ground. "What does this mean?" he asked, turning to a new boy who stood beside him. Prabhupāda's face was serious. The boy blushed. "I . . . *uh* . . . I don't know what it means." Prabhupāda remained thoughtful, waiting for an explanation. The devotees gathered around him. Looking intently down at the bird droppings, the boy thought the Swami might be expecting him to decipher some hidden meaning in the pattern of the droppings, the way people read the future in tea leaves. He felt he should say something: "It's the . . . *uh* . . . excreta, the defecations of . . . *uh* . . . birds." Prabhupāda smiled and turned toward the others for an answer. They were silent.

"It means," said Prabhupāda, "that these birds [he pronounced the word "*bards*"] have lived in the same tree for more than two weeks." He laughed. "Even the birds are attached to their apartments."

As they passed the shuffleboard courts and the old men playing checkers, Prabhupāda stopped and turned to the boys. "Just see," he said. "Old people in this country do not know what to do. So they play like children, wasting their last days, which should be meant for developing Kṛṣṇa consciousness. Their children are grown and gone away, so this is a natural time for spiritual cultivation. But no. They get some cat or dog, and instead of serving God, they serve dog. It is most unfortunate. But they will not listen. Their ways are set. Therefore we are speaking to the youth, who are searching."

When Prabhupāda and the boys passed a sloping green lawn just off Kezar Drive, the boys pointed out that this was the famous Hippie Hill. In the early morning the gently sloping hill and the big quiet meadow surrounded by eucalyptuses and oaks were silent and still. But in a few hours hundreds of hippies would gather here to lounge on the grass, meet friends, and get high. Prabhupāda advised the boys to come here and hold *kīrtanas*.

CHAPTER TWO

The Price Affair

Swamiji's disciples in New York were surprised to find that they could still carry on in his absence. At first, rising early, going to the storefront, and holding the morning *kīrtana* and class had been difficult. Without Swamiji everything had seemed empty. But he had taught them what to do, and gradually they realized that they should simply follow what he had shown them, or even imitate, as a child imitates his parents.

And it worked. At first they had been too shy to speak or lead the *kīrtana*, so they had played tapes of Swamiji's *kīrtanas* and classes. But when the evenings came and guests attended the temple, the devotees felt compelled to give "live" classes. Rāya Rāma, Brahmānanda, Satsvarūpa, and Rūpānuga took turns giving brief talks and even answering challenging questions from the same Lower East Side audiences that Śrīla Prabhupāda had lion-tamed for six months. Things were shaky and lacking without him, and yet in a sense he was still present. And the devotees found that everything—the chanting, the cooking, the taking of *prasādam*, the preaching—could still go on.

On January 19, just three days after his arrival in San Francisco, Prabhupāda had written back to his New York disciples. They were his spiritual children and were very dear to him. Although far from his homeland, India, he hadn't thought first of writing to anyone there. Since he was a *sannyāsī*, he had no interest in writing to any family members or relatives. And as for writing to his Godbrothers, there was not much importance in that, since they had repeatedly shown their reluctance to help. But being in a new city among new faces and having met with an initial fanfare of success, Prabhupāda had wanted to share the news with those most eager to hear from him. He had also wanted to reassure his disciples whom, after only a few months of training, he was expecting to conduct the Kṛṣṇa consciousness movement in New York.

> My dear Brahmananda
> Hayagriva
> Kirtanananda
> Satsvarupa
> Gargamuni
> Acyutananda
> Jadurani
>
> Please accept my greetings and blessings of Guru Gouranga Giridhari Gandharvika. You have already got the news of our safe arrival and good reception by the devotees here. Mr. Allen Ginsberg and about fifty or sixty others received us on the air port and when I arrived in my apartment there were some press reporters also who took note of my mission. Two three papers like the Examiner and the Chronicles etc have already published the report. One of the reports is sent herewith please find. I wish that 1,000 copies of this report may be offset printed at once and 100 copies of the same may be sent here as soon as possible.
>
> I understand that you are feeling my absence. Krishna will give you strength. Physical presence is immaterial; presence of the transcendental sound received from the spiritual master should be the guidance of life. That will make our spiritual life successful. If you feel very strongly about my absence you may place my pictures on my sitting places and this will be source of inspiration for you.
>
> I am very much anxious to hear about the final decision of the house. I wish to open the house by the 1st of March 1967 and arrangement may be done dexterously in this connection. I have not as yet received the tapes for Dictaphone and I have sent you tapes yesterday. Please offer my blessings to Sriman Neal.
>
> Sriman Rayarama is cooking well and distributing Prasadam to the devotees numbering sometimes seventy. It is very encouraging. I think this center will be very nice branch without delay. Everything is prospective. Hope you are well and awaiting your early reply.

The letter had helped—especially the second paragraph. Brahmānanda had posted it in the storefront. Now Swamiji had clearly enunciated that they were still with him and he was still in New York with them. It was something special—service to the spiritual master in separation—and even the devotees in San Francisco, who were with Swamiji every day, could not yet know its special taste. While the devotees in New York performed their daily duties, they often quoted from the letter and thought about it: "Krishna will give you strength. Physical presence is immaterial; presence of the transcendental sound received from the spiritual master should be the guidance of life. That will make our spiritual life successful."

Although Prabhupāda had written that they could place his photograph on his seat, no one had a photograph. They had to ask the devotees in San Francisco for one. A boy took some poor color snapshots and sent them to New York, and the devotees placed one at Prabhupāda's sitting place in his apartment. It helped.

For Prabhupāda also, the letter to his disciples in New York marked a milestone. This was the basis on which he hoped to conduct a world movement. He could travel from place to place and yet be simultaneously present in many places by his instructions.

Brahmānanda, as president of the New York temple, frequently phoned San Francisco. "The chanting is the focal point," he told Hayagrīva. "We can always sit and chant. We're beginning to understand what Swamiji meant when he said that worship in separation is more relishable."

And Śrīla Prabhupāda wrote to his New York disciples regularly, at least once a week. Brahmānanda got most of the business instructions: arrange to purchase a new building in New York, see Mr. Kallman and get copies of the *kīrtana* record, get a copy of the movie a filmmaker had made of the devotees, investigate the possibility of publishing *Bhagavad-gītā*. "If I am assisted by one expert type-writer. . . ," Prabhupāda wrote Brahmānanda, "we can publish every three months a book. And the more we have books the more we become respectable."

Satsvarūpa got a letter from Prabhupāda asking him to type the dictated tapes of the new book, *Teachings of Lord Caitanya.* Although Prabhupāda's typist, Neal, had gone to San Francisco, after a day he had disappeared.

"I think you have five tapes with you because I have got only three with me," Prabhupāda wrote. "See that the tapes do not miss." Satsvarūpa had written inquiring how he would be able to understand transcendental knowledge. "You are a sincere devotee of the Lord,"

Prabhupāda replied, "and certainly He will bless you with auspicious advancement in the matter of spiritual understanding."

Rāya Rāma got a letter encouraging him to continue publishing the magazine. "*Back to Godhead* will always remain the backbone of the society . . . your ambition should always be how to improve the quality. . . ."

Acyutānanda, one of the youngest devotees (only eighteen), was now working alone in the kitchen. In a letter Śrīla Prabhupāda wrote to five devotees, signing his name five times, he told Acyutānanda, "Since Kirtanananda is absent certainly you are feeling some strain. But the more you serve Krishna the more you become stronger. I hope you are being properly assisted by your other Godbrothers."

Prabhupāda advised Gargamuni, also eighteen, to cooperate with his older Godbrothers. Asking whether Gargamuni had gone to see his mother, Prabhupāda said he hoped she was all right. Since Gargamuni was the temple treasurer, Śrīla Prabhupāda advised him, "Checks should be drawn with full deliberation."

Prabhupāda wrote Jaduräṇī, "I always remember you as the nicest girl because you are so devoutly engaged in the service of Krishna." She had informed him that she had been cheated by a boyfriend, and Śrīla Prabhupāda replied, "Better you accept Krishna as your Husband, and He will never be unfaithful. . . . Devote yourself therefore 24 hours in the service of Krishna and see how you feel happy in all respects."

Rūpānuga had written Prabhupāda that the temperature in New York had dropped below zero and that there had been a two-day blizzard. Śrīla Prabhupāda wrote,

> Certainly this situation would have been a little troublesome for me because I am an old man. I think Krishna wanted to protect me by shifting me here at San Francisco. Here the climate is certainly like India and I am feeling comfortable but uncomfortable also because at New York I felt at Home on account of so many beloved students like you. As you are feeling my absence so I am feeling for you. But we are all happy on account of Krishna Consciousness either here or there. May Krishna join us always in His transcendental service.

The neophyte disciples in New York felt assurance from their spiritual master's words and by their own experience. Service in separation was a transcendental fact. They were improving in chanting on their beads, and the New York center was going on. "So long our *kīrtana* is all right," Prabhupāda wrote, "there is no difficulty at all."

But there was one difficulty. Attempts to purchase a new building, which had gone on smoothly while Prabhupāda had been present, had become a great problem as soon as he had left. Shortly after Śrīla Prabhupāda's departure for San Francisco, Brahmānanda had given Mr. Price a thousand dollars, and Mr. Price had promised to help the devotees get their building. When Prabhupāda heard this, he became perturbed.

> In the opinion of the devotees and the trustees here, $1000.00 has been risked without any understanding. I know that you are doing your best but still there has been an error of judgment. I am not at all displeased with you but they say that Mr. Price will never be able to secure financial help from any other source. He is simply taking time under different pretext, changing constantly. Therefore you should not pay even a farthing more than what you have paid. If he wants any more money you should flatly refuse.

Śrīla Prabhupāda remembered Mr. Price and their first meeting, at which the blond-haired, elegantly dressed businessman, his face tanned even in winter, had addressed him as "Your Excellency." That address alone had made Prabhupāda distrust him. There was a Bengali saying, Too much devotion denotes a thief. Prabhupāda knew that businessmen were prone to cheat and that an American businessman would be particularly difficult to deal with. Prabhupāda's American disciples were innocent children in worldly affairs. He was ready to instruct them step by step, but now, without consulting him, they had become involved in an unbusinesslike transaction, risking a thousand dollars of the Society's money without any written agreement.

Śrīla Prabhupāda had visited the building on Stuyvesant Street, and he wanted it. It was a historical, well-kept, aristocratic building, suitable for his New York headquarters. It was worth the $100,000 price—if they could afford it. But it was difficult for Prabhupāda to know from San Francisco what was going on between Brahmānanda and the businessmen.

And the difficulty increased as letters and phone calls from Brahmānanda introduced other persons involved. Aside from Mr. Price there was Mr. Tyler, the owner, and Mr. Tyler's lawyer, who seemed independent of Mr. Tyler, and finally there was ISKCON's lawyer, who also had a mind of his own.

Although Śrīla Prabhupāda's disciples usually surrendered to his direction, they seemed bent on listening to the businessmen's promises, even though their spiritual master had cautioned them not to. Prabhupāda became disturbed. His preaching in San Francisco was being threatened by fears that the businessmen would cheat his Society of what he had begun in New York.

With no responsible advisors to turn to, Śrīla Prabhupāda sometimes discussed the problem with Mukunda and other devotees in his room. They all agreed that the transaction seemed highly irregular; Brahmānanda was probably being led on by false promises.

Brahmānanda, however, saw Mr. Price as a rare person—a successful man who wanted to help the devotees. Although no other respectable businessman had ever shown interest, Mr. Price listened and sympathized. And he would greet the devotees with "Hare Kṛṣṇa!" Brahmānanda was well aware of the humble economic and social position of the devotees. They were almost all ex-hippies, and they were poor. But here was Mr. Price, a wealthy man with diamond cuff links who was always glad to see him, shake his hand, pat his back, and speak appreciatively of the religion of India and the moral behavior of the small band of devotees.

Mr. Price had received a group of devotees as guests in his apartment and said nice things about each one of them. He had said that Hayagrīva was an excellent writer, and that *Back to Godhead* was the best magazine on the market, and that its mimeographed appearance made it look even better than the slicks. He said he would give the devotees a movie projector. And he came close to saying that if he could liquidate some of his money he would *give* them the building.

Brahmānanda, who saw Mr. Price a few times a week, would come away intoxicated with high hopes. The Kṛṣṇa consciousness movement could rise to success through this wealthy man's patronage. After leaving Mr. Price's office, Brahmānanda would rejoin the devotees in the evening and tell them all that had happened. On nights when there were no public *kīrtanas*, the devotees would hold meetings—Swamiji had named them *iṣṭa-goṣṭhīs*—to discuss the instructions of the spiritual master.

And the *iṣṭa-goṣṭhīs* became dominated by talks of Mr. Price and the building.

One night Brahmānanda explained why he had given Mr. Price a thousand dollars: Mr. Price had asked for "something to work with." It was like earnest money, and it was also for a trip Mr. Price had to take to Pittsburgh to see whether he could release some of his wealth to use in Kṛṣṇa's service.

One of the boys asked whether there would be any receipt or written agreement. Swamiji had taught them to use receipts, at least amongst themselves. Gargamuni and Satsvarūpa, as treasurer and secretary, signed each voucher, and Gargamuni kept the vouchers on file. These included requests for items like "fifty cents for a hat" and "three dollars for sneakers." Brahmānanda said he had mentioned a written statement to Mr. Price but hadn't pressed the matter. Anyway, it wasn't necessary, or even desirable, since they were not simply conducting business with Mr. Price but cultivating a relationship. Mr. Price was a well-wisher, a friend, who was helping them as charity. He was going to do big things and use his influence to get the building. This one thousand dollars was just a gesture to show their interest and to show Mr. Price's friends the devotees weren't joking; they had some money.

In fact, the devotees had ten thousand dollars—five thousand in small donations and a five-thousand-dollar donation from a wealthy hippie. In addition to donations, the temple had a regular monthly income of eight hundred dollars—Brahmānanda's four-hundred-dollar paycheck from his job as a substitute teacher for the New York City public school system and the four-hundred-dollar paycheck Satsvarūpa earned as a caseworker for the welfare department.

But the devotees were in no position to buy *any* building, and they knew it—all the more reason, Brahmānanda explained at *iṣṭa-goṣṭhī*, why they had to depend on Mr. Price. After all, he reasoned, Swamiji himself had inspired them to look for a $100,000 building. Swamiji knew they couldn't pay for such a building, except in some extraordinary way. And Mr. Price, Brahmānanda figured, must be the way. Swamiji wanted the building. No sooner had he reached San Francisco than he had written back, "I am very anxious to hear about the final decision of the house. I wish to open the house by the 1st of March 1967 and arrangement may be done dexterously in this connection."

The assembled devotees listened to Brahmānanda's explanations, sympathized, and added their own understanding of how Kṛṣṇa and Swamiji were working. There were a few contrary remarks and opinions, but basically everyone agreed: Brahmānanda's dealings with Mr. Price were all right.

When Kīrtanānanda and Rāya Rāma returned to New York from San Francisco, they consulted with Brahmānanda. Then Brahmānanda went to Mr. Price, who promised that if somehow they couldn't get the building he would return at least $750. (The balance of the money represented travel in the devotees' interest.) But they would get the building, Mr. Price assured him.

Then Mr. Price told Brahmānanda the latest: he had found a wealthy financier, Mr. Hall, who had almost agreed to pay the full $100,000 for the building. Mr. Price was working on Mr. Hall, who happened to be his close friend. Prospects seemed good. But the devotees would also have to do their part, Mr. Price explained, by putting up five thousand dollars. Mr. Price would then arrange everything else.

Mr. Price set up a meeting with an architect on Park Avenue, and soon Brahmānanda and Satsvarūpa were sitting with Mr. Price and his architect friend, reviewing sketches. To give the building that authentic Indian-temple look, the architect proposed a facade with arches and, if they liked, domes. It was wonderful! Of course, they didn't dare ask him how much it would cost. But Mr. Price even hinted that the work might be done free. After Mr. Price served himself and his architect friend some liquor and offered some to the boys (although he knew they wouldn't accept it), the two men held up tinkling glasses, smiled, and politely toasted themselves and the boys, saying, "Hare Kṛṣṇa."

While going down on the elevator, Mr. Price spoke eloquently of the devotees' faith in God. He said that others might argue about the existence of God but the most convincing thing was the devotees' personal experience. "Your personal testimony," Mr. Price assured them, "is the best argument. It is a very powerful thing."

The boys nodded. Later among themselves they laughed about the liquor, but still they figured these men wanted to help.

When Śrīla Prabhupāda heard about the latest developments, he did not share his disciples' optimism. On February 3 he wrote Gargamuni:

> I had a talk with your brother Brahmananda yesterday on the dial. I am glad that Mr. Price has promised to return the amount of $750.00 in case no sale contract is made. But in any case, you should not pay any farthing more than what you have already paid, either to the Lawyer or to Mr. Price, unless there is actual sale contract made. It appears to me very gloomy about the transaction because there was no basic understanding before the payment of $1000.00 either to the Lawyer or to the Real estate. This is not businesslike. Unless there is a basic understanding where is the way of transaction? If there was no basic understanding, why so much waste of time and energy? I cannot understand. And if there was basic understanding, why is it changed so quickly? I am therefore perturbed in the mind. When there was no basic understanding, what was the need for appointing Lawyer? Anyway, it is my advice that you should consult me before issuing any further money. But I hope you will make the transaction successful without further delay.

Śrīla Prabhupāda had also instructed Gargamuni to protect the ten thousand dollars in the bank and never withdraw any sum that would leave a balance of less than six thousand. Prabhupāda had left one account for which the devotees were the signers, but he also had an account for which he controlled the funds. He now asked the devotees to put six thousand dollars from their account into his. He wrote Brahmānanda, "This $6000.00 will be transferred forthwith by me as soon as there is a <u>Sale contract</u> for purchase of the house."

On February 10 Prabhupāda wrote to Kīrtanānanda,

> Regarding the house, I was correct in my remarks that there was no definite understanding. . . . In such negotiations, everything is done in black and white. Nothing is being done in black and white but everything is being done with faith on Mr. Price.
>
> Let this understanding be completed within the 1st of March 1967 and close the chapter. I think this is my last word in this connection. You are all grown up boys and you use your discretion and you can now complete the transaction without prolonging it indefinitely. If, however, we are not able to purchase a house it does not mean closing our activity at 26 Second avenue. So there is no question of packing up and coming to S.F.

Then on February 15 Prabhupāda wrote Satsvarūpa,

> So far I can see from the correspondence of Brahmananda it is not possible for us to get the house for so many reasons. The main reason is that we have no money to pay cash and nobody is going to invest cash in that house because it is neither complete nor has any income. It is simply utopian to think of possessing the house and Mr. Price is simply giving us false hope.
>
> You are all innocent boys without any experience of the world. The cunning world can befool you at any time. So please be careful of the world in Krishna consciousness. When Krishna will desire, the house will come to us automatically.

Śrīla Prabhupāda's doubts were confirmed when Mr. Price wrote to him asking for money. If Mr. Price had so much money, Prabhupāda reasoned, why was Mr. Price asking *him* for money?

On February 17 Śrīla Prabhupāda wrote to Mr. Price to impress upon him that there would have to be a sale contract before ISKCON could actually purchase the building.

> If there is sale contract, my students here and in New York will be able to raise the fund very seriously. In the absence of any sale contract everything appears to be in the air and Mr. Tyler or his lawyer can change his word as he has already done.

Śrīla Prabhupāda's message was clear. Brahmānanda, however, complained of poor communications. Things were always changing, and Brahmānanda wasn't always able to get Swamiji's confirmation on the latest changes. Swamiji would write his instructions in a letter, and although the devotees had to obey whatever he said, the circumstances would often have changed by the time they received the letter. Swamiji would also sometimes change his opinion when he heard new information. Sometimes Brahmānanda would call San Francisco and Swamiji wouldn't be available. Brahmānanda didn't feel right about sending messages through the devotees in San Francisco, because he knew that the devotees there were skeptical about the whole transaction. If New York got the building, San Francisco would have to donate a thousand dollars. And the devotees in San Francisco, of course, had their own plans for how to spend money for Kṛṣṇa.

Mr. Price suggested to the devotees in New York that maybe the

Swami didn't understand American business dealings. With all respect, His Excellency couldn't be expected to know all the intricacies of finance in a foreign country. And His Excellency's request for a purchase contract was, as Mr. Price put it, "something that went out with hoop skirts." Brahmānanda and Satsvarūpa didn't know how to reply; the remarks seemed like blasphemy. But Brahmānanda and Satsvarūpa were already entangled in the promises Mr. Price had given and went on meeting with him. They would meet with Mr. Price and then ride back to Second Avenue on the subway, chanting Hare Kṛṣṇa.

Śrīla Prabhupāda wrote almost daily to various devotees in New York. On February 18, he wrote a letter to Brahmānanda with the word CONFIDENTIAL typed at the top of the page.

> Now if you think he is able to secure money for us, if you think that there is something hopeful by this time then you can continue the negotiation as he is doing. <u>But do not for Krishna's sake advance a farthing more on any plea by him</u>. He may be trying his best, but he is not capable to do this. That is my honest opinion.

While trying to avoid further losses in New York, Prabhupāda continued his active preaching in San Francisco. Mukunda and the others were lining up lots of engagements, and the reception was often enthusiastic. In the same confidential letter to Brahmānanda in which Prabhupāda put forward his strategies for negotiating with Mr. Price and company, he also wrote glowingly of "grand successful" meetings at various Bay-area colleges. The meetings were similar, he said, to the wonderful *kīrtanas* in Tompkins Square Park. This was the way to spread Kṛṣṇa consciousness, not by becoming entangled with treacherous real estate agents.

> I am enclosing herewith a copy of the letter received from Himalayan Academy. See how they are appreciating our method of peace movement. So in this way we have to forward our cause. No businessman will come forward to help us on utopian schemes as contemplated by Mr. Price. We have to try for ourselves. So the summary is to obtain a <u>hire purchase sale contract</u> from Mr. Tyler and popularize our movement by outdoor engagements as many as possible.

Śrīla Prabhupāda had done what he could. The boys were foolish, even to the point of not listening to him. But they had raised the money themselves. If despite his instructions they lost it, what further help could he give? So he simply went on with his San Francisco preaching and advised the boys in New York also to become convinced of achieving success through *kīrtana*.

CHAPTER THREE

New Jagannātha Purī

Śrīla Prabhupāda put on a sweater over his turtleneck jersey, wrapped his *cādar* around his shoulders, and left his apartment, accompanied by a few disciples. The weather was beautiful, and the blue, cloudless sky reminded him of India. An hour before, he had sent devotees ahead to start a *kīrtana*, and now one of the girls had come running back to him, excitedly knocking on his door and announcing, "Swamiji, there are so many people!"

The clay *mṛdaṅgas* he had ordered many months ago from Calcutta had recently arrived. Today would be one of the first times he would play a genuine clay *mṛdaṅga* in America. The boys and girls would like it. He had arranged for the drums to be wrapped in cloth and had cautioned the boys to be careful because the clay drums broke easily.

The walk to the park was short, and as usual Prabhupāda walked faster than his young followers. They walked down Frederick Street to Stanyan, where they turned the corner at the doughnut shop (frequented by the Hell's Angels and still sometimes visited by certain devotees). On Stanyan they hurried past the parking lot of Kezar Stadium, the stadium itself looming beyond. At the Wallen Street intersection Prabhupāda continued his rapid stride without stopping or even bothering to look at the light. One of the boys caught his arm: "Wait, Swamiji—the light." But Prabhupāda darted across the street.

As they continued down Stanyan toward Haight Street, the park appeared on the right. They entered, walking past a duck pond with a fountain and a willow tree on its center island. They walked past tall redwoods and eucalyptus trees, which lent fragrance to the surrounding area. There were also maple, oak, and ash trees and flowering shrubs, like azaleas. Prabhupāda said that the park resembled parks in Bombay and that the city was like a holy place because it was named after St. Francis.

They entered a fifty-foot-long tunnel with artificial stalactites hanging from the ceiling and came out onto a path heavily shaded by trees on either side. Just ahead was the meadow, covered with tiny daisies and clover and encircled by redwood and eucalyptus trees. Prabhupāda could hear the chanting, the *karatālas*, and the booming of the timpani. As he entered the meadow, he saw a sloping hill dotted with hundreds of young people—sitting, lying, lounging, smoking, throwing Frisbees, or walking around; and in the meadow below the hill was his *kīrtana*.

The meadow was a popular place. People walked through it on the way to the zoo or the tennis courts. But today many passersby had stopped and were listening in a group, about two hundred feet from the *kīrtana*. Closer in, about fifty feet from the *kīrtana*, was another group, listening more intently. And then there was the *kīrtana* party itself, Prabhupāda's disciples and dozens of young hippies, sitting tightly together and chanting. And others were standing nearby, clapping and swaying to the rhythm of the drum and *karatālas*.

Flags decorated the *kīrtana* area. Three feet by four feet, they had been made by devotees, and each bore the symbol of a different religion. A bright red flag with a yellow star and the crescent moon of Islam flew from a ten-foot bamboo pole stuck into the earth. Beside it waved a pale blue flag with a dark blue Star of David in the center. And beside that, a yellow flag bore the Sanskrit *oṁkāra*.

Prabhupāda's disciples, with their long hair and casual clothes, were indistinguishable from the other young dancers and singers except for the strands of large, red chanting beads around their necks. Some of the devotees danced, with arms upraised against the background of uninterrupted blue sky. Others played instruments. The *karatālas* and timpani were there, Hayagrīva had brought his cornet, and there were other instruments brought by devotees and hippies. Little children were taking part. Even a stray dog pranced in the innermost circle of the *kīrtana* party. On Sundays the meadow beneath Hippie Hill was always an open show, and today the *kīrtana* was the featured attraction.

Prabhupāda joined the *kīrtana*. Walking up suddenly, to the surprise and delight of the devotees, he sat down and began playing the *mṛdaṅga* and leading the singing in a loud voice.

Mukunda: *Although we had heard Swamiji play different drums before and some of us had played along with him, when he played the clay* mṛdaṅga *from India it was a completely different feeling. The feeling it created was akin to seeing an old friend after many, many years. It was so right and so natural. It was the very thing our* kīrtanas *had been missing, and it increased our feelings of ecstasy many times over. Obviously Swamiji was in greater ecstasy than ever. You could sense by the way he held the drum, by the ease with which he brought out its intricate rhythms to control the* kīrtana, *that this drum was like a long-lost friend to him. Swamiji playing that drum was the talk of the community. Now we knew what* kīrtana *really was, how it was supposed to sound, what it was really like.*

Prabhupāda was the center of attraction. Even his age and dress made him prominent. Whereas the others in the park were mostly young people dressed in denims or various hippie costumes, Prabhupāda was seventy and distinctly dressed in saffron robes. And the way the devotees had all cheered and bowed before him and were now looking at him so lovingly caused onlookers to regard him with curiosity and respect. As soon as he had sat down, some young children had gathered in close to him. He had smiled at them, deftly playing the *mṛdaṅga*, enthralling and entertaining them with his playing.

Govinda dāsī: *With Swamiji's arrival there was a mastery and an authority about the whole* kīrtana *that was absent before. We were no longer kids in San Francisco chanting Hare Kṛṣṇa. Now we had historical depth and meaning. Now the* kīrtana *had credentials. His presence established the ancient historical quality of the chanting. When Swamiji came, the whole disciplic succession came.*

After an hour of chanting, Prabhupāda stopped the *kīrtana* and addressed the crowd: "Hare Kṛṣṇa, Hare Kṛṣṇa, Kṛṣṇa Kṛṣṇa, Hare Hare/ Hare Rāma, Hare Rāma, Rāma Rāma, Hare Hare. This is the sound vibration, and it is to be understood that the sound vibration is transcendental. And because it is transcendental vibration, therefore it appeals to everyone, even without understanding the language of the sound. This is the beauty. Even children respond to it. . . ."

After speaking five minutes, Prabhupāda began the *kīrtana* again. One woman with long, uncombed red hair began dancing back and forth and chanting, her baby in her arms. A man and woman sitting side by side played together on the heads of a pair of bongos. Subala, in tight corduroy pants and a flowing white shirt, danced in a semblance of the step Swamiji had shown him, although Subala looked somewhat like an American Indian dancer. A little girl no more than four years old sat cross-legged, playing *karatālas* and chanting seriously. A suave-looking fellow wearing a vest and round sunglasses played castanets against his palm. Ravīndra-svarūpa sat rocking back and forth as he played the drone on the harmonium. Beside him, Hayagrīva chanted forcefully, his head and upper body lunging forward and back, his long hair and beard jutting out wildly, while nearby a girl stood with her right arm around one boy and her left arm around another, all three of them swaying back and forth, singing with peaceful, blissful smiles, enjoying the chanting and the sunshine. One girl sat silently meditating, while beside her a girl danced provocatively and a five-year-old beside the dancing girl played with two balloons.

Prabhupāda set his *mṛdaṅga* aside and stood, playing *karatālas* and swaying among the dancers, his feet moving in a stately measure. A big black man danced nearby, facing his white girl friend, both of them moving as if they were at the Avalon. The girl shook her body and head in wild abandon, and her long straight hair completely covered her face. Bright, blonde Nandarāṇī stood on Prabhupāda's right, playing *karatālas*. Sometimes Prabhupāda stopped singing and simply observed the scene, his mouth closed in a stern yet sublimely tolerant expression.

Some of the young people joined hands, forming a circle, and began to dance around and around in front of Swamiji. Then they encircled him, and as he looked on, still swaying and now clapping solemnly, they danced around him hand in hand, jumping and wriggling and chanting Hare Kṛṣṇa. The soft pink hue of his *khādī* robes contrasting with the pied dress of the hippies, Swamiji looked unusual and wonderful, watching and solemnly sanctioning the *kīrtana* performance.

The dancing was free form and sensuous. But that was the way these young people expressed their feelings—through their bodies. They bounced and bounded into the air. Sometimes the circle of dancers would break and become a single line, weaving in and out among the people sitting on the grass, in and out among the silk flags. A muscular boy held the hand of a girl wearing long dark braids and a black headband in American Indian style. At the end of the line, a boy held a girl's hand with his left hand while with his right he held a wooden recorder to his mouth and tooted as he weaved in and out of the crowd.

Prabhupāda became tired and sat beside the brass-bottomed timpani. Singing and playing *karatālas*, he sat grave and straight like an ancient sage. Nearby, a blonde woman sat in yogic posture, bending her body forward until her forehead touched the ground again and again, in supplication or exhibition. Another girl stretched out her hands imploringly in a mixed expression of inner feelings—physical and spiritual—while her golden earrings jangled. A Mexican in a checkered shirt beat a tom-tom. A white sheep dog wandered from person to person.

Swamiji looked kind and amused. The hippies found him beautiful. He remained gentlemanly, aloof amid the twisting, shaking, rocking, dancing young people. Amid their most sensual movements, he appeared not at all like them, for he moved in a stately, elderly way.

As he surveyed the activities in the meadow, he seemed deeply pleased to see the ring of dancers singing all around him, chanting Hare Kṛṣṇa. Although the enthusiasm of these hippies was often wild and sensual, the gathering assumed a wholesome sweetness due to the chanting of Hare Kṛṣṇa. For Swamiji the main thing was that the chanting was going on and on. Dressed in his saffron cloth that seemed to change colors subtly in the fading afternoon sunlight, he watched in a kindly, fatherly way, not imposing any restraint but simply inviting everyone to chant Hare Kṛṣṇa.

Twenty-five-year-old Linda Katz was walking in the park when she heard the sound of the *kīrtana*. In the crowd of hundreds of people gathered around the scene, Linda found it easy to go close without becoming conspicuous. She felt comfortable watching and even thought of joining the fun. Then she noticed the Swami leading the singing. She was startled, even a little frightened, having never before seen anyone so grave. He was striking.

And the dancers appeared beautiful to her. A girl with arms upraised and eyes closed seemed to be swinging like a tree in the wind. One of the men was tall and attractive, with golden, curly hair. And Linda saw a boy she knew from college in New York, a crazy boy who always wore a shocking-pink wool cap.

Linda had arrived in San Francisco from New York only a few days ago. She had no plans, except to study under a certain dance teacher and maybe get into some of the exciting things she had heard were going on in Haight-Ashbury. As a graduate student in ancient Greek literature at Columbia University, Linda had become attracted to Socrates, who had lived and died for truth. But she hadn't found any of her professors to be at all like Socrates. She had envisioned herself living a life of truth by pursuing scholarship, but it had become dry. The ancient civilization of Greece was a dead idea, not a living truth. It didn't touch the heart.

She had been aching for a new, exciting experience, and she was ready to throw herself into San Francisco's hippie society. She had come here alone, giving up her fashionable clothes and donning bell-bottoms and old shirts. But because she wanted to be serious, she felt awkward trying to fit in with the hippies. She felt that to belong she was supposed to wipe the serious look off her face and just smile mindlessly. So even in the society of San Francisco's hippies, she remained unsatisfied and lost.

The *kīrtana* in the park was the most beautiful sight Linda had ever seen. The dancers were swaying back and forth, their arms raised against the open sky, and in the middle of the dance was a dark, gray-haired wise person sitting and chanting. As she moved in closer, she began to sway with the devotees. Then she sat down and started chanting, wanting to find out what was going on.

After more than an hour of chanting, the elderly leader finally stopped the *kīrtana*, and Linda began talking to some of the devotees. Although the Swami had slipped away, some of his followers had remained, handing out flyers and invitations to the Sunday Love Feast and picking up the timpani and the flags. One of them asked her to come with them to the temple.

Linda found the devotees to be something like hippies, but not scruffy street people like most of the hippies she had met. They were attractive, not repellent. Madrases and plants decorated their little storefront temple. When she stopped before a painting of people singing and dancing, one of the devotees said, "This is Lord Caitanya and His associates." A devotee gave her some *prasādam*, and Linda left that night without meeting the Swami.

The next day, however, at seven in the morning, she returned, eager for another chance to see him. She thought he had noticed her at the park and might remember her. She had made a drawing of him, and she wanted to show him.

That morning, as Prabhupāda chanted prayers and led *kīrtana*, Linda didn't take her eyes off him. And when he asked everyone to chant Hare Kṛṣṇa with him on beads, she excitedly accepted a strand from one of the devotees and tried to chant like him. Then he began reading the Sanskrit verse to begin his lecture, and Linda was captivated by the sound. If she were to continue with her graduate program in Greek, she would study Sanskrit next; so she listened with keen interest, proud that perhaps no one else in the room could understand as well as she.

Later that same morning, she met Śrīla Prabhupāda upstairs in his apartment.

Linda: *In the first conversation I had with him, Swamiji summed up Greek civilization for me in a couple of sentences. He explained that* Śrīmad-Bhāgavatam *was the source of stories like the* Iliad *and the* Odyssey *and was the source of Platonic philosophy. I was thrilled. Of course, I believed him. I knew that whatever he was speaking was the truth. There was no doubt in my mind. And he didn't discourage my love for Socrates. He told me that Socrates was actually a devotee in disguise.*

Then he began telling me the story of Kṛṣṇa as the butter thief, and I said, "Oh, yes, I know that story. I saw a dance about Kṛṣṇa as the butter thief." He was very pleased, and he laughed. He said, "Oh, yes, you know?"

This encounter with Swamiji was like meeting an old friend, because I felt completely at home and protected. And I felt I had found what I was looking for. Here I could use my intelligence and ask the questions I had always wanted to ask in school.

Prabhupāda initiated Linda, giving her the name Līlāvatī. Seeing her eagerness to serve him personally, he decided to teach her to cook by having her prepare his lunch. He already had a little weekend cooking class in which he taught Jānakī, Govinda dāsī, Nandarāṇī, and others the art of cooking for Kṛṣṇa. Now he invited Līlāvatī to come. He would walk back and forth in the small room, showing the girls how to knead dough, cook *capātīs*, measure spices in the right palm, and cut vegetables and cook them in ghee with *masālā*. The foods were basic—rice, *capātīs*, cauliflower with potatoes—but he wanted to teach the girls precisely how to cook.

Mukunda: *One day, just out of curiosity, I went in to witness Swamiji's cooking classes. So I came in and stood at the doorway to Swamiji's kitchen. The women were there learning how to cook, and Swamiji said to me, "What are you doing?"*

"Oh," I said, "I just came to see my wife."

Then Swamiji said, "Are you going back to Godhead or back to wife?" Everyone was amused, and I realized I wasn't welcome, so I left.

The incident made me reflect on Swamiji's seriousness. For one thing, I learned that I should not be so attached to my wife, and secondly I learned that his relationship with the women and what he was teaching them was actually very sacred—not like the sometimes frivolous association between husband and wife. Because he spent many hours in the kitchen teaching them, they were very inspired.

Līlāvatī tended to be proud. Many of the devotees were not college graduates, and none of them were classical scholars. She sometimes typed for Swamiji, did his wash, or brought flowers to his room in the morning. And he had quickly chosen *her* to be his exclusive cook. After only a few days of cooking lessons, Swamiji had told her, "All right, you cook." And now he came in only occasionally to check on her. Once when he saw her rolling *capātīs*, he said, "Oh, you have learned very nicely."

Preparing Swamiji's meals just right—with the proper spicing, without burning anything, and on time—was a challenge. By the time Līlāvatī finished, she would be perspiring and even crying from tension. But when she brought in his lunch he would ask her to bring an empty plate, and he would serve her portions from his own plate and invite her to eat with him. For the first few days, Līlāvatī made remarks about the wonderful tastes of the *prasādam*, and Swamiji would smile or raise his eyebrows. But then she noticed that he never spoke while eating but seemed to be concentrating intensely as he sat, cross-legged, bending his body over the plate of *prasādam* and eating with his right hand.

One day, on Ekādaśī, Līlāvatī arrived late at Swamiji's apartment, thinking there would not be much cooking on a fast day. But when she entered the kitchen she found Swamiji himself busily cooking. He was heating something white in a skillet, vigorously stirring and scraping it from the bottom of the pan. "Oh," he said, "I was just wondering, 'Where is that girl?' "

Līlāvatī was too shy to ask what Swamiji was doing, so she simply busied herself cutting vegetables. "Today is a fast day," she said, as if chiding Swamiji for cooking.

"You have to understand—" he replied, "in Kṛṣṇa consciousness a fast day means a feast day. We are offering this to Kṛṣṇa." Līlāvatī continued to keep her distance from Swamiji's whitish, sticky-looking preparation until he completed it and placed it on the windowsill to cool. "Later it will harden," he said, "and we can cut it and serve it." And with that he turned and walked out of the kitchen.

When Līlāvatī finished cooking and served Swamiji his Ekādaśī lunch, he asked her to bring him some of "that thing" on the windowsill. He took a bite, seemed pleased, and asked Līlāvatī to call Mukunda and Jānakī to taste it.

Jānakī took a bite and exclaimed, "It's wonderful! Simply wonderful! Incredible! What is this?"

Turning to Līlāvatī, Swamiji asked, "What is in this preparation?"

"I don't know, Swamiji," she said.

"You don't know?" he replied. "You were standing right by me in the kitchen, and you don't remember?" Līlāvatī's face turned red.

"Oh, Swamiji," Līlāvatī replied, "I was very busy. I just didn't see."

"Oh, you are busy without intelligence," he replied, and he laughed for a long time, until Mukunda was also laughing. Līlāvatī felt even more humiliated.

Swamiji asked Jānakī if she could tell what was in the preparation. She couldn't, except that it was sweet. He then sent Līlāvatī downstairs to get Govinda dāsī and Gaurasundara. When they entered, Swamiji told Līlāvatī, "Go get some more of that simply wonderful thing."

Again, this time in front of four devotees, Swamiji asked Līlāvatī, "So what is in this preparation?" And again she defended herself; she had been too busy to notice. And again he laughed until everyone was laughing with him. He then asked Govinda dāsī to taste the "simply wonderful" and say what was in it. Immediately she guessed: sugar, butter, and powdered milk.

"Oh," Swamiji looked at Līlāvatī, "she is an artist. She is intelligent."

To Līlāvatī the whole episode was a devastating ordeal. Only later did she understand that Swamiji had been trying to teach her humility.

* * *

It was seven A.M. Śrīla Prabhupāda sat on his dais in the temple. Beside him, on an altar, stood the recently acquired statue of Kṛṣṇa. The child Kṛṣṇa stood two feet high, with His left hand on His hip, His right hand holding a rod. Guru dāsa had found Him at an import store and had begged the manager to sell Him, and after several visits the man had agreed—for thirty-five dollars. Prabhupāda had given Him the name Kartāmi-śāyī, "the boss." This morning, as Prabhupāda and Kartāmi-śāyī looked out at the devotees in the room, only about six people were present. The night before, the temple had been crowded.

"Where are the others?" Prabhupāda asked. And then he gave the answer himself: "They are sleeping? All this sleeping is not good." He took out his *karatālas* and began playing the one-two-*three* rhythm. Mukunda took up a *mṛdaṅga* and played along, trying to execute the rhythms Śrīla Prabhupāda had recently taught him.

Śrīla Prabhupāda had not even begun singing when the door opened and half a dozen barefoot hippies wandered in, reeking of marijuana. They glanced around, then sat down on the floor with the devotees as Prabhupāda began singing *Gurv-aṣṭakam*, the Vaiṣṇava prayers to the spiritual master.

Although none of his disciples knew the words, they loved to listen to Swamiji sing these morning prayers. Unhurriedly, he sang each verse, several times repeating each line, deliberately developing the mood of unadulterated service to the spiritual master.

Then one of the hippies, a boy with long, straight blonde hair and a red headband, began mumbling, fidgeting, and moaning. Someone softly asked him to be quiet. The boy paused but then moaned again. Swamiji and his followers were used to drugged hippies who stayed up all night and came to the morning program, sometimes disrupting things. Usually the visitors remained submissive. And even if they occasionally called out in a strange mood, they usually found peace in chanting Hare Kṛṣṇa and would try to blend with the energy of the devotees. But today's discordant visitor seemed agitated by the chanting, as if it were challenging him. Rather he sounded like *he* was challenging *it.*

The devotees began clapping in time with Prabhupāda's *karatālas,* and when Prabhupāda began singing Hare Kṛṣṇa, his half-dozen followers immediately joined him, chanting both lead and chorus. Prabhupāda looked at them gravely, encouraging the bedraggled early-morning band of youngsters, and they responded determinedly.

The guests sat in drugged contemplation, although one or two tried singing along. But the blonde boy with the red headband remained adamantly disharmonious, moaning defiantly, as if trying to throw off the effects of the chanting. Nonetheless, despite the boy's moaning, which was sometimes loud and savage, Prabhupāda kept singing, and the devotees kept chanting.

Mukunda and Hayagrīva exchanged anxious glances but tolerated the boy, unsure what else to do. Some of the devotees were disturbed and even frightened, but they had also heard Swamiji say in recent lectures that advanced devotees aren't shaken in any circumstances. Swamiji was their leader, not only in devotional prayers but also in how to respond to this intruder, so they waited and watched him for a sign.

Prabhupāda remained undisturbed. But although after twenty minutes the *kīrtana* was strong and determined, the blonde boy's madness was not going away. As the chanting built up momentum, he became more agitated. He screamed like a lost soul and hollered like a rock singer. He was becoming more and more troubled and angry.

When the devotees rose to their feet and began dancing, the boy began dancing too, but in his own way, crying and pounding his chest. Mukunda played louder on the drum. The sounds were discordant—a clash of individual madness and group chanting—until Prabhupāda finally brought the *kīrtana* to a close.

The devotees bowed their heads to the floor, and Śrīla Prabhupāda intoned the Sanskrit prayers honoring the spiritual masters, the Supreme Lord, and the sacred places. "All glories to the assembled devotees," he said.

They responded, "Hare Kṛṣṇa."

"All glories to the assembled devotees."

"Hare Kṛṣṇa."

"All glories to the assembled devotees."

"Hare Kṛṣṇa."

"Thank you very much," Prabhupāda said. And then, as was his morning custom, he announced, "Chant one round."

Everyone sat down, including the crazy hippie. The devotees put aside the drums and *karatālas*, reached for their large red beads, and began chanting *japa* in unison: "Hare Kṛṣṇa, Hare Kṛṣṇa, Kṛṣṇa Kṛṣṇa, Hare Hare/ Hare Rāma, Hare Rāma, Rāma Rāma, Hare Hare." Fingering one bead at a time, they uttered the *mantra*, then proceeded to the next bead.

Surprised at this turn of events, the blonde boy commented loudly, "Far out!" As rapid chanting filled the room, the boy jumped to his feet and shouted, "Come with me!" He whirled about, faced Śrīla Prabhupāda, and howled, "I AM GOD!" Then he began screaming long, loud, berserk cries: "*OWAHOOOO... WAHOOOO! AAAA!... OOOOOOOOOH!*" He sobbed, growled, grumbled, stomped his feet. Like a small child, he explored every sound his voice could make. Beating his fists on his chest again and again, he cried, "I am God!" And one of the boy's friends suddenly played a few notes on a panpipe.

But Śrīla Prabhupāda kept chanting *japa*, and the devotees also tried to continue chanting undaunted, while at the same time keeping an eye on the madman and wondering where it would all end. Then, with a final, violent ejaculation, the boy shrieked, "I AM GOD!" and in anger and disgust strode out of the room, slamming the door behind him, yelling as he ran down the street.

The proper *japa* peacefully engulfed the storefront, and Śrīla Prabhupāda's voice assumed its place more clearly above the voices of all the chanting devotees. After about ten minutes of chanting, Prabhupāda recited, *sarvātma-snapanaṁ paraṁ vijayate śrī-kṛṣṇa-saṅkīrtanam.* "Let there be all glory to the congregational chanting of Hare Kṛṣṇa, which cleanses the dirt from the mirror of the mind and gives a taste of the nectar for which we are always hankering."

As Prabhupāda put on his spectacles and opened the *Bhagavad-gītā* (he had been speaking each morning on the Sixth Chapter), the room settled and became silent for hearing his lecture. His students, some of whom had been imbibing his instructions for more than two months, listened attentively as he spoke the eternal *paramparā* message. It was Kṛṣṇa's timeless message, yet Swamiji was presenting it just for them as they sat on the rug early in the morning in the small storefront, 518

Frederick Street, in Haight-Ashbury.

Prabhupāda lectured on the transmigration of the soul. Foolish people, he said, aspire for material acquisitions. They don't know that these things are finished with the death of the body. Spiritual life, however, is of the utmost importance, because it is never lost. So even if Kṛṣṇa consciousness becomes inconvenient or uncomfortable, one should never give it up.

Śrīla Prabhupāda was again stressing that the devotee is never disturbed, a point that seemed especially relevant in the wake of this morning's interruption. A devotee, Prabhupāda explained, is always tolerant.

Prabhupāda told a story about the great devotee Haridāsa Ṭhākura, a contemporary of Lord Caitanya's, who endured severe beating at the hands of a Muslim magistrate. As Prabhupāda told the story, he improvised dialogue.

"Oh," the magistrate said to Haridāsa, "you are born in such a nice family, and you are chanting Hare Kṛṣṇa?"

And then Prabhupāda spoke for Haridāsa: "Sir, many Hindus also have become Muhammadan, so if some Muhammadan becomes Hindu, what is the harm?"

Prabhupāda didn't change the pitch or accent of his voice while taking different parts of the dialogue. But with a subtle storyteller's art, each voice became a distinct person.

The magistrate spoke threateningly. "Oh, you are arguing?"

Then Prabhupāda became the narrator: "So, it was decided that Haridāsa was to be punished. Give the dog a bad name and hang it."

Then Prabhupāda became Haridāsa's floggers, who despite repeatedly beating Haridāsa were unable to make him cry out in pain. Finally, exhausted, they spoke up. "Sir, the idea was that you would die, but now we see that you do not die. So now punishment is awaiting us."

Haridāsa: "What do you want?"

The floggers: "We want that you should die."

Narrator: "Then he played himself into *samādhi*, and the floggers brought him to the magistrate."

The magistrate: "Throw him in the water. Don't put him in the graveyard. He has become Hindu."

Śrīla Prabhupāda concluded his tale. "The others were flogging him, and he was chanting Hare Kṛṣṇa, Hare Kṛṣṇa, Kṛṣṇa Kṛṣṇa, Hare Hare/

Hare Rāma, Hare Rāma, Rāma Rāma, Hare Hare. He was undisturbed. He was steady. Therefore, Lord Kṛṣṇa says that a person who is spiritually advanced—for him there is no misery, even in this world, and what to speak of the other world."

A devotee suffers no loss, Prabhupāda explained. Even if he doesn't become perfectly Kṛṣṇa conscious, or even if he falls away, his next birth also will be human.

"There was a prince." Prabhupāda began a story to illustrate his point. "His name was Satyavān. But he was to die at a certain age, his horoscope said. But one girl named Sāvitrī—she fell in love with that boy. Now she wanted to marry. Her father told her, 'He'll die at certain age. You don't marry.' But she was bent. She married.

"In course of time, the boy died—say after four or five years—and the girl became widow. But she was so staunch lover that she won't let the dead body go away. And the Yamarāja, the . . . what is the English for one who takes away the body or the soul after death? So he came to take the soul away. So this chaste girl would not allow the husband's body to go away."

By Prabhupāda's voice and widening eyes, he appeared as Yamarāja, the lord of death, speaking to the widow Sāvitrī: " 'It is my duty that I should take. You give it up. Otherwise, you'll be also punished.' The girl gave up her husband, but followed behind Yamarāja." Then Prabhupāda's Yamarāja, by a slight dropping of his voice, became compassionate: " 'My dear girl, you go home. I give you benediction that you will have a son. Don't cry for your husband.' But Sāvitrī continued to follow Yamarāja. Yamarāja said, 'Why are you following me?' "

Then Prabhupāda's Sāvitrī spoke—not in a feminine voice, but with the reasoning and heart of Sāvitrī: " 'Now you are taking my husband. How can I have my son?' "

Prabhupāda spoke as narrator: "Oh, then he was in dilemma. He returned her husband.

"So, similarly, there is a technique. If you take to Kṛṣṇa consciousness, then your husband, or this human form of life, is guaranteed."

The devotees understood the gist of the story, but they weren't perfectly clear what their lives had to do with the woman in the story. Some, however, understood: if they took to Kṛṣṇa consciousness, their ill-destined lives could become auspicious.

"Yes," Śrīla Prabhupāda continued, "a spiritual life is the most auspicious life." He looked around emphatically at the devotees seated before him on the floor. "Anyone who has done something nice, auspicious thing—oh, it will never be vanquished. He will never be put into difficulty. It is such a nice thing."

He ended his lecture and asked for questions. A young woman raised her hand: "You say that people foolishly worship the photograph of someone who has already gone—you gave the example of George Washington or Gandhi. But can't the photo of a spiritual teacher be very helpful to teach others to love him?"

Prabhupāda: "Yes, those who are spiritually advanced—they are not different from their photograph. Just like here is the statue of Kṛṣṇa—He's not different from Kṛṣṇa. The original person Kṛṣṇa and this statue of Kṛṣṇa are the same. Just like we are chanting Hare Kṛṣṇa—Kṛṣṇa and the name of Kṛṣṇa are nondifferent. Do you realize it? If we are not getting some spiritual enlightenment by chanting Hare Kṛṣṇa, then do you think we are simply wasting our time? No. We're not wasting our time. We're actually getting spiritual ecstasy, because there is no difference. Similarly, a spiritually perfect person and his photograph is the same, because it is in the absolute stage. Is that clear?"

Govinda dāsī raised her hand: "You said that after leaving this body a person in Kṛṣṇa consciousness goes to a higher planet?"

Prabhupāda: "No. If you make perfection of Kṛṣṇa consciousness, then after leaving this body you go directly to Kṛṣṇa. But if you are not perfect, if you have simply executed a certain percentage only, then you'll get the chance of another human body. But one who has understood what is Kṛṣṇa—how Kṛṣṇa takes His birth, how Kṛṣṇa acts—he doesn't get any more material birth. Then? Where does he go? *Tyaktvā dehaṁ punar janma naiti mām eti.* 'He comes to Me.' That means in the supreme abode of Kṛṣṇa.

"Therefore, we should be very serious. Why should we wait for another birth, either in very pious family or rich family or in other planet? This human body can give you the highest perfection. But we have to be very serious and try for that perfection. But we are not serious. We are not very serious. Actually, human civilization means that people should be very serious to have perfection of this human body—that is perfect human civilization. That is missing at the present moment."

Śrīla Prabhupāda sat in silence for several minutes, not moving. No one in the audience made a sound. Finally he reached over for his *karatālas* and began loudly ringing them together and singing: *govinda jaya jaya, gopāla jaya jaya.* And the devotees joined him:

govinda jaya jaya
gopāla jaya jaya
rādhā-ramaṇa hari
govinda jaya jaya

It was Prabhupāda's desire to see his disciples raise their Kṛṣṇa consciousness to one hundred percent in their present lifetime. They could do it, too, because the chanting was absolutely potent. If there was something they didn't understand, he would explain it. Govinda dāsī hadn't understood; she had thought that a devotee was meant to go to a higher planet. But now she understood.

And he had told them to become more serious. He knew they sometimes went to the doughnut shop and even smoked cigarettes after *kīrtanas*, and he tolerated it. But he let them know that he really wanted them to be completely serious. Unless they were completely serious, they might have to go to a higher planet within the material universe; and what good was that? To rise to a human birth took many lifetimes. Human life was meant for perfection, so they should be serious. "But," he had said, "we are not serious."

After the *kīrtana*, Śrīla Prabhupāda left the storefront and returned to his apartment. Hayagrīva, turning to Haridāsa, asked why no one had thrown the crazy boy out. "In New York," Hayagrīva said, "Brahmānanda would have removed him at the first outburst."

"You have to be careful with the hippies here," Haridāsa explained. "*Tactful* is the word. In this neighborhood, if someone walks around high on LSD, people automatically assume that he is due all the respect of God and should be tolerated. They come in and jump up and down and scream, but we can't lay a hand on them, because they are LSD saints. If we had touched that boy this morning, the whole neighborhood would be down on us. The Diggers next door are pretty noisy, but they unplug their jukebox during lectures, and they've been very friendly, giving us clothing and helping us decorate the temple. Sometimes the Hell's Angels go over there and raise a lot of noise, and sometimes they even come in here. If they do, best to humor them. They are always trouble."

That very morning some Hell's Angels started a fight in the Diggers' store. The devotees could hear thuds and screams through the walls as a big black beat up three Hell's Angels. The brawl ended only after a police car and an ambulance arrived.

Afterwards, about a dozen people drifted into the temple, talking about the brawl. Harṣarāṇī put out extra plates for the guests.

* * *

One day in March eighteen-year-old Wayne Gunderson was walking down the street when a piece of paper, blowing along the sidewalk, caught on his foot. He tried to kick it off without breaking his stride, but it hung on. Then he stopped and tried to kick it off. He couldn't. He reached down and picked it off and found that it was a flyer—"Stay High Forever"—advertising lectures by Swami Bhaktivedanta at 518 Frederick Street.

Like so many others, Wayne, a mild-mannered young man who worked for the post office, had come to Haight-Ashbury to take part in the revolution. He attended rock concerts and be-ins, browsed through the books and posters in the psychedelic shops, shared an apartment with his girl friend and another couple, and took drugs. But he was quiet, polite, and solitary. He didn't dress like a hippie, but wore clean, conservative, casual clothes and a whimsical, odd-looking sports cap.

The flyer about the Swami seemed a timely coincidence, because Wayne had been planning to go to India to find a *guru*. He decided to go see Swami Bhaktivedanta on Frederick Street.

Wayne was surprised to find only a storefront. He was startled by the picture of the Swami in the window—no smiling, bearded *yogī*, but a shaven-headed swami with a stern look.

Wayne went in. It was a typical Haight-Ashbury scene, with hippies sitting around. But there were also a few people with big red beads strung like garlands around their necks. And up front he saw the Swami. Wayne was impressed as Prabhupāda began chanting Hare Kṛṣṇa, and he found the lecture firm and authoritative. The Swami stressed, "We are not these bodies." And when he spoke of Kṛṣṇa, he described Kṛṣṇa so personally that it was like being introduced to Kṛṣṇa.

After a few meetings, Wayne got up the nerve to ask a question: "Can one practice *haṭha-yoga* at the same time as Kṛṣṇa consciousness?"

"Oh, why do you want to spend so much time with that body?" Prabhupāda replied, and Wayne felt Prabhupāda's eyes look deep within him. "You are not that body." He said it so strongly that Wayne, who was easily hurt, felt like shrinking into the floor. "This body is not as important as the soul," Śrīla Prabhupāda explained. "So we shouldn't spend so much time with the body, exaggerating its needs." Then he smiled at Wayne. "Besides, all *yogas* culminate in Kṛṣṇa consciousness." And Wayne felt that smile lift him completely out of his diminished and crushed condition.

Several weeks later Wayne asked about initiation. When the devotees told him he should go up and see the Swami, Wayne went home and rehearsed his lines first. Anticipating what Prabhupāda would say, Wayne prepared his own responses and contrived the whole conversation. Then, nervously, he approached Prabhupāda's door.

But before he could even knock, the door opened, and there was Prabhupāda looking at him—not sternly, as in his picture, but kindly, as if expecting him. "Yes," Prabhupāda said, "come in." The incident completely shattered Wayne's planned approach. He concluded that Swamiji could read minds. So, trying to clear his mind of bad thoughts, he entered Prabhupāda's apartment.

Prabhupāda sat in his rocking chair, and Wayne, who usually sat on the floor, sat in the only other chair in the room. Wayne immediately felt uncomfortable, as he realized that it would be more proper to sit at Prabhupāda's feet. But feeling too weakhearted to alter the situation, he kept his seat, nervously fingering his sports cap. "Swamiji," he began, "I would like to be your disciple."

Prabhupāda immediately agreed. He asked whether Wayne could follow the four principles, and Wayne, although not even sure what the four principles were, said he could. Prabhupāda then asked him what principle was the most difficult for him to follow. "Well," he said, "I have difficulty with meat-eating." A lie—he was a vegetarian. But he was too shy to say that his real problem was uncontrolled sexual desire. Prabhupāda laughed, "Oh, that's no problem. We will give you *prasādam.* You can be initiated next week."

Wayne then asked if he would be able to go to India. He felt the Swami would be pleased to hear that his new follower wanted to go to his country. But Prabhupāda seemed displeased: "India? Why India?" Wayne thought. . . . The real reason he had wanted to go to India was to find a *guru.*

"Well," he said, "to learn Sanskrit."

"I will teach you Sanskrit," Prabhupāda replied. So there was no need to go to India. And he would be initiated by a genuine *guru* next week—right here in San Francisco.

Some devotees helped Wayne prepare for his initiation ceremony. Hayagrīva lent Wayne his *dhotī,* a piece of yellow cloth much too large for Wayne. Devotees set up a sacrificial arena in the storefront—a bed of earth, firewood, colored dyes, flowers.

During the ceremony Wayne was nervous. When Prabhupāda chanted the *mantras,* Wayne couldn't hear them exactly, so he just mimicked as best he could. And when Prabhupāda began the fire sacrifice, Wayne felt a little frightened because the initiation seemed such a serious commitment. He watched Prabhupāda gravely building the fire and saying the *mantras.* When Prabhupāda initiated Wayne with his new name, Upendra, Wayne didn't hear it clearly and began to worry. Then the ceremony ended, and Prabhupāda stood up and abruptly left the storefront.

Upendra: *Someone reminded me that I should go upstairs and give Swamiji an offering. So I decided to give him a baby blanket and a beach towel. It wasn't that I lacked money, but these things had some sentimental value to me, so I wanted to give them to Swamiji. I went upstairs to his room, and he was sitting at the foot of his mattress. I came in and bowed down and presented him with the baby blanket and beach towel. He held them up in his fingers and looked at them both in each of his hands. He said, "These things are useless," and he tossed them down on the floor. I was hurt, and I had nothing to say. I just sat there. After a while, I excused myself and went back to my apartment.*

The next day, I went to see Swamiji during his evening visiting time, and he had the beach towel and baby blanket out on the floor like rugs so that his guests who came to visit could have something to sit on. I felt satisfaction that he had found some use for my offerings.

Prabhupāda said that Upendra was not living up to his vows, since he was still living with his girl friend. Upendra felt guilty about breaking the principles forbidding illicit sex and intoxication, but he just couldn't follow them. He wanted to tell Swamiji but couldn't bring himself to do it. Besides, he thought, even if he confessed, how could he stop? Upendra's girl friend didn't like Kṛṣṇa consciousness, didn't want to meet Swamiji, and didn't want to come to the temple. So Prabhupāda decided that instead of marrying Upendra to her, he would save Upendra from her.

Prabhupāda decided to make Upendra a *brahmacārī.* Although Śrīla Prabhupāda had about twenty-five San Francisco disciples, hardly any were *brahmacārīs.* Practically the only solid one was Jayānanda, who was a little older than the rest. Jayānanda worked all day driving a cab, chanting Hare Kṛṣṇa even while driving. And when he was off work he would be at the temple, cooking or doing any service he could find or sitting with Prabhupāda in his apartment with the other devotees. He was known for his serious *japa.* Sitting cross-legged, eyes squeezed tightly shut, he would hold his strand of beads up in both hands and rock forward almost to the floor and back, chanting intensely, oblivious of the outside world. He was serious. And that was the only way one could remain a *brahmacārī.* In New York Prabhupāda had about a dozen *brahmacārīs,* but a more permissive attitude among his followers in San Francisco made *brahmacārī* life more difficult.

In the original Vedic society of ancient India, *brahmacārī* life began at the age of five. Parents would send their son to live with the *guru* at the *gurukula,* where the boy would receive basic education, spiritual instruction, and strict moral discipline under the *guru.* Even Lord Kṛṣṇa, in His transcendental pastimes on earth, had attended a *gurukula* and very humbly served His spiritual master.

The basic principle of *brahmacārī* life was celibacy. By practicing celibacy, the *brahmacārī* would develop great powers of memory and sensory control. And if such a trained *brahmacārī* later decided to take a wife, his sex life would be regulated, not licentious. But although *brahmacārī* life was necessary for a healthy society, Prabhupāda had seen within his own lifetime the rapid deterioration of *brahmacarya* almost to nonexistence.

And in America the situation was of course much worse. *Śrīmad-Bhāgavatam* tells of a young *brāhmaṇa,* Ajāmila, who fell from spiritual life because he had seen a drunken man embracing a half-naked prostitute. In America to see a half-naked prostitute in public was not uncommon. As soon as a *brahmacārī* walked out on the street, he would confront so many allurements. But Prabhupāda was convinced that *brahmacārīs* could protect themselves even in America if they regularly chanted Hare Kṛṣṇa and sincerely tried to follow the rules and regulations. Kṛṣṇa would protect them.

Prabhupāda had decided to ask Upendra to come and live with him as his personal servant. Prabhupāda's former servant, Raṇacora, had recently left his position. Although supposedly a *brahmacārī*, he had never been a serious *brahmacārī*. He had even seduced one of the young women devotees in New York. Prabhupāda had found out and had asked the girl why she had indulged in sex with Raṇacora if she wasn't planning to marry him. Prabhupāda's "Why?" had so disarmed the girl that she had been unable to answer. Prabhupāda had admonished her, "You girls should not make yourselves so cheap," and had given Raṇacora another chance.

But Raṇacora never became serious. After playing the drums during the big *kīrtana* at the Avalon Ballroom, Raṇacora had become fascinated with the dance hall. He would sneak out from his service, lie to Prabhupāda about his absence, and go looking for girls at the Avalon. One day he never returned. As one of the devotees reported to Prabhupāda, "He just disappeared into the strobe lights." Raṇacora did come back once—to ask Prabhupāda for money so that he could return to his home in New York.

Upendra, despite his weaknesses, was spontaneously attracted to Prabhupāda and liked to be with him whenever he could. Sometimes Upendra would go up to the apartment with one or two other devotees and just sit in front of Prabhupāda as Prabhupāda sat on the thin pillow behind his low desk. Sometimes Prabhupāda would continue reading or writing, and Upendra would sit and bask in his presence, simply watching him work. After ten minutes or so, Prabhupāda would look up and say, "All right, that is enough," and the boys would bow and leave. Upendra would also go to see Prabhupāda taking his lunch, and Prabhupāda would take some rice and vegetable from his plate, put them on a *capātī*, and offer them to Upendra. Although the *prasādam* was similar to the *prasādam* the devotees ate downstairs, Upendra thought that it tasted much better.

One day when Upendra was alone with Prabhupāda in his room,

Prabhupāda asked, "You are living with a young girl and people who take intoxicants?" For the second time, Upendra was convinced that Swamiji could read his mind and knew his entire life.

"Yes," Upendra admitted, "but I am not having—"

Prabhupāda interrupted: "That is not good."

"Swamiji, I am not having any sexual connections."

"Where there is a boy and where there is a girl," Prabhupāda said, "there is sex. You must come and live with me."

Upendra was delighted: "Yes, I'll come immediately."

He took a few belongings from his apartment, left everything else with his girl friend, and moved into the front room of Prabhupāda's apartment. He was now Swamiji's personal servant.

Prabhupāda requested him to keep his job at the post office. Around midnight, as soon as Upendra got off work, he would return to the apartment. (Prabhupāda always left the door unlocked for him.) Usually, soon after Upendra locked the door, crawled into his sleeping bag, and fell asleep he would be awakened by Prabhupāda speaking into his dictating machine, composing *Teachings of Lord Caitanya.* Upendra would nod off again and sleep until six.

Upendra relished this close association with his spiritual master and became always cheerful. "I just want to be Swamiji's dog," he would often tell the other devotees.

One time Upendra was reading to himself from *Śrīmad-Bhāgavatam:*

> The whole subject matter is so presented through the lips of Srila Sukadeva Goswami that any sincere audience who will lend his ears submissively to this message of the transcendental world, will at once relish the transcendental mellows distinguished from the perverted mellows of the material world. The ripen fruit is not dropped all of a sudden from the highest planet of *Krishna Loka* but it has come down carefully being handled by the chain of disciplic succession without any change or disturbance in the formation of the soft and ripen fruit.

"You don't have any questions?" Prabhupāda asked.

Upendra looked up from the book: "No, Swamiji, I accept everything you say." Prabhupāda began rocking strongly in his rocking chair and smiled as Upendra kept reading. Then Prabhupāda taught Upendra the proper way to hold a book while reading—with the palms of both hands "up and off the lap." This advice gave Upendra greater enthusiasm to please his spiritual master by reading his books.

Upendra was still bothered by sexual desires. He thought that maybe he should get married. But he was confused about what a Kṛṣṇa conscious marriage was supposed to be. How could you be married, he puzzled, if you don't love the girl you want to marry? And how could you love her without having sex with her? He wanted to ask Swamiji about this, but he kept it to himself, waiting for an opportunity and for the courage. Then one day he entered Prabhupāda's room as Prabhupāda paced back and forth from one end of the room, with its three large bay windows overlooking Frederick Street, to the other end, where his rocking chair sat. Now, Upendra decided, he could ask his question.

"Swamiji," he began, "may I ask a question?"

"Yes," Śrīla Prabhupāda replied, stopping his pacing.

"If a boy is separate from a girl, then how can he learn to love her?"

Prabhupāda began to walk back and forth again, chanting on his beads. After a moment he turned and said softly, "Love? Love is for Kṛṣṇa." And he walked toward the window and looked down at the street below. "You want a girl? Pick one." He pointed toward some women passing on the street. "There is no love in this material world," he said. "Love is for Kṛṣṇa."

Gradually, under Śrīla Prabhupāda's pure influence, Upendra began to feel less agitated by sexual demands. He came to understand that he was not a material body but a spiritual soul, that the soul's eternal nature was to love Kṛṣṇa, and that for a pure devotee—for Swamiji—love *was* for Kṛṣṇa.

More and more, Upendra just wanted to be the servant of Swamiji. He thought of what foods to buy for him and how to make things comfortable for him. It was in this mood of wanting to serve Swamiji that Upendra visited the Psychedelic Shop one day. He had heard they had recently received some prints from India, so he went in and browsed through the prints, picked out some pictures of Lord Kṛṣṇa, and took them to Swamiji.

In Prabhupāda's room, along with other devotees, Upendra unrolled the prints one by one on Prabhupāda's desk, waiting to see Prabhupāda's response. As Upendra watched, it seemed to him that Swamiji was looking at photos of his personal friend. He was pleased with the pictures. Hayagrīva commented that the religious art of the Indian prints was a bit garish, but Prabhupāda explained that the technique didn't matter. The important thing was that the pictures were of Kṛṣṇa and were executed according to Vedic descriptions. For the devotee they were beautiful; they were nondifferent from Kṛṣṇa.

Prabhupāda selected as his favorite a picture of Lord Kṛṣṇa standing and playing His flute in the moonlight, the River Yamunā flowing by. In this picture Kṛṣṇa was known as Govinda. Prabhupāda held the picture up and quoted a verse:

smerāṁ bhaṅgī-traya-paricitāṁ sāci-vistīrṇa-dṛṣṭiṁ
vaṁśī-nyastādhara-kiśalayām ujjvalāṁ candrakeṇa
govindākhyāṁ hari-tanum itaḥ keśi-tīrthopakaṇṭhe
mā prekṣiṣṭhās tava yadi sakhe bandhu-saṅge 'sti raṅgaḥ

He then took a sheet of paper and began writing, while the devotees watched him intently, listening to the scratching of the pen on the page. Then he read aloud: "My dear friend, if you still have an inclination to enjoy material life, society, friendship, and love, then please do not see the boy named Govinda, who is standing in a three-curved way, smiling and skillfully playing on His flute, His lips brightened by the full moonshine."

"Yamunā, you can write this nicely?" Prabhupāda knew that Yamunā was a trained calligrapher. He asked her to print the verse and display it, along with the picture, by his sitting place in the temple. He wanted to be able to look at it during *kīrtanas.*

Upendra thought and prayed, "If I can just fix myself steadily in serving Swamiji, who has such love for Kṛṣṇa, then I too will become transcendental." He felt that since it was not possible for him to see Govinda the way Swamiji saw Him, he should serve Swamiji, the pure devotee of Govinda, and in that way become pure. "I just want to become Swamiji's dog," Upendra said as he left the apartment.

* * *

In New York the boys had their orders from Prabhupāda not to give any more money to Mr. Price unless there was a purchase contract. Prabhupāda still wanted the building. He had written to Brahmānanda on March 4, "I hope when I go to New York next I shall enter the new house forthwith." And he had written Rāya Rāma on March 7, "I am very glad to learn that Brahmananda, yourself and all others have the transcendental courage to take all risks for Krishna and this act will enhance your glory in Krishna consciousness." But he wanted them not to be cheated by false promises.

Meanwhile, Mr. Price was asking the devotees to turn over $5,000 to his financier friend, Mr. Hall, who would then add $20,000 and make the down payment to the owner, Mr. Tyler. Mr. Price wanted Brahmānanda to get the point across to His Excellency that negotiations had to be done in this fashion, and right away, if they seriously wanted to get the house.

Brahmānanda wrote to Prabhupāda, asking him to advise the bank to transfer $5,000 into the account controlled by the boys, the trustees of the International Society for Krishna Consciousness. Prabhupāda gave permission and asked that the check be signed by the president and secretary, because "Brahmananda and Satsvarupa are the main support for purchasing this house, and Kirtanananda is a supplement to this from his kitchen department." But he said that the check should be made to the seller, Mr. Tyler, not to the financier, Mr. Hall. "The money and the society is yours," Śrīla Prabhupāda acknowledged. "You can spend in any way but it is my duty to give you advice as ever well-wisher."

Then Mr. Price invited Brahmānanda to meet Mr. Hall; and he suggested that Brahmānanda come prepared with a check for $5,000. On the way, Mr. Price explained that Mr. Hall was perhaps the biggest real estate dealer in Manhattan—a multi-multimillionaire. He owned skyscrapers. Everything he owned was big. When Brahmānanda entered Mr. Hall's office, he thought it was right out of a Hollywood movie—a conference room ten times bigger than the Second Avenue temple room. And seated at the head of the large oval table was Mr. Hall himself. The room was in semidarkness, with a few spotlights on Mr. Hall, who sat before a battery of telephones. Even as they began to discuss, Mr. Hall paused several times, picking up phones and talking to persons in various places across the country.

"Young man," Mr. Hall said to Brahmānanda, "we are helping you get the house. It is a beautiful house, a New York City landmark." Then Mr. Hall's girl friend called from a boat in the Caribbean. He talked to her for a while and then returned to Brahmānanda and Mr. Price, who sat in the shadows at his conference table.

Mr. Hall had a big contract he wanted Brahmānanda to sign. Brahmānanda knew that Swamiji wanted a contract—and here it was. He also knew that if he signed over the $5,000 he would have no other money and no extra income; and he knew they knew it. But Swamiji wanted the building. Swamiji himself had looked at $100,000 buildings and had offered to buy them, even though he had very little money to back his offers up. And Brahmānanda always did whatever Swamiji said. To sign this contract, Brahmānanda concluded, was an act of faith in Swamiji and Kṛṣṇa. He didn't analytically ask "Where will the rest of the money come from?" To do so, he thought, would be like doubting Swamiji.

So here he was in this big-time financier's office. It was awesome. The millionaires were going to help. Mr. Price was at Brahmānanda's elbow. Mr. Hall was telling Brahmānanda that everything was all right: "We are going to get you this house." Now it was actually going to happen. Here was one of the biggest men in Manhattan offering to help. And whereas Brahmānanda had no money, Mr. Hall would be able to pick up the place very easily from the owner. Glancing quickly over the contract, Brahmānanda signed. It was a deal. And he gave them the check for $5,000.

As soon as Brahmānanda and Mr. Price left Mr. Hall's office, there was a distinct change in Mr. Price. Although still acting as Brahmānanda's friend, he now said, "Gee, you know, now you have to get this money." As they walked together on the uptown streets, Mr. Price cheerfully pushed the whole thing onto Brahmānanda. That was the change: before, Mr. Price had been saying that he and Mr. Hall were going to do it, but now he said that it was all up to the devotees. Brahmānanda asked about the legal position. Mr. Price explained that only the Kṛṣṇa Society was bound. But what about the promises? What about Mr. Hall's being so rich and wanting to help them and Mr. Price's wanting to help? Mr. Price assured Brahmānanda that he and Mr. Hall did want to help. They were doing everything they could. But Brahmānanda and the other devotees should also do everything they could and come up with the $20,000 to complete the down payment by the end of the month. And what if they couldn't? Mr. Price made it very clear: "If you don't pay the balance in a month, then you lose your deposit."

By the time Brahmānanda reached 26 Second Avenue he realized he had been cheated. He was crushed. He turned to the other devotees and told them what had happened, but they could only return, "Why did you do it?" Brahmānanda phoned Śrīla Prabhupāda in San Francisco. Now that his eyes had been opened about Mr. Price, Brahmānanda was blunt about his mistake, and he told Prabhupāda that he had given away the $5,000.

"All of it is gone?" Śrīla Prabhupāda asked.

"Yeah," Brahmānanda replied. He heard Prabhupāda hang up the phone. Brahmānanda had been about to explain the whole thing, but Swamiji had just hung up without a word. Brahmānanda placed the receiver back on the hook. He was shaken.

The next day the trustees held a special meeting. The boys sat around in the front room of Prabhupāda's apartment trying to decide what to do. Gargamuni again called Prabhupāda, who advised them to stop the check at the bank. "Swamiji's as smart as a fox," Rāya Rāma smiled. Gargamuni phoned the bank. But it was too late; the check had already been cashed.

They consulted Mr. Goldsmith, their friendly lawyer. He said it sounded like a weak legal case. Price and Hall hadn't legally bound themselves to pay anything if the devotees failed to pay; and if the devotees couldn't pay the $20,000 balance by the end of the month, they would lose their $5,000 deposit. They could sue for fraud, but court fees would be costly.

Then, one by one, Brahmānanda, Satsvarūpa, Kīrtanānanda, Rāya Rāma, Gargamuni, and the others began to look at the letters from Prabhupāda and discuss how he had warned them to avoid being cheated. Their greatest blunder, they began to realize, was disobeying his instructions. He had told them not to trust the promises of these businessmen, and he had told them that the check should be made only to the owner, not to the financier.

Within a few days, further instructions from their spiritual master came in the mail. There were admonishments, but hearing from him, even if he was chastising them, was better than the pain of his hanging up the phone without a word. "But you have not followed my instructions and now you are in trouble," he wrote to the boys.

He wrote Rāya Rāma,

> You are all foolish boys. I repeatedly warned you, even at the last point, that we should not pay the check unless there was agreement between

> Mr. Tyler and Mr. Hall. The agreement was signed like a marriage ceremony without the presence of the bride-groom. The mistake was there, and now you are repenting.

To Satsvarūpa he wrote,

> You have asked me whether the San Francisco branch will pay some money for purchasing the house. But where is your house and where is the purchase? So far it is talks of Mr. Price and company in which you innocent boys have been entrapped. I do not know how I can help you in your great blunder. I can only hope that Krishna will help you.

Unlike the boys and their lawyers, Prabhupāda thought that the legal case against the businessmen would be a strong one.

> I am not a Lawyer but this is common sense affair. Mr. Hall has taken the money, and he must finance to purchase the house. If he has no money to finance then it is a cheating case clear and simple.

The culprits, he said, should be brought to criminal court; their conspiracy and fraud were obvious and could be proven.

> From the telephonic conversation of Brahmananda it appears to be an organised cheating case and you have to face with courage without excusing any one of them. We are not revengeful but we cannot lose Krishna's money for nothing.

The boys had already blundered so much that Prabhupāda doubted whether they could tackle the cheaters. But he said they had to try: "Let us have the house or return back the money. In default, there is clear case of cheating. Now you can do as you like."

Śrīla Prabhupāda wrote the boys' lawyer, relating the history of the case. He also wrote a letter to the financier, the owner, and Mr. Price, threatening to expose everything, including what he alone had seen: that the lawyers involved were also implicated. Brahmānanda could barely understand what was going on, but it appeared that Swamiji was going to get results. The boys were fools, certainly, but the businessmen were certainly cheaters. And Swamiji claimed that he could prove it in court.

While admonishing his blundering disciples and going fiercely after the cheaters, Śrīla Prabhupāda still remained the ultimate shelter for his foolish boys. In a letter to the six trustees of his New York branch, he shed transcendental light into their gloomy minds.

> Forget the chapter. Take it for granted that Krishna has taken away this money from you for your deliberate foolishness. In future be very cautious and abide by the orders of Krishna. If you abide by the orders of Krishna, He can give you things that you may need. Be cheerful and chant Hare Krishna without any lamentation. As I have told you several times, that my Guru-maharaj used to say that this world is not a fit place for a gentleman. His version is corroborated by the following verse of Srimad-Bhagavatam. It is said like:
>
> Yasya asti bhagavati akincana bhakti
> Sarvai gunais tatra samasate sura.
> Harau abhaktasya kuto mahat guna
> Manorathen asato dhavato bahi
>
> "A person who is not in Krishna consciousness has no good qualifications. However so called gentleman one may be or academically educated he may be he is hovering over the mental plane and therefore he must commit nuisance being influenced by the external energy. A person who has however unflinching faith in the Supreme Personality of Godhead has all the good qualifications of the demigods." In other words you should not keep your trust on so called gentlemen of the world however nicely dressed he may be. In the matter of discharging our mission of Krishna consciousness we have to meet so many so-called gentlemen but we must be very cautious for dealing with them as we are cautious in dealing with serpents.

Now, more than ever, the boys in New York wanted Swamiji to come back. Although most of the talk in the temple was still about real estate, they were holding regular *kīrtana* and lecture programs, and two new boys had joined. Jadurāṇī had finished some new paintings of Lord Viṣṇu, which now hung in the temple, and she was waiting anxiously for Swamiji to come and see them. Some devotees had made a new speaker's seat in the temple for Swamiji. They knew they were fools, but they asked him please to come back. He agreed. He set April 9 as the date for his return to New York. But meanwhile he still had much to do in San Francisco.

* * *

One day Mālatī hurried into Śrīla Prabhupāda's apartment, took a small item out of her shopping bag, and placed it on Prabhupāda's desk for his inspection. "What is this, Swamiji?"

Śrīla Prabhupāda looked down and beheld a three-inch wooden doll with a flat head, a black, smiling face, and big, round eyes. The figure had stubby, forward-jutting arms, and a simple green and yellow torso with no visible feet. Śrīla Prabhupāda immediately folded his palms and bowed his head, offering the little figure respects.

"You have brought Lord Jagannātha, the Lord of the universe," he said, smiling and bright-eyed. "He is Kṛṣṇa. Thank you very much." Śrīla Prabhupāda beamed with pleasure, while Mālatī and others sat amazed at their good fortune of seeing Swamiji so pleased. Prabhupāda explained that this was Lord Jagannātha, a Deity of Kṛṣṇa worshiped all over India for thousands of years. Jagannātha, he said, is worshiped along with two other deities: His brother, Balarāma, and His sister, Subhadrā.

Excitedly, Mālatī confirmed that there were other similar figures at Cost Plus, the import store where she had found the little Jagannātha, and Śrīla Prabhupāda said she should go back and buy them. Mālatī told her husband, Śyāmasundara, and together they hurried back and bought the two other dolls in the set.

Śrīla Prabhupāda placed the black-faced, smiling Jagannātha on the right. In the center he placed the smallest figure, Subhadrā, who had a red, smiling mouth and a rectangular black and yellow torso. The third figure, Balarāma, with a white, round head, red-rimmed eyes, and a happy red smile, had the forward-jutting arms like Jagannātha and a blue and yellow base. Prabhupāda placed Him next to Subhadrā. As Prabhupāda looked at them together on his desk, he asked if anyone knew how to carve. Śyāmasundara said he was a wood sculptor, and Prabhupāda asked him to carve three-foot-high copies of the little Jagannātha, Balarāma, and Subhadrā.

More than two thousand years ago, Śrīla Prabhupāda told them, there was a king named Indradyumna, a devotee of Lord Kṛṣṇa. Mahārāja Indradyumna wanted a statue of the Lord as He had appeared when He and His brother and sister had traveled on chariots to the holy field of Kurukṣetra during a solar eclipse. When the king requested a famous artist from the heavenly planets, Viśvakarmā, to sculpture the forms, Viśvakarmā agreed—on the condition that no one interrupt his work. The king waited for a long time, while Viśvakarmā worked behind locked doors. One day, however, the king felt he could wait no longer, and he broke in to see the work in progress. Viśvakarmā, true to his word, vanished, leaving behind the uncompleted forms of the three deities. The king was nevertheless so pleased with the wonderful forms of Kṛṣṇa, Balarāma, and Subhadrā that he decided to worship them as they were. He installed them in a temple and began worshiping them with great opulence.

Since that time, Śrīla Prabhupāda continued, Lord Jagannātha has been worshiped all over India, especially in the province of Orissa, where there is a great temple of Lord Jagannātha at Purī. Each year at Purī, during the gigantic Ratha-yātrā festival, millions of pilgrims from all over India come to worship Lord Jagannātha, Balarāma, and Subhadrā, as the deities ride in procession on three huge carts. Lord Caitanya, who spent the last eighteen years of His life at Jagannātha Purī, used to dance and chant in ecstasy before the Deity of Lord Jagannātha during the yearly Ratha-yātrā festival.

Seeing this appearance of Lord Jagannātha in San Francisco as the will of Kṛṣṇa, Prabhupāda said that they should be careful to receive and worship Lord Jagannātha properly. If Śyāmasundara could carve the forms, Prabhupāda said, he would personally install them in the temple, and the devotees could then begin worshiping the deities. San Francisco, he said, could be renamed New Jagannātha Purī. He chanted, *jagannāthaḥ svāmī nayana-patha-gāmī bhavatu me.* "This is a *mantra* for Lord Jagannātha," he said. "*Jagannātha* means 'Lord of the universe.' 'O Lord of the universe, kindly be visible unto me.' It is very auspicious that He has chosen to appear here."

Śyāmasundara bought three large blocks of hardwood, and Prabhupāda made a sketch and pointed out a number of details. Using the small statues, Śyāmasundara calculated ratios and new dimensions and began carving on the balcony of his apartment. Meanwhile, the devotees bought the rest of the tiny Jagannāthas from Cost Plus, and it became a fashion to glue a little Jagannātha to a simple necklace and wear Him around the neck. Because Lord Jagannātha was very liberal and merciful to the most fallen, Śrīla Prabhupāda explained, the devotees would soon be able to worship Him in their temple. The worship of the forms of Rādhā and Kṛṣṇa in the temple required very high, strict standards, which the devotees were not yet able to meet. But Lord Jagannātha was so merciful that He could be worshiped in a simple way (mostly by chanting Hare Kṛṣṇa), even if the devotees weren't very much advanced.

Prabhupāda set March 26, the appearance day of Lord Caitanya, as the day for installing the deities. The devotees would have a big feast and begin worshiping Lord Jagannātha. Prabhupāda said they would have to build an altar, and he told them how to prepare it.

While Śyāmasundara hurried to finish his carving, a small splinter lodged itself in his hand, and the wound became infected. Finally Śyāmasundara got blood poisoning and became so sick that he had to go to the hospital. Lord Jagannātha was taking away the reactions to Śyāmasundara's previous sinful activities, Prabhupāda said.

On March 26, the appearance day of Lord Caitanya, Prabhupāda said that during the morning they would stay together in the temple, read about Lord Caitanya, and hold *kīrtana*, and in the evening they would have a ceremony for installing Lord Jagannātha. Having fasted until moonrise, they would then break fast with a *prasādam* feast.

When Śrīla Prabhupāda entered the temple that morning, he saw the work the devotees had done. The new altar stood in the rear of the room, above where his dais had been, and his dais was now on the right side of the room, against the wall. From his seat he would be able to see the altar very easily. The altar was a simple redwood plank seven feet above the floor and fixed between two thick redwood pillars. A canopy covered the place where the deities would stand. Below the altar hung Haridāsa's painting of Lord Caitanya and His associates dancing during *kīrtana*, and behind the painting was a madras backdrop. About three feet above the floor, a shelf below the painting held candlesticks and would be used for articles to be offered to the deities.

Prabhupāda took his seat. As usual, he led *kīrtana* and then chanted one round of *japa* with the devotees. Then he had Hayagrīva read aloud from the biographical sketch of Lord Caitanya from the first volume of *Śrīmad-Bhāgavatam.* But many devotees were sleepy, despite Hayagrīva's reading loudly with force and elocution. Although Prabhupāda was listening attentively and wanted the others to sit with him and hear about Lord Caitanya, when he saw that so many were dozing he stopped the reading and held another *kīrtana.* Then he chanted *japa* with them for about fifteen minutes.

"All right," he said. "We will read again. Who will read?" Līlāvatī's hand flew up urgently. "All right." He had her sit near his dais, and someone placed a microphone before her. Līlāvatī's reading presented a contrast to the deep tones of Hayagrīva. But she was another scholarly voice. Her careful pronunciation of the Sanskrit words and phrases was pleasing to Śrīla Prabhupāda, and he several times commented, "Oh, very nice." Līlāvatī was thrilled and read on intensely, determined to keep everyone awake.

That evening, devotees and hippie guests filled the room to capacity. Prabhupāda was present, and the mood was reverential and festive. It was a special event. The just-finished deities sat on the altar, and everyone was glancing at them as they stood on their redwood shelf beneath a yellow canopy, their features illumined by spotlights. The deities wore no clothes or ornaments, but were freshly painted in bright black, red, white, green, yellow, and blue. They were smiling. Śrīla Prabhupāda was also glancing at them, looking up to their high altar.

Prabhupāda lectured about the four social and four spiritual orders of life described in the Vedic literatures. According to one's quality and work, he said, each person has a certain occupational duty. "But the ultimate goal of that duty," he explained, "is to satisfy the Supreme Lord." It doesn't matter if one is lowborn or poor. "Material qualification has nothing to do with spiritual evolution. Spiritual evolution is that with your talent, with your capacity, with your work, you have to satisfy the Supreme Lord."

Prabhupāda gave the example of Śrīdhara, an impoverished devotee of Lord Caitanya's who earned the equivalent of less than five cents a day yet offered half his earnings in worship of the Ganges. If one were rich, however, one should still give half his wealth to the service of the Lord. Prabhupāda cited Rūpa Gosvāmī, who had given fifty percent of his wealth for Kṛṣṇa consciousness, given twenty-five percent for his family, and saved twenty-five percent for emergencies. Suddenly Prabhupāda began speaking about the money his disciples in New York had lost: "And twenty-five percent for himself so that in times of emergency . . . because as soon as money is gone out of my hand, I have no control. We have recently lost $6,000—not here, in our New York. So as soon as the check is out of hand, now it is gone. It is gone. . . ."

Prabhupāda gestured to indicate money flying like a bird out of his hand. At this reference to the troubling, entangling affair with Mr. Price and the foolish boys and their hard-earned money gone, Prabhupāda paused for a moment. Then he continued with the lecture.

"Paying attention to Bhagavān, the Supreme Person, is practical," Śrīla Prabhupāda said. "Here is Kṛṣṇa. Kṛṣṇa's form is there. Kṛṣṇa's color is there. Kṛṣṇa's helmet is there. Kṛṣṇa's advice is there. Kṛṣṇa's instruction is there. Kṛṣṇa's sound is there. Everything Kṛṣṇa. Everything Kṛṣṇa. There is no difficulty.

"But if you turn your attention to the impersonal and to the Supersoul in the heart, as the *yogīs* do, then it is very difficult. It is very difficult. You cannot fix your attention to the impersonal. In the *Bhagavad-gītā* it is said that, *kleśo 'dhikataras teṣām avyaktāsakta-cetasām:* 'Those who are attached to the impersonal feature of the Absolute Truth—their business is very troublesome.' It is not like chanting, dancing, and eating—this is very nice. But *that* is very troublesome. And even if you speculate on the impersonal, the result that is achieved by working hard for many, many lives is that you will have to also eventually come to Kṛṣṇa."

Śrīla Prabhupāda continued describing Kṛṣṇa as the Supreme Personality of Godhead, citing evidence from scriptures like *Bhagavad-gītā* and *Brahma-saṁhitā.* The first step in spiritual life, he explained, was to hear from Kṛṣṇa Himself. But Prabhupāda warned that if one heard the class and then went outside and forgot, he could not improve. "Whatever you are hearing, you should say to others," Prabhupāda said. And he gave the example of how disciples were writing in *Back to Godhead* what they had heard from their spiritual master. And to speak or write what one has heard, a person has to be thoughtful. . . .

"You are hearing about Kṛṣṇa, and you have to think. Then you have to speak. Otherwise, it will not work. So, *śrotavyaḥ kīrtitavyaś ca dhyeyaḥ pūjyaś ca.* And you should worship. Therefore, you require this

Deity for worshiping. We have to think of, we have to speak, we have to hear, we have to worship (*pūjyaś ca*). And should we do this occasionally? No. *Nityadā:* regularly. Regularly. This is the process. So anyone who adopts this process—he can understand the Absolute Truth. This is the clear declaration of the *Śrīmad-Bhāgavatam.* Thank you very much. Any question?"

A young boy raised his hand and began earnestly: "Well, you mentioned about how we should follow the supreme law, how we should be like what your spirit tells you? Or what you, your supreme, whatever it tells you? I mean . . . whatever it tells you? I mean, if you meditate a lot, you feel you should do . . . something. . . ."

Prabhupāda: "It is not *something.* It must be actual fact."

Boy: "Yeah, I mean like . . ."

Prabhupāda: "So, there is no question of *something.*"

Boy: "Well, I see . . ."

Prabhupāda: "*Something* is vague. You must speak what is that something."

Boy: "Well, let's say, be . . . uh . . ."

Prabhupāda: "That you cannot express. That means you have no idea. So we have to learn. This is the process. I am speaking of the process. If you want to have knowledge of the Absolute Truth, the first thing is faith. Then you must be thoughtful. Then you must be devoted, and you must hear from authentic sources. These are the different methods. And when you come to the ultimate knowledge—from Brahman platform to Paramātmā platform, then to the Supreme Absolute Personality of Godhead—then your duty shall be to satisfy the Supreme Personality of Godhead. That is the perfection of your active life. These are the processes. And it is concluded that everyone, never mind what he is—his duty is to satisfy the Supreme Personality of Godhead.

"And how can we satisfy? We have to hear about Him, we have to speak about Him, we have to think about Him, we have to worship Him—and that is *regularly.* This will help you. But if you have no worship, if you have no thought, if you have no hearing, if you have no speaking, and you are simply thinking of *something, something, something*—that *something something* is not God."

Boy: "I mean, well, you know, I'm so young. I didn't know what I meant. I don't know what . . ."

Prabhupāda: "*Don't know.* That I am speaking—that you have to *know* by these processes. We are all 'don't knows.' So we have to *know.* This is the process."

Young woman: "Since we don't yet understand the supreme law, because we are young and just new to this, then how can we speak about it?"

Prabhupāda: "Therefore you have to hear! The first thing is *śrotavyaḥ:* you have to hear. Unless you hear, how can you speak? We are therefore giving you facility to hear. You hear, and then you can speak. Then you can think. We are giving all facility to hear, to speak, to think, to worship. This is the Society's work. Unless you hear, how can you speak? The first task is given: *śrotavyaḥ.* Then *kīrtitavyaś ca dhyeyaḥ pūjyaś ca nityadā.* These are the processes. You have to hear. And hearing, you have to repeat, chant. And then you have to think. You have to worship. These are the processes."

Upendra: "Swamiji . . . so we have to hear, I understand. But do we speak, or do we first listen for a long time and then speak?"

Prabhupāda: "No. Why a long time? Suppose you hear two lines. You repeat that two lines. And aside from everything else, you hear Hare Kṛṣṇa. So you can chant Hare Kṛṣṇa. What is the difficulty there? *Śrotavyaḥ kīrtitavyaś ca.* You have to hear and chant. So if you cannot remember all the topics which we are speaking from the *Bhagavad-gītā* or *Śrīmad-Bhāgavatam,* you can at least remember this: Hare Kṛṣṇa. Therefore, it is the easiest process. You hear Hare Kṛṣṇa and chant Hare Kṛṣṇa. The other things will come automatically.

"Now, this is possible for everyone. Even the child can repeat Hare Kṛṣṇa. What is the difficulty? You hear Hare Kṛṣṇa and chant Hare Kṛṣṇa. We are not giving you very difficult or troublesome task. Then everything will follow. We are giving you everything. But if you feel in the beginning it is difficult, then you can do this—this is very nice—chant Hare Kṛṣṇa. You are doing that, actually. Hearing and chanting—this process will help you. It is the basic principle of advancement in spiritual life. Without hearing, we shall simply concoct, waste our time, and mislead people. We have to hear from the authoritative sources."

Śrīla Prabhupāda paused. The philosophical talk had been rigorous, lasting about forty-five minutes. He wasn't tired—he could have gone on—but now he wanted to conduct the deity installation. Everything necessary for spiritual life was here: the temple, the devotees, the books, the

Deity, *prasādam*. He wanted these young people to take advantage of it. Why should they remain living like animals and thinking of spiritual life as a vague groping for "something"? They should take advantage of Kṛṣṇa's mercy and be successful and happy. And for this, Prabhupāda was their tireless servant.

Prabhupāda: "So, Hayagrīva? Come here." Prabhupāda had had the devotees arrange for a large candle on a plate. The ceremony he had planned would be a simple one, with devotees and guests one after another coming up and offering the flame in circles before the Jagannātha deities. "This should be lighted up," Śrīla Prabhupāda said, "and when there is *kīrtana*, one must be doing like this before the Deity." (Śrīla Prabhupāda moved his hands around in a circle before the Deity.) "You see?"

Hayagrīva: "Yes, yes."

Prabhupāda: "Yes, with the *kīrtana*. And then when one person is tired he should hand it over to another person, devotee. When he is tired he should give to another—as long as the *kīrtana* will go on. This should be done with the *kīrtana* just now. Do you follow? Yes. You begin, and when you are tired you hand over to another. It will go on like that."

Śrīla Prabhupāda, from his seat, guided Hayagrīva in approaching the Deity with the lit candle. Some of the girls tittered with nervous expectation. "Before the Deity," Śrīla Prabhupāda said. "All right. Now better begin *kīrtana*."

Prabhupāda began playing *karatālas* and singing the Hare Kṛṣṇa *mantra* to the popular melody he had introduced in America. "Just in front," he called out, gesturing to Hayagrīva to stand more directly before the deities. Devotees and guests began rising to their feet and dancing, arms raised, bodies swaying rhythmically back and forth as they faced the bright, personal forms of the deities and chanted. Colored lights within the canopy began flashing intermittently blue, red, and yellow, highlighting the extraordinary eyes of Lord Jagannātha, Subhadrā, and Balarāma. Mukunda, who had arranged the lights, smiled and looked to Swamiji, hoping for approval. Prabhupāda nodded and continued forcefully singing Hare Kṛṣṇa.

The young hippies were enthusiastic in singing and dancing, knowing that the *kīrtana* usually lasted an hour. Some had grasped the Swami's words when he had spoken of fixing the mind on the personal form of the Supreme Lord; and they had understood when he had looked up at the deities and said, "Here is Kṛṣṇa." Others hadn't followed, but thought that it was just great and blissful to sing Hare Kṛṣṇa and look at the grinning, big-eyed deities up on the altar, amid the flowers and billowing incense.

Prabhupāda watched with pleasure as one person after another took a turn at offering the candle before Lord Jagannātha. This was a simple procedure for installing the Deity. Although in big temples in India the installation of the Deity was a complex, exact procedure, requiring several days of continuous rituals directed by highly paid priests, in San Francisco there were no *brāhmaṇa* priests to pay, and the many other standards would be impossible to maintain.

For non-Hindus to handle Lord Jagannātha and conduct His worship would be considered heresy by the caste-conscious *brāhmaṇas* of India. Except for Prabhupāda, none of the persons present would have been allowed even to enter the temple at Jagannātha Purī. The white man, the Westerner, was not allowed to see Lord Jagannātha except once a year as He rode in His cart during the Ratha-yātrā festival. But these restrictions were social customs, not the scriptural injunctions. Śrīla Bhaktisiddhānta Sarasvatī had introduced Deity worship and initiation for anyone, regardless of caste, race, or nationality. And Bhaktivinoda Ṭhākura, Śrīla Bhaktisiddhānta Sarasvatī's father, had longed for the day when the people of the West would mingle with their Indian brothers and chant Hare Kṛṣṇa.

Śrīla Prabhupāda had come to the West to fulfill the desires and the vision of his spiritual master and of Bhaktivinoda Ṭhākura by creating Vaiṣṇavas among the Westerners. Now, if the Westerners were to become actual devotees, they would have to be given the Deity worship. Otherwise it would be more difficult for them to become purified. Śrīla Prabhupāda was confident in his spiritual master's direction and in the scriptures. He had faith that Lord Jagannātha was especially merciful to the fallen. He prayed that the Lord of the universe would not be offended by His reception at New Jagannātha Purī.

When the *kīrtana* ended, Prabhupāda asked Haridāsa to bring him the candle. Prabhupāda passed his hands across the flame and touched them to his forehead. "Yes," he said, "show everyone. Each and every one. Whatever they can contribute. Here, take it like this and show everyone." He indicated that Haridāsa should present the candle before each person in the room so that all present could touch their hands to the flame as he had shown and then touch their foreheads. As Haridāsa went from person to person, a few devotees dropped some coins on the plate, and others followed.

Śrīla Prabhupāda explained further: "The *Bhāgavatam* has recommended hearing, chanting, thinking, and worshiping. This process which we just now introduced on the advent of Jagannātha Svāmī means that now this temple is now completely fixed. So this is the worshiping process. This is called *ārati*. So at the end of *kīrtana*, this *ārati* will go on. And the worshiping process is to take the heat of the light and, whatever your condition is, pay something for the worship. So this simple process, if you follow, you just see how you realize the Absolute Truth.

"Another thing I request you: All the devotees—when you come to the temple, you bring one fruit and one flower. If you can bring more fruit, more flower, it is very good. If not, it is not very expensive to bring one fruit and one flower. And offer it to the Deity. So I will request you, when you come to the temple you bring this. Whatever fruit it may be. It does not mean that you have to bring very costly fruit. Any fruit. Whatever you can afford. One fruit and one flower."

He paused, looking around the room: "Yes, now you can distribute *prasādam*."

The guests sat in rows on the floor, and the devotees began serving *prasādam*, offering the first plate to Prabhupāda. The food preparations were those Prabhupāda had personally taught the devotees in his kitchen: *samosās, halavā, puris*, rice, several cooked vegetables, fruit chutney, sweets—all the Sunday specials. The guests loved the *prasādam* and ate as much as they could get. While the devotees, especially the expert women, served more and more *prasādam*, the guests relaxed and enjoyed an evening of feasting and convivial conversation. After Prabhupāda tasted all the preparations, he looked up with raised eyebrows: "Very nice preparations. All glories to the cookers."

A few minutes later, as the feasting continued, Śrīla Prabhupāda spoke into the microphone, "*Jagannāthaḥ svāmī nayana-patha-gāmī bhavatu me*. Howard, repeat this."

Hayagrīva swallowed, cleared his throat, and spoke up: "*Jagannāthaḥ svāmī nayana-patha-gāmī bhavatu me*."

Prabhupāda: "Yes, this should be chanted. *Jagannāthaḥ svāmī nayana-patha-gāmī bhavatu me.*"

A boy asked what it meant. Hayagrīva replied, "Oh . . . uh, Lord of the universe, please be present before me."

When Prabhupāda noticed an older, respectably dressed man leaving the room without receiving a feast plate, Prabhupāda became concerned: "Oh, why is he going away? Ask him to come."

A boy ran after him, opening the temple door and calling, "Please don't leave. Swamiji requests . . ."

As the man reentered the storefront, Prabhupāda requested, "Please, please, take *prasādam.*" And turning to the servers, he instructed, "Give him *first.*" And so the feasting continued beneath the altar of Lord Jagannātha and under the auspices of His servant, Śrīla Prabhupāda.

The next day, acting on a whim, the devotees took the Jagannātha Deity off the altar and carried Him to Golden Gate Park for a *kīrtana.* Within minutes, hundreds gathered in the meadow below Hippie Hill, dancing and chanting around Lord Jagannātha. After several hours, the devotees returned Him to the altar.

Prabhupāda disapproved: "The Deity should never leave the temple. The deities don't go out to see the people, except on special occasions. They are not for parks for birds to drop stool on. If you want to see the deities, you have to visit *them.*"

Lord Jagannātha's presence quickly beautified the temple. Devotees made garlands for Him daily. Jadurāṇī's paintings of Lord Viṣṇu arrived from New York, and Govinda dāsī had painted a large portrait of Śrīla Prabhupāda, which now hung beside his seat. Devotees also put Indian prints of Kṛṣṇa on the walls. The lights flashing upon Lord Jagannātha made His eyes seem to pulsate and His colors move and jump, and He became a special attraction in the psychedelic neighborhood of Haight-Ashbury.

As Prabhupāda had requested, devotees and guests began bringing offerings before the altar of Lord Jagannātha. Hippies would come by and leave whatever they could: a stalk of wheat, half a loaf of bread, a box of Saltines, a piece of fudge, or candles, flowers, or fruit. Hearing that before using something for yourself you should first offer it to God, some hippies began bringing their new clothes and offering them with a prayer to Lord Jagannātha before wearing them. These hippies didn't follow Lord Jagannātha's instructions, but they wanted His blessings.

Each night, the devotees performed the *ārati* ceremony just as Prabhupāda had taught them, taking turns offering a candle before Lord Jagannātha. When the devotees asked whether they could add anything to the ceremony, Prabhupāda said yes, they could also offer incense. He said there were many more details of Deity worship, numerous enough to keep the devotees busy twenty-four hours a day; but if he were to tell them everything at once, they would faint.

Speaking privately in his room to one of his disciples, Prabhupāda said that during *kīrtana* in the temple he thought of Lord Caitanya dancing before Lord Jagannātha. He told how Lord Caitanya had traveled to Purī and danced before Lord Jagannātha in such ecstasy that He had been unable to say anything more than "Jag—, Jag—." Lord Caitanya had been thinking, "Kṛṣṇa, for so long I wanted to see You. And now I am seeing You." When Lord Caitanya had lived in Purī, as many as five hundred men at a time would visit Him, and every evening there would be a huge *kīrtana* with four parties, each with four *mṛdaṅga* players and eight *karatāla* players. "One party this side, one party this side," Prabhupāda explained. "One party back side, one party front side. And Caitanya Mahāprabhu in the middle. They would all dance, and the four parties would chant, "Hare Kṛṣṇa, Hare Kṛṣṇa, Kṛṣṇa Kṛṣṇa . . .' That was going on every evening so long He stayed at Jagannātha Purī."

The devotees understood that there was a great difference between themselves and Swamiji. He had never been a hippie. He wasn't at home amid the illusion of Haight-Ashbury's LSD, psychedelic posters, rock musicians, hippie jargon, and street people. They knew he was different, though sometimes they forgot. He spent so much time with them every day—eating with them, joking with them, depending on them. But then sometimes they would remember his special identity. When they chanted with him in the temple before Lord Jagannātha, he, unlike them, would be thinking of Lord Caitanya's *kīrtanas* before Lord Jagannātha in Purī.

When Lord Caitanya had seen Jagannātha, He had seen Kṛṣṇa, and His love for Kṛṣṇa had been so great that He had gone mad. Prabhupāda thought of these things to a degree far beyond what his disciples could understand—and yet he remained with them as their dear friend and spiritual instructor. He was their servant, teaching them to pray, like him, to be able to serve Kṛṣṇa: "O Lord of the universe, kindly be visible unto me."

* * *

Govinda dāsī had a question for Swamiji. He had mentioned briefly that Lord Caitanya used to cry in separation from Kṛṣṇa and had once even thrown Himself into a river, crying, "Where is Kṛṣṇa?" She was unsure whether her question would be proper, but she waited for an opportunity to ask it.

One evening after the lecture, when Prabhupāda asked for questions and there were none, Govinda dāsī thought, "This is my chance." But she hesitated. Her question wasn't on the subject of his lecture, and besides, she didn't like to ask questions in public.

"No question?" Śrīla Prabhupāda looked around. Govinda dāsī thought Swamiji seemed disappointed that there were no questions. He had said several times that they should ask questions and clear up any doubts. Again he asked, "Have you got any questions?"

Govinda dāsī: "Uh, well, could you tell about Lord Caitanya asking . . ."

Prabhupāda: "*Hmm?*"

Govinda dāsī: ". . . asking where is Kṛṣṇa?"

Prabhupāda: "*Hmm?*"

Govinda dāsī: "Could you tell about Lord Caitanya asking where is Kṛṣṇa and falling in the water? Or would that be not . . ."

Prabhupāda smiled. "Yes, yes. Very nice. Your question is very nice. Oh, I am very glad.

"Lord Caitanya—He was the greatest symbol of *kṛṣṇa-bhakti*, a devotee of Kṛṣṇa. So just see from His life. He never said that, 'I have seen Kṛṣṇa.' Never said, 'I have seen Kṛṣṇa.' He was *mad* after Kṛṣṇa. That is the process of Caitanya philosophy. It is called *viraha. Viraha* means 'separation' . . . 'separation': 'Kṛṣṇa, You are so good, You are so merciful, You are so nice. But I am so rascal, I am so full of sin, that I cannot see You. I have no qualification to see You.' So in this way, if one feels the separation of Kṛṣṇa—'Kṛṣṇa, I want to see You, but I am so disqualified that I cannot see You'—these feelings of separation will make you enriched in Kṛṣṇa consciousness. Feelings of separation. Not that 'Kṛṣṇa, I have seen You. Finished. All right. I have understood You. Finished. All my business finished.' No! *Perpetually*. Think of yourself that 'I am unfit to see Kṛṣṇa.' That will enrich you in Kṛṣṇa consciousness.

"Caitanya Mahāprabhu displayed this—these feelings of separation. This is Rādhārāṇī's separation. When Kṛṣṇa went from Vṛndāvana to His place, His father's place, Rādhārāṇī was feeling in that way—always mad after Kṛṣṇa. So Kṛṣṇa Caitanya, Caitanya Mahāprabhu, took the separation feeling of Rādhārāṇī. That is the best way of worshiping Kṛṣṇa, becoming Kṛṣṇa conscious. So you know that Lord Caitanya fell on the sea: 'Kṛṣṇa, if You are here. Kṛṣṇa, if You are here.'

"Similarly, the next devotees, Lord Caitanya's direct disciples, the Gosvāmīs—Rūpa Gosvāmī, Sanātana Gosvāmī—they also, the same disciplic succession, they also worship Kṛṣṇa in that separation feeling. There is a nice verse about them."

Śrīla Prabhupāda sang:

he rādhe vraja-devike ca lalite he nanda-sūno kutaḥ
śrī-govardhana-kalpa-pādapa-tale kālindi-vanye kutaḥ
ghoṣantav iti sarvato vraja-pure khedair mahā-vihvalau
*vande rūpa-sanātanau raghu-yugau śrī-jīva-gopālakau**

"These Gosvāmīs also, later on when they were very much mature in devotional service—what were they doing? They were *daily* in the Vṛndāvana *dhāma*, just like a *mad*man: 'Kṛṣṇa, where You are?' That is the quality.

---

*"I offer my respectful obeisances to the six Gosvāmīs, namely, Śrī Rūpa Gosvāmī, Śrī Sanātana Gosvāmī, Śrī Raghunātha Bhaṭṭa Gosvāmī, Śrī Raghunātha dāsa Gosvāmī, Śrī Jīva Gosvāmī, and Śrī Gopāla Bhaṭṭa Gosvāmī, who were chanting very loudly everywhere in Vṛndāvana, shouting, 'Queen of Vṛndāvana, Rādhārāṇī! O Lalitā! O son of Nanda Mahārāja! Where are you all now? Are you just on the hill of Govardhana, or are you under the trees on the bank of the Yamunā? Where are you?' These were their moods in executing Kṛṣṇa consciousness."

"It is a very nice question."

Śrīla Prabhupāda paused and uttered a thoughtful "*Mmm.*" He remained silent. They also remained silent, watching him. He sat cross-legged on the black velvet pillow on the redwood dais. His hands were folded, his eyes closed. And he became overpowered by inner feelings of ecstasy. Although the simple devotees present could not know what was happening, they could *see* him enter a deep inward state. They could feel the atmosphere transform into awesome devotional stillness. They kept their eyes fixed on him.

A minute and a half passed. Śrīla Prabhupāda uttered another thoughtful "*Mmm*" and opened his eyes—they were filled with tears. He reached over and grasped his *karatālas*, which rattled in his hand. But he moved no further. Again he withdrew from external consciousness.

Another minute of silence passed. The minute seemed extremely calm, yet intense and long. Another minute passed. After almost four minutes, Prabhupāda cleared his throat and struck the *karatālas* together, beginning the slow rhythm. A devotee began the one-note drone on the harmonium. Prabhupāda sang: *govinda jaya jaya gopāla jaya jaya/ rādhā-ramaṇa hari govinda jaya jaya*, building the chanting to a lively pace. After about ten minutes the *kīrtana* stopped, and Prabhupāda left the room.

As the devotees rose and began their various duties—some leaving out the front door behind Prabhupāda and going to the kitchen, others coming together for conversation—they all knew that their spiritual master had been intensely feeling separation from Kṛṣṇa. They had no doubt that it was a deep ecstasy, because just by being in his presence during that long and special stillness they also had felt a glimmer of the same love for Kṛṣṇa.

* * *

On the invitation of his disciples, Śrīla Prabhupāda agreed to hold a *kīrtana* on the beach. On a Tuesday night, with no *kīrtana* or lecture scheduled in the temple, he got into the back seat of one of the devotees' cars. About a dozen initiated followers and a couple of dogs got into other cars, and together they traveled to the beach. When they arrived, some devotees went running across the beach, gathering driftwood and building a fire in the shelter of a sand dune.

The late afternoon air was cool, and there was a seaside wind. Prabhupāda was dressed in a long checkered coat over a hooded sweatshirt. During the *kīrtana* he clapped and danced while the devotees joined hands, forming a circle around him. As the sun was setting, all the devotees faced the ocean, raising their arms and singing as loudly as they could, "*Hariiii* Bol!" But with the surf pounding in on the coast and with the great expanse of windy air around them, their *kīrtana* sounded very small.

Gathering around the fire, the devotees buried foil-wrapped potatoes and foil-wrapped apples filled with raisins and brown sugar under the coals. It was their idea, but Prabhupāda was happy to comply with their ideas of California *kīrtana* fun.

Haridāsa and Hayagrīva had composed a song about the sage Nārada Muni, and they sang it for Prabhupāda.

> Do you know who is the first eternal spaceman of this universe?
> The first to send his wild, wild vibrations
> To all those cosmic superstations?
> For the song he always shouts
> Sends the planets flipping out.
> But I'll tell you before you think me loony
> That I'm talking about Narada Muni,
> Singing
> HARE KRISHNA HARE KRISHNA
> KRISHNA KRISHNA HARE HARE
> HARE RAMA HARE RAMA
> RAMA RAMA HARE HARE

Prabhupāda laughed. He liked anything that had chanting in it. And he asked them to compose more such songs for their countrymen.

Walking together along the beach, they came upon an old dilapidated Dutch windmill. "Mukunda," Prabhupāda said, "you should approach the government and tell them that we will restore this windmill if they let us build a temple on this site." Mukunda took it as a joke at first, but then he saw that Prabhupāda was completely serious. Mukunda said he would inquire about it.

Prabhupāda, in his oversized checkered coat buttoned up to the neck, was the beloved center of the devotees' outing. After their walk, he sat with them on a big log, eating baked potatoes smeared with melted butter; and when he finished he threw his remnants to the dogs.

As the night grew dark, stars appeared high over the ocean, and the devotees stood close around Prabhupāda for a last *kīrtana.* Then, just as in the temple, they bowed down, and Prabhupāda called out the prayers to the Lord and the disciplic succession. But he ended: "All glories to the assembled devotees! All glories to the assembled devotees! All glories to the Pacific Ocean!"

They all laughed. Swamiji was doing what his disciples wanted: enjoying an evening *kīrtana*-cookout at the beach with them. And they were doing what he wanted: chanting the *mahā-mantra,* becoming devotees of Kṛṣṇa, and becoming happy.

* * *

Hayagrīva sat facing Prabhupāda, alone with Prabhupāda in his room. A few days before, Hayagrīva had shown Prabhupāda a play about Lord Caitanya he had found in the library, and Prabhupāda had said it wasn't bona fide. So Prabhupāda decided to prepare an outline for a bona fide play and have Hayagrīva write it. "I will give you the whole plot complete," Śrīla Prabhupāda said. "Then all you will have to do is execute it."

Prabhupāda was in a relaxed, jolly mood, intent on relating the events of Lord Caitanya's life. He had prepared an outline of twenty-three scenes, and now he wanted to expound each one. Hayagrīva had barely enough time to understand what Prabhupāda was about to do and almost no time to prepare himself for note-taking as Prabhupāda began describing the first scene.

"First scene," he began, "is that people are passing on the road with *saṅkīrtana,* just as we do. There is a very nice procession with *mṛdaṅga* and *karatālas* and that bugle, and all people are doing *saṅkīrtana* in the ordinary way. We have to make a nice procession.

"The second scene shows Kali as decorated blackish with royal dress and very ugly features. And his queen is another ugly-featured lady. So they are disturbed. They will talk amongst themselves that, 'There is the *saṅkīrtana* movement now, so how shall we prosecute our business in this Age of Quarrel, Kali-yuga?' In that scene there will be in one corner two or three people drinking. The scene will be like that. The Age of Quarrel personified and his consort are sitting in the center. In one corner someone is taking part in drinking, and in another part somebody is illicitly talking of lust and love with a woman. In another section there is slaughtering of a cow, and in another section, gambling. In this way, that scene should be adjusted. And in the middle, the ugly man, Kali, and the ugly woman will talk that, 'We are now in danger. The *saṅkīrtana* movement has been started. What to do?' In this way, you have to finish that scene.

"Then the third scene is very nice—*rāsa* dance."

Hayagrīva interrupted. He had some of his own ideas about what he called "the dramatic point of view." "I think," Hayagrīva said, strongly articulating his words, "this can apply for the whole world, in the sense that the names may be Indian but I think the exhibition you described of the assembly of Kali and his consort Sin and the exhibition of illicit sex and the slaughterhouse can all be from Western prototypes."

Śrīla Prabhupāda said that he had no objection to Hayagrīva's suggestion but that he didn't want people to think he was singling out Westerners, as if they were the only ones who committed illicit sex. Hayagrīva was about to reply but decided that this was no time to quibble; Swamiji was eager to go on describing the pastimes of Lord Caitanya.

Prabhupāda: "*Rāsa* dance means Kṛṣṇa and Rādhārāṇī in the center and the *gopīs* are surrounding. You have seen that surrounding scene when they were dancing with us the other day in the park hand to hand?"

Hayagrīva: "Yes, yes."

Prabhupāda: "So one Kṛṣṇa and one *gopī*—they are dancing. That should be the scene. Then the *rāsa* dance should be stopped, and Kṛṣṇa will talk with the *gopīs*. Kṛṣṇa will say to the *gopīs* that, 'My dear friends, you have come to Me in the dead of night. It is not very good, because it is the duty of every woman to please her husband. So what your husband will think if you come in such dead of night? So please go back.'

"So in this way the *gopīs* will reply that, 'You cannot request us to go back, because with great difficulty and with great ecstatic desire we have come to You. And it is not Your duty to ask us to go back.' In this way, you arrange some talking that Kṛṣṇa is asking them to go back but they are insisting, 'No, let us continue our *rāsa* dance.'

"Then when the *rāsa* dance is finished, the *gopīs* will go, and then Kṛṣṇa will say, 'These *gopīs* are My heart and soul. They are so sincere devotees they do not care for family encumbrances or any bad name. They come to Me. So how shall I repay them?' He was thinking, 'How shall I repay their ecstatic love?' So He thought that, 'I cannot repay them unless and until I take up their situation to understand Me. But I Myself cannot understand Me. I have to take the position of the *gopīs*—how they are loving Me.'

"So with that consideration He took the form of Lord Caitanya. Therefore, Kṛṣṇa is blackish, and Lord Caitanya is the color of the *gopīs*. The whole life of Lord Caitanya is the representation of the *gopīs'* love toward Kṛṣṇa. That should be painted in the picture of this scene. Do you have anything to ask?"

Hayagrīva: "This is His determination to incarnate as Lord Caitanya?"

Prabhupāda: "Lord Caitanya, yes."

Hayagrīva: "In order to . . . ?"

Prabhupāda: "In order to appreciate Kṛṣṇa in the form of a *gopī*. Just like I have got dealings with you. So you have got your individuality, and I have got my individuality. But if I want to study how you are so much obedient and loving to me, then I have to go to your position. It is very natural psychology. You have to paint in that way."

Prabhupāda described and explained one story after another, most of them new to Hayagrīva. Hayagrīva couldn't properly spell or even pronounce the names; he didn't know who Lord Caitanya's mother was or whether Nityānanda was a devotee. And when Prabhupāda told the story of Kṣīra-cora Gopīnātha, the Deity who stole condensed milk for His devotee, Hayagrīva got confused and thought Prabhupāda had said that Lord Caitanya had stolen the condensed milk.

Prabhupāda: "No. Oh. You did not hear? Caitanya, after seeing the Deity, He was sitting and seeing, and meantime Nityānanda Prabhu narrated the story how the Deity's name became Kṣīra-cora Gopīnātha. You do not follow me?"

Hayagrīva groped, "Nityānanda?"

Prabhupāda: "Nityānanda was going with Lord Caitanya . . ."

Hayagrīva: "Nityānanda was narrating this to Lord Caitanya?"

Prabhupāda: "Yes, the Deity was known as Kṣīra-cora Gopīnātha. The story"—Prabhupāda repeated for the third time—"was narrated that formerly He stole one pot of condensed milk for His devotee."

Hayagrīva: "Now, what direct relationship does this have to Lord Caitanya?"

Prabhupāda: "Lord Caitanya visited this temple. Anyone in those days going to Jagannātha Purī from Bengal had to pass that way. And on the way, the Kṣīra-cora Gopīnātha temple is there. So everyone used to visit. Formerly, Mādhavendra Purī also visited, and for him the Deity stole the condensed milk. From that time, the Deity is known as Kṣīra-cora Gopīnātha. That story was narrated to Caitanya Mahāprabhu. So while sitting before the Deity, the story was narrated, and Caitanya Mahāprabhu relished that God is so kind that sometimes He steals for His devotee. This is the significance. So here the scene should be arranged that it is a very nice temple, the Deity is within, and Lord Caitanya has entered while chanting Hare Kṛṣṇa. And then He saw the worship, *ārati.* These things are to be shown in this scene. And a little story about Him, that's all."

When Prabhupāda told of Lord Caitanya's visit to the Sākṣi-Gopāla temple, Hayagrīva again got lost. "Do you follow?" Prabhupāda asked.

"No," Hayagrīva chuckled. "No."

Eventually, Hayagrīva stopped asking questions and interrupting. Although he had very little knowledge of the identity or meaning of the characters, as soon as he had heard a little about them he had been trying to adjust and rearrange their activities from the "dramatic point of view." Prabhupāda had raised no objections to Hayagrīva's inquiries. In fact, Prabhupāda had invited them, so that Hayagrīva could understand how to present the play. Hayagrīva, however, decided to first try to hear what Prabhupāda was saying.

By the end of the first hour of their talk, Prabhupāda had narrated many scenes from the first half of Lord Caitanya's life: His teasing the *brāhmaṇas* by the Ganges at age five, His civil disobedience movement against the Muhammadan magistrate, His accepting the renounced order at age twenty-four, His last meeting with His beloved mother, His traveling to Purī and touring South India, His meeting and instructing disciples like Sārvabhauma, Rāmānanda Rāya, and Rūpa Gosvāmī and Sanātana Gosvāmī.

Finally Prabhupāda's morning schedule permitted him to go no further. It was time for him to bathe and take lunch. The next day they would meet again.

At the next session Hayagrīva listened more carefully, and the transcendental scenes came quickly, one after another. As Prabhupāda described each scene, speaking the words and thoughts of Lord Caitanya and His associates, Prabhupāda seemed to be seeing the scenes enacted before him. He especially became moved when he spoke of Lord Caitanya and Haridāsa Ṭhākura.

"The life of Haridāsa Ṭhākura," Prabhupāda said, "is that he was born in a Muhammadan family. Some way or other he became a devotee, and he was chanting three hundred thousand times: 'Hare Kṛṣṇa, Hare Kṛṣṇa, Kṛṣṇa Kṛṣṇa, Hare Hare/ Hare Rāma, Hare Rāma, Rāma Rāma, Hare Hare.' And Caitanya Mahāprabhu made him the *ācārya*, the authority of chanting. Therefore, we glorify him—*nāmācārya* Haridāsa Ṭhākura *ki jaya*—because he was made the *ācārya*, the authority of chanting Hare Kṛṣṇa.

"When Lord Caitanya took *sannyāsa*, Haridāsa Ṭhākura decided, 'My dear Lord, You are leaving Navadvīpa. Then what is the use of my life? Either You take me or let me die.'

"So Caitanya Mahāprabhu said, 'No. Why shall you die? You come with Me.' So He took him to Jagannātha Purī. In Jagannātha Purī, because he considered himself born of a Muhammadan family, Haridāsa did not enter the temple. But Caitanya Mahāprabhu gave him a place at Kāśīnātha Miśra's house. There he was chanting, and Caitanya Mahāprabhu was sending him *prasādam*. In that way he was passing his days. And Caitanya used to come and see him daily."

Śrīla Prabhupāda wanted a scene for the passing away of Haridāsa Ṭhākura.

Hayagrīva: "Is this the same Haridāsa the Muhammadans threw into the river?"

"Yes," Prabhupāda said.

Then very casually Hayagrīva mused aloud, "So he finally met his end there in the fifth scene?"

Prabhupāda hesitated. Here again Hayagrīva revealed his lack of transcendental knowledge, talking as though Haridāsa's passing away was the same as an ordinary man's meeting his end.

"All right," Hayagrīva cued him, "what is this particular incident?"

Prabhupāda: "The particular incident is significant. Caitanya Mahāprabhu was a *brāhmaṇa*, and He was a *sannyāsī*. According to social custom, He should not even touch a Muhammadan. But this Haridāsa Ṭhākura was a Muhammadan, and yet at his death He took the body Himself and danced. And He put him in the graveyard and distributed *prasādam*.

"Because Haridāsa was a Muhammadan, he did not enter the temple of Jagannātha Purī, because the Hindus were very strict. Haridāsa was a devotee, but he thought: 'Why should I create some row?' So Caitanya Mahāprabhu appreciated Haridāsa's humble behavior. Although he had become a devotee, he was not forcibly going to the temple. But then Caitanya Mahāprabhu Himself was daily coming and seeing him. While going to take bath in the sea, He will first of all see Haridāsa: 'Haridāsa, what you are doing?' Haridāsa will offer his respect, and He will sit and talk for some time. Then Caitanya Mahāprabhu will go and take His bath.

"In this way, one day when He came He saw Haridāsa not feeling very well: 'Haridāsa, how is your health?'

" 'Yes, sir, it is not very . . . after all, it is the body.'

"Then the third day He saw that Haridāsa is going to leave his body today. So Caitanya Mahāprabhu asked him, 'Haridāsa, what do you desire?' Both of them could understand. Haridāsa said that, 'This is my last stage. If You kindly stand before me.' "

Śrīla Prabhupāda became caught in the intense spiritual emotions of the scene, as if it were happening before him. He closed his eyes: "*Mmm.*" He stopped talking. Then he began again slowly, haltingly. "So Caitanya Mahāprabhu stood before him . . . and he left his body." Prabhupāda sighed and became silent. Hayagrīva sat staring at the floor. When he glanced up, he saw that Swamiji was crying.

Prabhupāda quickly summed up a few last scenes and ended his outline. "Now you write," he told Hayagrīva, "and I shall make some addition or alteration. This is the synopsis and framework. Now you can proceed." Hayagrīva left the room. The material was lengthy, and whether he would ever write the play was doubtful. But he was thankful to have received this special discourse.

* * *

Sitting on a bridge table in the student lounge, chanting into a little microphone while his followers played their instruments, Prabhupāda began the *kīrtana* at Stanford University. At first there were about twenty students, but gradually more entered the lounge and gathered around. Everyone was chanting. Then suddenly the lounge became transformed, as more than two hundred Stanford students, most of them completely new to the Hare Kṛṣṇa *mantra*, danced and chanted with as much enthusiasm as the most uninhibited Haight-Ashbury crowd. Prabhupāda led the *kīrtana* for more than an hour.

In his talk afterwards he explained what they had all just experienced: "This Hare Kṛṣṇa dance is the best process for getting out of this illusion that 'I am this body.' Our Society is trying to distribute to the world the priceless gift of the Lord. You did not understand the words, but you still felt the ecstasy to dance."

Prabhupāda took questions from the audience. Everything proceeded in a standard fashion until someone asked whether college students should respond to the military draft. Prabhupāda replied that since they had elected their own government, there was no use complaining if the government told them to go to war. But some of the students—the same students who had chanted and danced only minutes before—began to shout, "No! No!" Prabhupāda tried explaining his point, but they raised their voices in anger until the hall became a bedlam of shouting. Finally Śrīla Prabhupāda picked up his *karatālas* and began chanting again, and the dissenters left.

The next day, the *Palo Alto Times* ran a front-page story with headlines and a photo of the *kīrtana.*

Ancient trance dance features swami's visit to Stanford

> Hold on there a minute, all you "with it" people. There's a new dance about to sweep the country. It's called "the swami."
>
> It's going to replace the frug, watusi, swim and even the good old barn stomp.
>
> Why? Because you can do any old step to it and at the same time find real happiness. You can rid yourself of the illusion that you and your body are inseparable. . . .
>
> The chant started quietly but gained volume as more people joined in.

> After half an hour, a long-haired youth with three strings of red beads around his neck stood up and began to dance to the music. He closed his eyes in ecstasy and held his hands palms up shoulder high.
>
> Two girls soon followed him. One had a string of bells around her neck.
>
> A bearded fellow with a fluorescent pink skull cap joined in, still beating on his tambourine.
>
> The Swami cut in a microphone in front of him, and the added volume provoked others to chant and stomp more loudly.
>
> A pretty girl in a sari danced as if in a hypnotic trance.
>
> A short dark man neatly dressed in suit and tie threw off his shoes and joined in. A young math professor did likewise. A pretty, blond, 3-year-old girl rocked and swayed in one corner.
>
> Suddenly most of the audience was dancing and chanting. The pace grew faster and faster. Faces streamed with sweat; the temperature soared.
>
> Then it all stopped.

Śrīla Prabhupāda was pleased with the article and asked for some photocopies of it. "What are they calling the dance?" he laughed. "The Swami?" Across the top of the *kīrtana* photo he typed, "Everyone joins in complete ecstasy when Swami Bhaktivedanta chants his hypnotic Hare Kṛṣṇa."

The devotees got Prabhupāda an engagement at a YMCA, where the audience consisted almost entirely of children. The devotees had decorated the hall with posters of Kṛṣṇa and had hung a big sign with the *mahā-mantra* on it. The children chanted along with Prabhupāda during *kīrtana.* Just before the lecture, Guru dāsa reminded him, "Maybe the talk should be simple, since they are all between nine and fourteen years old." Prabhupāda nodded silently.

"Is there a student here who is intelligent?" Prabhupāda began. No one responded. After a moment a twelve-year-old boy, urged by his teachers and fellow students, raised his hand. Prabhupāda motioned for him to come forward. The boy wore thick glasses, short pants, and a blazer, and his hair was combed back very neatly. Pointing to the boy's head, Prabhupāda asked, "What is that?"

The boy almost scoffed at the simpleness of the question: "My head!"

Prabhupāda then pointed to the boy's arm and said quietly, "What is that?"

"My arm!" the boy said.

Prabhupāda then pointed to the boy's foot: "What is that?"

"My foot," the boy answered, still looking incredulous.

"Yes," Śrīla Prabhupāda said. "You say this is *my* head, *my* arm, *my* foot—*my* body. But where are *you*?" The boy stood perplexed, unable to answer Prabhupāda's simple question.

"We say *my* hand," Śrīla Prabhupāda continued, "but who is the owner of my hand? We say *my* hand, so that means someone owns my hand. But where does the owner live? I do not say '*I* hand,' I say '*my* hand.' So my hand and I are different. I am within my body, and you are within your body. But I am not my body, and you are not your body. We are different from the body. Real intelligence means to know who *I* am."

Haight-Ashbury's Psychedelic Shop, a popular hippie gathering place, had extended to Prabhupāda many invitations to come and speak. After the Mantra-Rock Dance the hippies there had put a sign in the window: A Night of Consciousness. Also in response to the Mantra-Rock Dance, they had opened a meditation room in the rear of their store. But since the hippies at the Psychedelic Shop were almost always intoxicated, Prabhupāda's followers had said that it wouldn't be a good idea for Prabhupāda to go. But the hippies kept entreating. Finally the devotees relented, advising Prabhupāda it might be all right for him to go.

So one Saturday night, Prabhupāda and two devotees walked over to Haight Street, to the Psychedelic Shop. Young people crowded the streets: hippies sitting along the sidewalk selling hashish pipes and other dope paraphernalia; homosexuals; wildly costumed hippies with painted faces; small groups smoking marijuana, drinking, singing, and playing guitars—a typical evening on Haight Street.

At the Psychedelic Shop, marijuana and tobacco smoke hung heavy in the air, mingling with the smell of alcohol and bodies. Prabhupāda entered the meditation room, its ceiling and walls covered with madrases, and sat down. The room was full of hippies, many lying down, heavily intoxicated, looking up at him with half-closed eyes. He spoke in a low voice, but his presence somehow held their attention. Although lethargic, the group was appreciative, and after Prabhupāda had finished, those who were still conscious expressed their approval.

* * *

On Saturday, April 1, near the end of his stay in San Francisco, Prabhupāda accepted an invitation from Lou Gottlieb, head of Morning Star Ranch, a nudist hippie commune. Morning Star was a bunch of young people living in the woods, the devotees explained to Prabhupāda. The hippies there had spiritual aspirations. They grew vegetables and worshiped the sun. They would hold hands and listen to the air. And naturally they were involved in lots of drug-taking and free sex.

When Lou came in the morning to pick up the Swami, they talked, and Prabhupāda gave him a *rasagullā* (a sweet made of bite-sized balls of curd simmered in sugar water). After a few minutes together in Prabhupāda's room, they started for Morning Star, sixty miles north of San Francisco.

Lou Gottlieb: *I told Swamiji to fasten his safety belt. He said no. He said Kṛṣṇa will handle it, or something. So on the way out I was showing off all my vast erudition in having read a biography of Ramakrishna. That's when Bhaktivedanta gave the best advice to the aspirant I ever heard. We were talking about Ramakrishna and Vivekananda and Aurobindo and this and that. So he said, "You know," putting a gentle hand on my knee, "when you have found your true path, all further investigation of comparative religion is merely sense enjoyment."*

Situated in a forest of redwoods more than two hundred feet tall, Morning Star Ranch occupied what had once been an egg farm. Some of the land had been cleared for farming. There were a few tents, some unsubstantial little huts, a couple of tree houses, but the only decent, insulated building was Lou's place, an old chicken house. The commune had about one hundred full-time members, with the number of residents rising to as many as three hundred on the weekends in warm weather, when people would come out to work in the garden or just walk around naked and get high.

Prabhupāda arrived at one in the afternoon on a beautiful sunny day. He first wanted to rest, so Lou offered his own house. Walking to Lou's place, Prabhupāda noticed a few nude men and women hoeing in the garden. One of the workers, a short, stocky young man, Herbie Bressack, stopped his work in the garden and came to greet the Swami.

Herbie: *Lou Gottlieb introduced us. We were planting potatoes at the time. He said, "This is Swami Bhaktivedanta." I came out of the garden and shook Swamiji's hand. I said, "Hello, Swami." He asked me, "What are you doing?" I told him that I was just planting potatoes. He then asked me what I was doing with my life. I didn't answer.*

After resting for a few minutes, Prabhupāda was ready for the *kīrtana.* He and Lou went to a hilly pasture where the hippies had placed a wooden seat for Prabhupāda before a bower of wild flowers arranged like a bandshell. Prabhupāda took his seat and began chanting. The commune members, all of whom had been anticipating the Swami's visit, gathered eagerly for the group meditation.

Mike Morissey: *Some people had clothes on, some people didn't. Some were dancing around. But Swamiji wasn't looking at our bodies, he was looking at our souls and giving us the mercy we needed.*

The *kīrtana* was well received. One of the members of the commune was so enthralled by the *kīrtana* that he decided to put on his clothes and go back to San Francisco with the Swami. Prabhupāda spoke very briefly, and then he prepared to leave, shaking hands and exchanging courtesies as he walked to the car.

Although Śrīla Prabhupāda hadn't spoken much philosophy, his *kīrtana* left a deep impression on the hippies at Morning Star. While leaving he had told one of the young men, "Keep chanting this Hare Kṛṣṇa *mantra* here." And they did.

Lou Gottlieb: *The Swami was an extremely intelligent guy with a job to do. There was no sanctimony or holy pretention, none of that eyes-lifted-silently-to-the-sky. All I remember is just a very pleasant, incredibly safe feeling. There's no doubt that the* mahā-mantra*—once you get the* mantra *into the head, it's there. It never stops. It's in the cells. It awakens the DNA or something. Shortly thereafter, half of the people at Morning Star got seriously into chanting. Those that did were extremely sincere God seekers. Their aspiration was a thousand percent sincere, considering the circumstances in which they were found. They were all dopers, that's for sure, but they definitely gave that up once they got in touch with the* mahā-mantra.

* * *

His top cloth wrapped loosely around his shoulders, Prabhupāda stood a last moment by the open door of the car and looked back in farewell to the devotees and the storefront temple. It was no longer a mere storefront but had become something worthy: New Jagannātha Purī.

Śrīla Bhaktisiddhānta Sarasvatī had asked him to come here. Who among his Godbrothers could imagine how crazy these American hippies were—hallucinating on drugs, crying out, "I am God!" So many girls and boys—unhappy, mad, despite their wealth and education. But now, through Kṛṣṇa consciousness, some were finding happiness.

The first day he had arrived the reporter had asked him why he had come to Haight-Ashbury. "Because the rent is cheap," he had replied. His desire was to spread the movement of Lord Caitanya; why else would he have come to such a dilapidated little storefront to live next to a Chinese laundry and Diggers' Free Store? The reporters had asked if he were inviting the hippies and Bohemians to take to Kṛṣṇa consciousness. "Yes," he had said, "everyone." But he had known that once joining him, his followers would become something different from what they had been before.

Now the devotees were a family. If they followed his instructions they would remain strong. If they were sincere, Kṛṣṇa would help them. Lord Jagannātha was present, and the devotees would have to worship Him faithfully. They would be purified by chanting Hare Kṛṣṇa and following their spiritual master's instructions.

Prabhupāda got into the car, accompanied by some of his disciples, and a devotee drove him to the airport. Several carloads of devotees followed behind.

At the airport the devotees were crying. But Prabhupāda assured them he would return if they would hold a Ratha-yātrā festival. "You must arrange a procession down the main street," he told them. "Do it nicely. We must attract many people. They have such a procession yearly in Jagannātha Purī. At this time the Deity may leave the temple."

He would have to return, he knew, to tend the delicate devotional plants he had placed in their hearts. Otherwise, how could he expect these neophytes to survive in the ocean of material desires known as Haight-Ashbury? Repeatedly he promised them he would return. He asked them to cooperate among themselves—Mukunda, Śyāmasundara, Guru dāsa, Jayānanda, Subala, Gaurasundara, Hayagrīva, Haridāsa, and the girls.

Only two and a half months ago he had arrived here at this very terminal, greeted by a throng of chanting young people. Many were now his disciples, although just barely assuming their spiritual identities and vows. Yet he felt no compunctions about leaving them. He knew that some of them might fall away, but he couldn't stay with them always. His time was limited.

Śrīla Prabhupāda, the father of two small bands of neophytes, tenderly left one group and headed East, where the other group waited in a different mood, a mood of joyful reception.

CHAPTER FOUR

"Our Master Has Not Finished His Work"

There was no warning that Śrīla Prabhupāda's health would break down; or, if there were, no one heeded it. As he moved from his devotees in San Francisco to his devotees in New York, no one passed any words that Swamiji should slow down. After the five-and-a-half-hour jet flight, Prabhupāda spoke of a "blockading" in his ears, but he seemed all right. He didn't rest, but went straight through the festive airport reception into three hours of strong lecturing and chanting in the storefront at 26 Second Avenue. To his New York disciples he appeared dazzling and lovable, and by his presence, his glances, and his words, he increased their Kṛṣṇa consciousness. To them his advanced age, now nearing seventy-two years, was but another of his transcendental features. He was their strength, and they never thought to consider *his* strength.

In the temple, speaking from a new dais behind a velvet-covered lectern, Prabhupāda said, "In my absence things have improved." New paintings hung on the freshly painted white walls. Otherwise, it was the same tiny storefront where he had begun his International Society for Krishna Consciousness.

He had written them that he wanted to enter the new building on his return, but they had failed. And they had foolishly lost six thousand dollars. But without dwelling on this, Prabhupāda made a more important observation: his disciples, despite the physical absence of their spiritual master, had made progress by following his instructions.

As he sat looking happily at the freshly painted walls and the bright faces of his disciples, Prabhupāda explained how one obtained expertise in Kṛṣṇa consciousness by submissively following the spiritual master. He gave the example that although an engineer's apprentice may not be expert, if he turns a screw under the direct supervision of the expert engineer *he is acting as an expert.* Many of the devotees were relieved to hear this. They knew that giving up material desires was difficult and that they weren't going to become completely pure devotees overnight. Brahmānanda had even written a poem stating that if, after many lifetimes, he could chant one round of the Hare Kṛṣṇa *mantra, with attention,* he would consider this the greatest success. But Prabhupāda was explaining that even if they weren't expert in love of Kṛṣṇa, if they worked under an expert they were also acting as experts.

The next morning, with the fanfare of Prabhupāda's arrival past, it became apparent just how dependent the devotees were on their spiritual leader. The attendance was down to the dozen or so regulars, and Prabhupāda silently entered the storefront and began to lead the chanting. But when the moment came for the devotees to sing in response and Prabhupāda heard their first chorus, he looked out to them, startled and compassionate. Now he could hear: they were weak—more like croaking than singing. They *had* deteriorated in his absence! The *kīrtanas* had changed while he had been away, and now he was hearing what the devotees were like: helpless souls croaking without joy or verve.

Śrīla Prabhupāda lectured from *Caitanya-caritāmṛta.* "When flying from San Francisco I noticed that the plane was flying above an ocean of clouds. When I came from India by boat I saw an ocean of water, and on the plane I saw an ocean of clouds extending as far as you can see. Above the clouds is the sun, but when we come down through the clouds and land, everything in New York is dim and clouded. But the sun is still shining. Those clouds cannot cover the whole world. They cannot even cover the whole United States, which is no more than a speck in the universe. From an airplane we can see skyscrapers as very tiny. Similarly, from God's position, all this material nonsense is insignificant. As a living entity, I am very insignificant, and my tendency is to come down. But the sun doesn't have the come-down tendency. It is always above the clouds of *māyā. . . .*"

A new boy raised his hand: "Why is it that one person, one soul, comes to Kṛṣṇa and another doesn't?"

Prabhupāda replied with another question: "Why is one soul in the

Bowery and another has come to the Kṛṣṇa temple?" He paused, but no one could reply. "Because one wants to be here and the other doesn't," he explained. "It is a question of free will. If we use it properly, we can go to Kṛṣṇa. Otherwise we will stay down in the material world."

Everyone had something to ask Swamiji. Throughout the day, devotees would be in and out of his room, asking practical and philosophical questions. And they took up their old ways of reciprocating with him. Once again Prabhupāda was telling Acyutānanda what to cook for lunch and explaining to him that an expert servant learns to anticipate what the master wants even before he asks for it.

Satsvarūpa came in to show Prabhupāda the latest typed manuscripts for *Teachings of Lord Caitanya.* Although there was no difference in Satsvarūpa's assignment, now that he was face to face with Prabhupāda he realized he had to type and edit more seriously. He asked whether he could resign from his job at the welfare office. Prabhupāda said no.

Jadurāṇī continued painting in the outer room of Prabhupāda's apartment. Casting shyness aside, she asked him many questions about how to paint Kṛṣṇa. "How is Lord Viṣṇu situated in the heart?" she asked. "Is He sitting, or standing, or what?"

Prabhupāda replied, "Oh, for that you have to meditate for thousands of years." Jadurāṇī stared at him in dismay. Then Prabhupāda said, "He is standing," and she went off happily to paint.

When Jadurāṇī complained of weak health, Prabhupāda asked Acyutānanda to see that she got milk twice a day. Looking through the window that opened into the outer room, where typing, painting, and sometimes even construction went on, Prabhupāda watched Jadurāṇī one day as she worked on a painting of Lord Caitanya's *saṅkīrtana* party. Just as she started to paint the words of the *mahā-mantra* across the bottom of the painting, Prabhupāda called through the window, "Don't put the *mahā-mantra* there."

"But you told me to put it there," she said.

"I've changed my mind. Hare Kṛṣṇa should not be below Caitanya Mahāprabhu."

One by one, Prabhupāda saw all his old New York followers: Gargamuni, the temple treasurer, who reported good sales of the Hare

Kṛṣṇa record and incense; Rāya Rāma, editor of *Back to Godhead*, who talked about his indigestion; and Rūpānuga, who had a good job but was having difficulty convincing his wife about Kṛṣṇa consciousness. Even Mr. Chutey, the landlord, dropped by with complaints about the boys' behavior.

Prabhupāda also met Michael Blumert, a newcomer. Michael had been seeing a psychiatrist as a result of devastating drug experiences. When he had begun coming to the temple, his mother and father had thought the Swami another evil force. On meeting Swamiji, however, Mrs. Blumert accepted his authenticity, although her husband remained doubtful. "Mr. Blumert," Śrīla Prabhupāda said, "your wife is more intelligent." Mr. Blumert said he wanted his son to help the world in a more practical way—by becoming a doctor. Prabhupāda argued that there were already so many doctors but still people were suffering. A Kṛṣṇa conscious person, however, could relieve a person's suffering completely; so the work of Kṛṣṇa consciousness was more valuable. Mr. Blumert was unconvinced, but he agreed to let Michael stay with the devotees and drop going to the psychiatrist. He came to respect the Swami, even though disagreeing with him.

With Brahmānanda, Prabhupāda discussed the urgent problem of obtaining a permanent visa. Prabhupāda had repeatedly extended his visa ever since he had entered the country in 1965. Now immigration officials denied him any further extensions. He didn't want to leave the U.S., but the only way he would be able to stay would be to get permanent residency. He had applied, but so far with no success. "Your government doesn't want me to stay," he had said, "so I may have to go back to India."

Swamiji's going back to India was a frightening prospect. His disciples had barely been able to accept that he could leave them for preaching elsewhere in the U.S. If he were to go back to India! They feared they might fall back into the material world. He was sustaining their spiritual life. How could they go on without him? And Prabhupāda felt the same way.

Brahmānanda managed to find a lawyer to delay the proceedings of the immigration office. The threat of deportation passed. Prabhupāda spoke of going to Montreal and getting permanent residency there, but his main intention was to stay in America and cultivate what he had begun.

Brahmānanda reported to Prabhupāda about printing the *Bhagavad-*

gītā. The manuscript was ready, and they were considering the costs and where to print it, even though they didn't have enough money to publish the book themselves. They hadn't seriously attempted the arduous process of finding a publisher, but Prabhupāda pushed Brahmānanda to do so: "The only hope is that I have my books."

Brahmānanda also talked with Prabhupāda about the six thousand dollars he had lost to Mr. Price. Prabhupāda insisted that they prosecute the culprits. He sent Brahmānanda to speak with various lawyers and also to tell Mr. Price and Mr. Tyler that "His Excellency" was back and would take them to court.

At that they relented. Mr. Tyler refunded most of the $5,000 deposit, and Mr. Price returned $750 of the $1,000 he had wheedled out of Brahmānanda. The legal services had cost more than a thousand dollars—so that was lost—but Prabhupāda said that when dealing with a tiger you can expect to get scratched.

In a letter to Kīrtanānanda in Montreal, Prabhupāda described the successful termination of the Price affair: "You will be glad to know that I have been able, by Grace of Krishna, to recover $4227 . . . out of the $5000.00 gone in the belly of Sir Conman Fraud (Price). . . ."

There were signs that Prabhupāda should be cautious about his health. He had gone through difficulty while appearing on the Allen Burke TV show. Allen Burke was known for sitting back, smoking a cigar, and saying outrageous, even insulting, things to his guests; and if a guest became offended, Mr. Burke would provoke him all the more. It was a popular show.

Before they went on the air, Mr. Burke had asked Prabhupāda's permission to smoke a cigar, and Prabhupāda had graciously consented. Mr. Burke had introduced his guest as "a real swami." When he had asked Prabhupāda why he was against sex, Prabhupāda had said he wasn't; sex should be restricted to marriage for raising Kṛṣṇa conscious children. But Mr. Burke had persisted, wanting to know what was wrong with sex outside of marriage. The real purpose of human life, Śrīla Prabhupāda had replied, was self-realization. When one's mind is preoccupied with capturing new sex partners, keeping the mental peace necessary for self-realization becomes impossible. Mr. Burke had agreed. In fact, his manners had been the best ever. And at the end he had called

Prabhupāda "a very charming gentleman."

It was on his way home to the temple that Śrīla Prabhupāda had said that the TV lights had caused him so much pain in his head that at one point he had thought he wouldn't be able to continue.

Then one day Rūpānuga, sitting close to Prabhupāda's dais during a lecture, noticed Prabhupāda's hand shaking as he spoke. Kīrtanānanda had been there when months ago, the morning after they had made the record, Prabhupāda had slept late and complained of his heart skipping and of not being able to move. "If I ever get badly sick," Śrīla Prabhupāda had told Kīrtanānanda, "don't call a doctor. Don't take me to a hospital. Just give me my beads and chant Hare Kṛṣṇa."

Swamiji's disciples were reluctant to restrain him. Kīrtanānanda had tried. At the Avalon, when Swamiji had been dancing and jumping and streaming with perspiration, Kīrtanānanda had insisted that the *kīrtana* stop. But the others had called him paranoid.

Besides, Swamiji didn't like to be restrained. And who were *they* to restrain *him*? He was Kṛṣṇa's empowered representative, able to surmount any difficulty. He was a pure devotee. He could do anything. Hadn't he often described how a pure devotee is transcendental to material pangs?

Swamiji had written a letter consoling a disciple's ailing grandmother.

> All our ailments are due to the external body. Although we have to suffer some time from bodily inconveniences specially in the old age, still if we are God conscious, we shall not feel the pangs. The best thing is therefore to chant the holy Name of the Lord Constantly.

The devotees figured that although Swamiji might give good instructions to someone's old grandmother, nothing like what had befallen her was ever going to affect him. Of course, he referred to himself as an old man, but that was mostly in lectures to show the inevitability of old age.

To the devotees, Prabhupāda's health appeared strong. His eyes shone brightly with spiritual emotions, his complexion was smooth and golden, and his smile was a display of health and well-being. One time, one of the boys said that Swamiji's smile was so virile that it made him think of a bull and iron nails. Swamiji was taking cold showers, going on early-morning walks around the Lower East Side, playing *mṛdaṅga*, eating well. Even if his disciples wanted to slow him down, what could they do?

Some of his disciples had actually tried to prevent him from attending the controversial Cosmic Love-In at the East Village Theater, but not because of his health; they had wanted to protect his U.S. residency case. Śrīla Prabhupāda had been invited to attend the Love-In, a fund-raising show for Louis Abolafia, the "Love and Peace" presidential candidate. Allen Ginsberg, Timothy Leary, and others were attending, along with a full line-up of rock bands. But when Prabhupāda's lawyer heard that he was going, he said it might jeopardize the visa case. Some of the boys took up the lawyer's opinion and opposed Prabhupāda's plan. Prabhupāda agreed that it might be best if he didn't go. But on the day of the Cosmic Love-In he changed his mind and decided to go anyway. "I came to this country to preach Kṛṣṇa consciousness," he declared. Now it was time to speak against these LSD leaders who claimed to be spiritualists. He had been saying that although he wanted to go, he wouldn't go if his disciples forbade him. But in the end he simply said he was going. And that was that.

During the last week of May, Śrīla Prabhupāda began to feel exhausted. He spoke of heart palpitations. Hoping that the symptoms would clear up in a day or two, Kīrtanānanda requested Prabhupāda to rest and see no visitors. But Prabhupāda's condition became worse.

Kīrtanānanda: *Swamiji began to complain that his left arm wasn't functioning properly. And then he began to develop a twitching in his left side, and his left arm would twitch uncontrollably. It seemed to pain him in some mysterious way, internally or psychologically.*

Acyutānanda: *It was Sunday, two days before Memorial Day, and we had arranged a large program in the afternoon in a hall uptown. I went up to get Swamiji, since all the devotees were ready. Swamiji was lying down, and his face was pale. He said, "Feel my heart." And I felt a quivering vibration in his chest.*

I went down, but didn't want to alert everyone and panic them. I went to Kīrtanānanda and quietly said, "The Swami is having some kind of mild heart palpitations." And immediately we both flew back up. Swamiji said, "Just massage here." So I rubbed him on the chest, and he showed me how. He said, "The others go, and Acyutānanda can stay here. If anything happens, he can call you."

So the others went and did the program, and I waited. Once or twice he called me in and had me quickly rub over his chest. Then he looked up, and his color had come back. I was staring with my mouth open, wondering what to do. He looked at me and said, "Why are you sitting idle? Chant Hare Kṛṣṇa." During the evening, palpitations again occurred, so I slept in the room next to his. And late at night he called me in and again had me massage.

Kīrtanānanda: *It was on Tuesday afternoon, Memorial Day, and I was sitting with Swamiji in his room. While* kīrtana *was going on downstairs, the twitching began again. The Swamiji's face began to tighten up. His eyes started rolling. Then all of a sudden he threw himself back, and I caught him. He was gasping: "Hare Kṛṣṇa." And then everything stopped. I thought it was the last, until his breathing started again, and with it the chanting. But he didn't regain control over his body.*

Brahmānanda: *I was there along with Kīrtanānanda. It was on Memorial Day weekend. We couldn't understand what was wrong with Swamiji. He couldn't sit up, he was moaning, and nobody knew what was happening. We nursed him—myself and Kīrtanānanda—trying all different things. I had to go out and buy a bedpan for him.*

Prabhupāda's left side was paralyzed. He asked that a picture of his spiritual master be put on the wall in front of him. Thinking that Prabhupāda was preparing to leave his body and wanted to meditate at the last moment on his spiritual master, Acyutānanda taped it to the door facing Prabhupāda.

Devotees entered the front room of the apartment, and Prabhupāda told them to chant Hare Kṛṣṇa. Then he told them to pray to Kṛṣṇa in His form of Nṛsiṁhadeva.

Satsvarūpa: *Swamiji said we should pray to Lord Nṛsiṁha and the prayer should be "My master has not finished his work." At different times he would allow us to take turns and massage different parts of his body. Then he had us go downstairs and hold* kīrtana *through the night.*

Jadurāṇī: *He taught us the prayers to Lord Nṛsiṁhadeva. He said the words one by one, and I wrote them down. I called up the temples in San Francisco and Montreal and told them the prayer. Swamiji said, "You should pray to Kṛṣṇa that, my spiritual master has not yet completed his work, so please let him finish."*

Dāmodara: *I went into the temple. No one was downstairs, so I just sat down to chant some rounds. Then a devotee came down looking very dis-*

turbed, so I asked what was going on. When he told me, I rushed upstairs. Everyone was sitting around in the second room, where they could see into Swamiji's room through the window in the wall. They were all chanting on their beads. Jadurāṇī was handing out little slips of paper with writing on them. Swamiji, she explained, wanted us to chant these prayers.

Brahmānanda: *We brought the painting of Lord Nṛsiṁha into Swamiji's room, and we were all chanting. When Swamiji had to use the bedpan in front of Lord Nṛsiṁha's painting, he begged forgiveness of Lord Nṛsiṁha. He could understand that Lord Nṛsiṁha was sitting right in front of him. I saw it as a painting, but Swamiji saw it as Lord Nṛsiṁha Himself sitting there.*

It was getting worse—total weakness and everything. I couldn't get a doctor, because it was Memorial Day and everything was closed. I even called my family doctor, but he wasn't in. Everyone had gone on vacation, because on Memorial Day everyone leaves the city. I couldn't get anyone. I was calling hospitals, doctors—trying this and that. But I couldn't get anyone. Finally I got a doctor by calling an emergency number for the New York City medical department. The doctor came. He was an old geezer with a real loud voice. When he saw Swamiji he said, "I think the old man is praying too much. I think he should get some exercise. He should go out for a walk in the morning."

Acyutānanda: *The doctor didn't know very much. He said that Swamiji had a cold. I said, "What do you mean? His heart is palpitating."*

"Hmm, *I don't know what to do. Does he take any whiskey?"*

I said, "He doesn't even drink coffee or tea."

"Ohhhh, *very good, very good. Well, I think he has just got a cold."*

Dvārakādhīśa dāsa: *He came and took a look at the place, and you could tell right away he didn't like what he saw. He thought we were just a bunch of hippies. He couldn't wait to get out of the place. But he said, "Oh, he's got influenza." That was a ridiculous diagnosis. And then he said, "Give me my money." We paid him, the doctor left, and Swamiji got worse.*

The devotees called a second doctor, who came and diagnosed Śrīla Prabhupāda as having had a mild heart attack. He said that Prabhupāda should at once go to the hospital.

Max Lerner (a lawyer friend of the devotees): *I got a call one day that the Swami had had a mild heart attack and I could be of some help. At that time they were going to take him to Bellevue Hospital, but I suggested that at least I could try to get him into a private hospital. After several hours of talking and negotiating with people at the hospital, we were able to get Swamiji into Beth Israel Hospital.*

Brahmānanda: *The day after Memorial Day we had to arrange for an ambulance. Beth Israel had no ambulance, so I called a private ambulance company. It was all arranged with the hospital that Swamiji would arrive at nine o'clock that morning. But the ambulance didn't come until about noon. During this time Swamiji kept moaning. Then finally the ambulance came, and they were horrible guys. They treated Swamiji like a bundle of cloth. I thought it would have been better if we had taken Swamiji in a cab.*

Except for Kīrtanānanda, who stayed in Prabhupāda's hospital room as a nurse, no one else was allowed to stay. They all went back to the temple to chant through the night, as Prabhupāda had requested. Kīrtanānanda phoned Hayagrīva in San Francisco and told him what had happened—how Swamiji had suddenly fallen back and cried out, "Hare Kṛṣṇa!" and how there had been nothing for about thirty seconds . . . and then a big gasp: "Hare Kṛṣṇa! Hare Kṛṣṇa!" Kīrtanānanda told Hayagrīva that the devotees in San Francisco should chant all night and pray to Lord Nṛsiṁhadeva:

tava kara-kamala-vare nakham adbhuta-śṛṅgaṁ
dalita-hiraṇyakaśipu-tanu-bhṛṅgaṁ
keśava dhṛta-narahari-rūpa jaya jagadīśa hare

Lord Nṛsiṁhadeva, the half-man, half-lion incarnation of Lord Kṛṣṇa, had appeared in another age to save His pure devotee Prahlada and kill the demon Hiraṇyakaśipu. Prabhupāda had asked his disciples to pray to Lord Nṛsiṁhadeva by chanting the special *mantra* and thinking, "Our master has not finished his work. Please protect him." The boys went back to the temple and chanted together, but after a few hours they fell asleep. They wanted to rest so that they could go to the hospital the next day.

Haridāsa: *When we heard about it in San Francisco, there was grief, and people were crying. There was a tremendous love and thinking about Swamiji and just concentration, a mass concentration of pulling him through, giving him strength and summoning the help of Kṛṣṇa and Lord Caitanya and everybody we could possibly call upon to lend their energies. People came into the temple doing rosaries, and whatever faiths or beliefs or trips they were on they were directing that toward a healing. They were all chanting with us.*

Hayagrīva: *It's a night I'll never forget. We turn on the altar lights behind the Jagannāthas, light candles, and chant in the flickering shadows. It is solemn chanting and even more solemn dancing. News quickly spreads down Haight Street, and soon the temple is crowded with others come to chant with us through the night.*

Mukunda and Jānakī phoned New York. But there is no additional information. Kīrtanānanda is spending the night in the hospital beside Swamiji's bed. No one else is being allowed in. Hospital regulations. Yes, everyone in New York is chanting.

We chant past midnight. Most of the guests leave, but none of us yet feel sleepy. The chanting overtakes us in waves. My mind wanders to Swamiji, to New York, to the future, to the past. . . . I have to yank it back into the room to confront the present, to realize why we are here chanting, to petition Śrī Kṛṣṇa to spare our master a little longer to allow him to spread Lord Caitanya's glorious saṅkīrtana *movement around the world.*

The chanting is always here, insistent.

By two A.M. I begin to tire. I change instruments just to keep awake, sometimes playing mṛdaṅga, *sometimes cymbals or harmonium. Many dance to stay awake. The girls serve* prasādam*—sliced apples. It is dangerous to sit next to the wall—an invitation to doze off. We are so frail.*

Hare Kṛṣṇa soothes. The chanting releases us from so much needless fretting. Through it we can relieve tensions, grieve, plead, and hope.

It is between three and four A.M. The most ecstatic hour, the brāhma-muhūrta *hour before the dawn. If he is alive at this hour, surely he will live.*

We sing. We chant on beads. Constant Hare Kṛṣṇa. We chant through the usual seven A.M. kīrtana *hour and into the morning. We chant fourteen hours without cessation. We cleanse the dust from the mind's mirror. We see Kṛṣṇa and Swamiji everywhere. Surely now he is well!*

During the night, Śrīla Prabhupāda's heart pained him. The next day he remained in critical condition. He could speak but softly and was too exhausted to converse. Skeptical of the doctors, he diagnosed himself: a heart attack affecting part of his brain, thus paralyzing the left side of his body. Massage, he said, was the cure.

On the morning of June 1, other disciples joined Kīrtanānanda in Prabhupāda's room and by taking shifts were able to give Prabhupāda a constant massage. They took turns massaging his head, chest, and legs as he directed. This simple act drew each of them into an intimate relationship with him.

When Prabhupāda heard that not only in New York but in San Francisco also the devotees had chanted and prayed all night, he expressed satisfaction, not by his usual hearty smile but by a very slight nodding and an approving sound. Despite his weakness, he was fully conscious.

The doctors, or more often their aides, took blood, gave injections, and investigated. Their diagnosis wasn't conclusive; they had plans for experiments. Then suddenly a doctor came in and announced their next move: a spinal tap. Prabhupāda was too weak to discuss the pros and cons of a spinal tap. He had put himself in the care of his disciples and Kṛṣṇa.

The doctor didn't want to be impeded. He explained why a spinal tap was necessary, but he wasn't asking for consultation or permission. Everyone—except for Kīrtanānanda, who insisted on staying—had to leave the room while the doctor performed the spinal tap. Neither Prabhupāda, who was too weak, nor his boys, who were uncertain how to act on his behalf, opposed the doctor. The devotees filed out of Prabhupāda's room while the doctor readied the largest, most frightening needle they had ever seen.

When they were allowed back, one disciple asked cautiously, "Did it hurt, Swamiji?" Śrīla Prabhupāda, his golden-skinned form wrapped in white hospital garments and lying between the white sheets, turned slightly and said, "We are tolerant."

Rūpānuga: *When Swamiji was first admitted to the hospital, it was very hard for me. I didn't know how I should act. I didn't have much experience with this kind of emergency. I was very uncertain as to what service to do for Swamiji. It was a frightening experience.*

Swamiji's life was at stake, yet his disciples didn't know what to do to save him. He lay on the bed as if at their mercy. But the hospital staff considered him their property—an old man with heart trouble, a subject of investigation. And for Swamiji's disciples this was a hundred times worse than dealing with Mr. Price and company. Now it was not just a matter of risking money but of risking Swamiji! Should they allow the EEG? What was an EEG? Was an operation necessary? An operation! But Swamiji had said that he should never even be brought to a hospital. "Give me massage," was all he had said, and "Chant Hare Kṛṣṇa."

When Śrīla Prabhupāda mentioned his preference for the Āyur Vedic medical treatments available in India, some of the devotees suggested they bring a doctor from India. After considering the expense, Prabhupāda decided to send a letter first. Unable to sit up or write, he slowly dictated a letter to Sri Krishna Pandit, who had given him quarters for several years in his temple in Delhi. Satsvarūpa read it back to Prabhupāda and then typed it right there in Prabhupāda's hospital room.

> I am writing this letter from the hospital. All of a sudden I have developed some headache, as well as throbbing of the chest. When I rub my chest I feel some sensation in my left hand and when I rub my left hand I feel sensation in my chest. My left hand no more works independently. I therefore ask you if there is any good Vedic physician in Mathura who can send me some medicines, that is, you purchase and send them by air mail to our temple: ISKCON, 26 2nd Ave., New York, N. Y. The symptom is predominantly when I get severe pain within my head. And the trembling of the left hand is coming every ten or fifteen minutes. I am afraid if this is not a disease like Lakhya; the boys are taking utmost care of me, there is no scarcity of care. But still after all, this body is subject to death. I came here with a great mission to execute my Spiritual Master's order but my heart is stabbing me. Of course, I'm not afraid of Maya, I know Maya cannot touch me, but still if I die in this condition, my mission will remain unfulfilled. Please therefore pray to Prabhu Lord Chaitanya and Vrindaban Bihar, to rescue me this time, my mission is still not finished. I wish

to live for a few more days. They're prepared to call an experienced Ayur Vedic physician who treats such diseases but I've not allowed the boys. But if necessary, if you can give me an expert physician who can travel here we can send necessary money for his coming here or arrange for air ticket. You can consult the man in charge of Dacca Shakti.

At last I may inform you that I am inclined toward Ayur Vedic treatment. You can consult the Ayur Vedic physician in Vrindaban who is a Goudiya Vaishnava. He knows me very well. He sells my books also.

Two things are to be done if it is possible; to send me proper medicines and directions, that will be nice. But if I require to return that also I can do. Please try to reply as soon as possible in English because my students cannot read Hindi. So long as I'm in bed it's not possible to read letters. You can treat this letter very urgently. Consult necessary physicians and let me know what I am to do. In Mathura there are undoubtedly many Ayur Vedic physicians and many quacks also. Try to avoid the quacks. I would have returned to India immediately but the doctors say it is risky. If need be, I shall return as soon as I get strength to take the strain of the journey.

I repeat my symptoms so that you can take necessary care. All of a sudden I developed some throbbing between the heart and stomach about 4 days ago. I was so exhaustive, it was like fainting—then I consulted a doctor who came and gave me medicine but it was of no good effect therefore my students at once transferred me to the hospital where they're spending more or less 400 rupees daily. There is no question of neglect. All scientific treatment is going on. But I think Ayur Vedic medicine will be proper. Therefore I request you to take immediate steps and reply me.

I hope this letter will convince you the actual position. While reading this letter you may consult some friend who knows English very well so that he'll read it correctly and reply correctly. There is no scope for corresponding in Bengali or in Hindi.

By Kṛṣṇa's grace, on the afternoon of Śrīla Prabhupāda's second day in the hospital he showed slight improvement. His heart was still causing him pain, his facial expression remained grave, with never a smile, but he was a bit stronger. The interns, nurses, and doctors came and went on schedule, treating him—impersonally. One doctor did seem a little interested in what Prabhupāda was all about, and at Prabhupāda's request, Kīrtanānanda played a taped lecture for the doctor. He listened politely, but then said, "It doesn't ring a bell."

The doctor said that he wanted to run a few more tests and that Swamiji might be able to leave after a few weeks—if all went well. Śrīla Prabhupāda tried speaking to the doctor, wanting to explain about Kṛṣṇa. Jadurāṇī had brought two of her paintings to the hospital room—one of Rādhā and Kṛṣṇa and the other of the fierce half-lion, half-man incarnation, Lord Nṛsiṁha, tearing apart the demon Hiraṇyakaśipu. Speaking in a very low voice, Prabhupāda said that these two pictures show how God is many-sided: "Here He is in His loving exchange, and here also we see that anger comes from Kṛṣṇa, or God."

The doctor politely said that he had his own philosophy and that Swamiji shouldn't be preaching while in such weak health; he should rest. Advising the disciples not to allow their *guru* to speak, the doctor excused himself and continued his rounds.

Śrīla Prabhupāda, with his slight improvement, expressed more disapproval of being in the hands of the hospital personnel. They weren't able to do anything, he said. Kṛṣṇa was in control: "If Kṛṣṇa wants to kill you, then no one can save you. But if Kṛṣṇa wants to save you, then no one can kill you."

Dāmodara: *I was there when a doctor came in to check his reflexes. There was the usual tapping with a little rubber hammer on his knee—that kind of thing. Swamiji was visibly annoyed with this man's coming in and tapping him all over. He was capable of diagnosing and giving the prescription for the cure, and it annoyed him that these men, who obviously didn't know what they were doing, were coming in and interfering with the process of recuperation.*

Acyutānanda: *The nurse would always let the door slam, and every time it slammed Swamiji would wince. He said, "Tell her not to slam the door." She would say, "Okay," and then she would let it slam again.*

Śrīla Prabhupāda began sitting up in bed and taking *prasādam* from the temple, supplemented by some of the vegetarian items on the hospital menu. He would say a prayer and offer the hospital food to the picture of his spiritual master. The devotees would sit at his feet, watching him as he then mixed with his right hand the carrots, peas, and mashed potatoes. And he would always distribute some of his food into the hands of his disciples.

Jadurāṇī: *We brought him many different kinds of fruit. We told him we had brought apples, but he was so tired he only said, "Oh" and seemed disinterested. We told him we had brought oranges, but again—"Oh." He gave so many tired "Oh"s he seemed disinterested. Finally I said, "We brought you watermelons," and immediately his face lit up—*"Ohhh!"

Rotating in four-hour shifts, two devotees at a time were always with Prabhupāda. Although awake, he would remain silent for long intervals; but massaging always continued, except when he was asleep. Gradually, the paralysis on his left side went away.

Once while Śrīla Prabhupāda was sitting up in bed, one boy massaging his leg and another softly, almost consolingly, stroking the back of his neck, Prabhupāda remarked that if he were not sick he would have considered the massaging and rubbing too familiar.

Dāmodara: *I was massaging Swamiji's temples with one hand, my thumb on one temple and other fingers on the other temple. As I was massaging, Swamiji kept saying, "Harder! Harder!" and I would squeeze harder. I thought, "Gee, I don't know if I should squeeze so hard, because he's sick." But he kept insisting: "Harder! Harder!"*

Puruṣottama: *I was massaging Swamiji's head, and I started singing the chant* śrī kṛṣṇa-caitanya. *When I started singing, a very beautiful smile came on his face. Although I did it only briefly, he took pleasure in hearing. He seemed to take it that I was ministering to him just by singing* śrī kṛṣṇa-caitanya.

As Śrīla Prabhupāda gained strength, his disciples were ready with questions. Puruṣottama asked, "Swamiji, in the scriptures when it describes the lotus feet of Kṛṣṇa, what does that mean—lotus feet?"

Prabhupāda then sang a verse:

samāśritā ye pada-pallava-plavaṁ
mahat-padaṁ puṇya-yaśo murāreḥ
bhavāmbudhir vatsa-padaṁ paraṁ padaṁ
padaṁ padaṁ yad vipadāṁ na teṣām

Then he asked the three devotees present to repeat each line after him again and again, until they had learned both the tune and the words. "In this verse from *Śrīmad-Bhāgavatam,*" Śrīla Prabhupāda explained, sitting up in his bed, "the time of death is compared to crossing a vast ocean. It is very fearful. One doesn't know where he will go in the next life. And at every step there is danger in the material world. But for one who has taken shelter at the lotus feet of Lord Kṛṣṇa, that vast, dangerous ocean of birth and death becomes shrunk up to no more than the impression made in mud by a calf's hoofprint. There is danger, but the devotee doesn't care for it. Just like if a gentleman is riding by in a carriage and he passes a small puddle, he considers it insignificant. So do you understand now what 'lotus feet' means?" It was clear.

Then Puruṣottama asked another question: "Why do people say that God has no name?" Śrīla Prabhupāda replied by asking why, since God is everything, He should not have a name. "In fact," he said, "all names are describing Kṛṣṇa." Prabhupāda asked Puruṣottama what his name had been before initiation.

"Paul," he said.

"What does *Paul* mean?" Prabhupāda asked.

"It means 'little.' "

"Yes," Prabhupāda said, "that is Kṛṣṇa. He is the smallest of the small."

Satsvarūpa then volunteered his name, Stephen, which means "crown."

"Yes," Prabhupāda replied, "Kṛṣṇa is the king."

But discussions were rare. Usually the hours were quiet. Prabhupāda rested, and the devotees on watch sat in chairs on opposite sides of his bed, reading or chanting softly on their beads. Late one afternoon, as the Manhattan sky turned to twilight, Prabhupāda sat up after having been silent for an hour and said, "I don't know Kṛṣṇa, but I know my Guru Mahārāja."

One day Brahmānanda began giving Prabhupāda a minute breakdown of the financial condition of the New York temple. In the midst of the detailed report, Brahmānanda suddenly stopped, looked up at Prabhupāda, and said, "Do you want me to tell all the details? I thought you would want me to let you know. I mean, you should know." Prabhupāda replied that if Brahmānanda could take care of everything without his knowing the details, that would be all right.

Suddenly one morning, Swami Satcidananda, the famous *haṭha-yoga guru*, entered Prabhupāda's room, grinning through his big gray beard.

He was dressed in a saffron silk *kurtā* and *yogī* pants and accompanied by one of his young American male disciples. Śrīla Prabhupāda sat up in bed, smiling at the pleasant surprise. They had not met before. Śrīla Prabhupāda offered Swami Satcidananda a seat at his bedside and asked Jadurāṇī to stand and give her seat to Swami Satcidananda's disciple.

Prabhupāda and Swami Satcidananda spoke in Hindi, and no one else in the room could follow their conversation. At one point, however, Śrīla Prabhupāda held up his hand and looked at it with indifference and then with disgust. Although his words were Hindi, the gesture and sardonic expression conveyed his meaning: the body was material and therefore could not be expected to be well.

Prabhupāda asked Acyutānanda to read aloud from a particular purport of the *Śrīmad-Bhāgavatam.*

> If there is enough milk, enough grains, enough fruit, enough cotton, enough silk and enough jewels then why the people need for economic development in the shape of machine and tools? Can the machine and tools supply vigour and vitality to the man and animals? Can the machinery produce grains, fruits and milk or jewellery or silk? Is not jewellery and silk, varieties of food stuff prepared with ghee and grains or milk and fruits sufficient for man's pure luxurious and healthy life? Then why there is artificial luxurious life of cinema, cars, radio, flesh and hotels? Has this civilisation produced any good result more than the dog's mentality of quarreling with one another individually and nationally? Has this civilisation enhanced the cause of equality and fraternity by sending thousands of men in the hellish factory and the war fields at the whims of a particular man?

When Prabhupāda offered to play the record he and his disciples had made, Swami Satcidananda politely agreed. But when Prabhupāda offered to play the other side of the record, Swami Satcidananda said he had to leave. He offered Prabhupāda some fruits, and Prabhupāda, after accepting them, told his disciples, "Distribute these, and give him some of our fruit in exchange."

As Swami Satcindananda rose to leave, Śrīla Prabhupāda suddenly got out of bed and stood shakily. "No, no, no." Swami Satcidananda protested. "Don't disturb yourself." And then he was gone, escorted by Acyutānanda. Śrīla Prabhupāda lay back in bed.

"Is he a swami?" Jaduranī asked.

"Why not?" Prabhupāda replied. But after a few moments he added, "*Swami* means one who knows Kṛṣṇa." There was no more talk about it, but Prabhupāda was pleased by the unexpected visit.

The constant coming and going of Śrīla Prabhupāda's young followers, wearing *tilaka* on their foreheads and carrying watermelons, special food, flowers, and paintings of Kṛṣṇa, created a special interest among the hospital staff. Sometimes workers would ask questions, and sometimes the devotees would talk with them about the Hare Kṛṣṇa movement. Once a nurse came by Prabhupāda's room and asked, "In the caste system in India, what is the name of the highest caste? What are they called?"

"Kṛṣṇa conscious," Prabhupāda firmly replied. He asked a disciple to give the nurse *prasādam.*

On June 5 Prabhupāda received an affectionate letter signed by all his disciples in San Francisco. After reading how they had stayed up all night chanting and praying for his recovery, he dictated a short letter.

> My dear boys and girls,
>
> I am so much obliged to you for your prayers to Krishna to save my life. Due to your sincere and ardent prayer, Krishna has saved my life. I was to die on Tuesday certainly but because you prayed sincerely I am saved. Now I am improving gradually and coming to original condition. Now I can hope to meet you again and chant with you Hare Krishna. I am so glad to receive the report of your progressive march and hope there will be no difficulty in your understanding Krishna consciousness. My blessings are always with you and with confidence you go on with your chanting Hare Krishna Hare Krishna Krishna Krishna Hare Hare Hare Rama Hare Rama Rama Rama Hare Hare.

The following day a tape arrived from Mukunda: a recording of the San Francisco devotees singing *śrī rāma jaya rāma jaya jaya rāma* and other *bhajanas.* Prabhupāda dictated another letter, saying that as soon as he got strength for traveling he would come again to San Francisco.

"In the meantime," he wrote, "I shall be very glad to know what arrangements you are going to do for the Ratha-yātrā festival. Make it a grand procession and unique introduction in the United States."

Some of Swamiij's disciples gathered in the storefront at 26 Second Avenue one night. Sitting around on the faded rug, they discussed the meaning of Swamiji's illness. He had said that when the heart attack had come, it had been meant for his death; therefore he had called out loudly, "Hare Kṛṣṇa!" thinking that the moment of death had come. Kīrtanānanda remembered that Swamiji had once told him that when he was on the boat coming to America the captain's wife had read his palm and said that if he survived his seventy-first year he would live to be a hundred.

Madhusūdana asked, "How could a pure devotee be subject to a death blow?" Kīrtanānanda replied that it was impersonal to think that because Swamiji was a pure devotee nothing could happen to him and that they should not even worry about him. Of course, the apparent suffering or even the passing away of a pure devotee wasn't the same as an ordinary man's. Swamiji had given the example of the cat: sometimes she carries her kittens in her mouth, and sometimes she catches a mouse in the same jaws. The mouse feels the jaws of death, but the kitten feels safety and affection. So although Swamiji's death call might have appeared similar to an ordinary man's, for Swamiji there had been no fear or danger.

As the disciples discussed their realizations, they began to clear away their doubts about why such an apparent setback had come upon their spiritual master. Satsvarūpa mentioned the letter he had typed for Swamiji at the hospital. In the letter Swamiji had said he was not afraid of *māyā* and could not be touched by *māyā*. But he had also referred to being stabbed by his heart. Brahmānanda said that Swamiji had once told him that a spiritual master may suffer for the sins of his disciples, because he has to take their *karma*. Swamiji now had about fifty disciples, so maybe that had been the cause of his heart attack. They talked about the importance of being very strict and not committing any sins with which to burden their spiritual master.

Another reason for Swamiji's illness, Kīrtanānanda said, was that

Kṛṣṇa had arranged it to engage them all in intimate service to Swamiji. By serving a pure devotee, one gains the favor of Kṛṣṇa, and Kṛṣṇa was letting them all become purified by massaging and serving Swamiji so intimately.

Satsvarūpa recalled that Swamiji had said in a letter to the devotees in San Francisco that he was supposed to have died but their prayers had saved him. Swamiji had told Kīrtanānanda that Kṛṣṇa had heard the devotees' prayers and had granted their wishes. Kṛṣṇa was allowing Swamiji to go on with his mission of spreading Kṛṣṇa consciousness in the West. It wasn't on his own behalf that Swamiji wanted to live, but to continue his mission.

Everyone agreed with Kīrtanānanda that it was a form of impersonalism for them to think that because Swamiji was a pure devotee he didn't need their loving care. They should continue to care for Swamiji even after he got better. He had put himself in their care, and they had to reciprocate accordingly. Swamiji had said they were like fathers to him; so they should not allow him to play the drum long and vigorously, to sing in the park for hours, to stay up talking late at night, or to do anything that might endanger his health.

Rāya Rāma said that Swamiji had asked him to reply to several letters from devotees on the West Coast and explain that he would probably never again be able to take on the strain of public lectures; the *saṅkīrtana* movement now rested on their shoulders. Rāya Rāma had explained in his letters that it was Kṛṣṇa's grace that Swamiji was still with them and able to advise them when things got rough; but now they must increase their efforts to distribute Kṛṣṇa consciousness to the world.

The talk turned to the need for them to realize Swamiji's instructions and become strong devotees. Everyone agreed that they could do this by studying Swamiji's books more carefully and always acting according to his instructions.

When they told Prabhupāda about their philosophical discussions, he replied only briefly: "Kṛṣṇa heard all your sincere prayers, and He thought, 'All right, let him stay and do his nonsense—so many devotees are praying on his behalf.' "

* * *

Before Prabhupāda's illness, the devotees had planned a big event in Tompkins Square Park for Sunday, June 4. The parks department had given them the use of a loudspeaker system and the stage in the band shell. Mr. Kallman, producer of the Hare Kṛṣṇa record, had encouraged them to advertise and had gotten in touch with the TV stations. The devotees had begun making Hare Kṛṣṇa *mantra* signs so that everyone, even the TV viewer, could chant.

Although now unable to go, Śrīla Prabhupāda said they should still have their festival; he would compose a special address for Kīrtanānanda to read to the public. From his hospital bed he dictated the short speech: "An Address to American Youth," by A. C. Bhaktivedanta Swami.

On June 4, several hundred people gathered around the band shell in Tompkins Square Park, while the devotees played harmonium, *karatālas*, and *mṛdaṅgas* and chanted Hare Kṛṣṇa over the P.A. system. Many people in the crowd chanted along, playing their own instruments and even joining the devotees onstage.

Kīrtanānanda stood before the microphone and announced that Bhaktivedanta Swami, although ill at Beth Israel Hospital, had prepared a message for everyone. Many among the Lower East Side crowd were acquainted with Bhaktivedanta Swami and his chanting of Hare Kṛṣṇa. They listened as Kīrtanānanda read.

My dear young beautiful boys and girls of America,

I have come to your country with great hope and a great mission. My Spiritual Master, Om Vishnupad Paramahansa Paribrajaka Acharya Sri Srimad Bhaktisiddhanta Saraswati Goswami Maharaja, asked me to preach this cult of Lord Sri Chaitanya Mahaprabhu in the Western world. That was the seed-giving incident. Gradually the seed fructified, and I was prepared to come to the Western world. Still, I do not know why I was so much attracted by the land of America. But from within Krishna dictated that instead of going to Europe I should better go to America. So you can see that I have come to your country under order of superior authority. And even after arriving here, when I perceived that some of the youngsters are being misled, confused and frustrated—this is not the condition of your country only, but in every country, the young people are neglected, although it is they who are the flower and future hope of everyone—so I thought to myself that if I go to the American youth with my message and they join with me in this movement, then it will spread all over the world, and then *all* the problems of the world will be solved. How I would like to be with you in person today, but Krishna has prevented that, so please pardon me and accept my blessings in this written form.

This process of samkirtan—this singing and dancing—is so nice because from the very beginning it places everyone on the spiritual platform. There are different platforms or levels to our existence: the bodily platform, the mental platform, the intellectual platform, and the spiritual platform. When you stand on the spiritual platform, then all the problems created by the necessities of the body, mind, intellect, and ego become solved. Therefore I appeal to you to join this movement most seriously. The process is very simple: we ask everyone to come join with us in chanting, hear something of the philosophy of life taught by Lord Krishna, take a little prasadam (foodstuff that is prepared and offered to the Lord), and peacefully, with refreshed mind, go home. That is our mission.

We do have certain restrictions; practically, they are not restrictions, but something better in place of something inferior. The other day, Mr. Alan Burke questioned me on his television program, "Swamiji, why do you insist on marriage?" And I answered him, "Unless one becomes peaceful in home life, how can he make any advance in any other area of life or knowledge? Therefore everyone should get married—just to be happy and peaceful." You are all beautiful, nice, educated boys and girls—why shouldn't you get married and live happily? If you live peacefully regulated lives, eating nothing but Krishna prasadam, then the tissues in your brain will develop for spiritual consciousness and understanding.

However, if you are not agreeable to these simple restrictions, still I request you to join the chanting with us. Everybody can do that, and that will gradually clarify everything, and all problems will be solved, and you will find a new chapter of your life. Just this week I have received a letter from a girl in New Jersey who has had such an experience. She writes:

"Dear Swamiji,

"You don't know me by name, but I am the girl who joined your parade in Washington Square this past Saturday.

"When I first saw your group I thought you were all crazy. Either that or on dope of some kind. After listening and talking with some of you I realized that it was neither of those. You people plainly believed in what you were doing and I admired you for that much; but my curiosity drove me further and I had to find out why. So I followed you, and as I did, the chant you sang began to take hold. The next thing I knew I felt free of myself and I was singing too. I didn't know where I was or where I was going but I was too elated to care. It wasn't until we stopped that I learned where I was.

"By that time I had picked up bits and pieces of what Krishna Consciousness was about. One of your members asked me to visit your temple and I followed you still further, hoping to discover just what it was that made you feel so strong about something I'd never heard of.

"After having taken a meal with you and reading your literature I left; but not alone. I took with me a new awareness of life. It occurred to me how futile my desires for the material things in life were: that a new dress, or big house, or color television were not important. If only people would open their eyes to the endless number of pleasures God has already given us, there would be no need for looking any further.

"You people are truly lucky. You may have had to do without many things, but because of this you are able to enjoy the simple God-given treasures of the world. Because of your beliefs, you are the wealthy; and I thank you for sharing a bit of that wealth with me."

So we invite you to please chant with us—it is such a nice thing. Come to our temple if you like, take a little prasadam, and be happy. It is not very difficult if you just chant this HARE KRISHNA, HARE KRISHNA, KRISHNA KRISHNA, HARE HARE, HARE RAMA, HARE RAMA, RAMA RAMA, HARE HARE. That will save you. Thank you very much, and God bless you.

* * *

Śrīla Prabhupāda was eager to leave the hospital. For several days he had wanted to go. "They are simply sticking needles," he complained. And each day was putting his Society into further debt. The devotees had rented a small seaside house in Long Branch, New Jersey, where Prabhupāda could go to recuperate. Kīrtanānanda, they decided, would be Prabhupāda's cook, and Gaurasundara and his wife, Govinda dāsī, were arriving from San Francisco to do the housekeeping and help. But the doctor wanted Prabhupāda to stay for another brain wave test and more observation.

One day while Brahmānanda and Gargamuni were visiting Prabhupāda, the doctor entered and announced that the Swami would have to go downstairs for an X ray.

"No needle?" Prabhupāda asked.

"Yes," the doctor replied, "it's all right."

When the nurse brought in a bed on wheels, Prabhupāda said he wanted Gargamuni to push it. He then sat on it cross-legged and put his hand in his bead bag, and Gargamuni, following the nurse, wheeled him out the door, down the hall, and onto the elevator. They went down to the third floor and entered a room. The nurse left them alone. Gargamuni could sense Prabhupāda's uneasiness. He was also nervous. It was such an unlikely place for him to be with his spiritual master. Then a different nurse entered, with a needle: "Time to give the Swami a little injection."

"No." Prabhupāda shook his head.

"I'm sorry," Gargamuni said flatly. "We're not going to do it."

The nurse was exasperated but smiled: "It won't hurt."

"Take me back," Prabhupāda ordered Gargamuni. When the nurse insisted, Gargamuni acted rashly—his usual tendency—and stepped between the nurse and Śrīla Prabhupāda.

"I'm ready to fight if I have to," Gargamuni thought. "I won't let you do it," he said and wheeled the bed out of the room, leaving the nurse behind.

Gargamuni was lost. He was somewhere on the third or fourth floor, faced with corridors and doors. And Prabhupāda's room was on the sixth floor. Unsure where he was going, Gargamuni wheeled through the corridors with Prabhupāda sitting cross-legged, chanting on his beads.

Brahmānanda arrived at the X-ray lab seconds after Gargamuni's escape. The nurse and an intern complained to him about what had happened.

Brahmānanda: *They considered this a theft. Swamiji was their property. As long as he was in the hospital, he was theirs to do whatever they pleased with. Gargamuni had stolen Swamiji away from them.*

Gargamuni got to the elevator. He had difficulty maneuvering the bed and in his haste bumped into the wall. He forgot what floor Swamiji was on. He only knew that he was protecting Swamiji, who wanted to be taken away.

When Gargamuni finally reached Prabhupāda's room, 607, an intern was there and spoke angrily. "I don't care," Gargamuni said. "He doesn't want any more needles or tests. We want to leave." Brahmānanda arrived, calmed his younger brother, and helped Prabhupāda back into bed.

Prabhupāda said he wanted to leave. When the doctor came in, Prabhupāda sat up and spoke decisively. "Doctor, I am all right. I can go." And he shook the doctor's hand to show him he was hale and hearty. The doctor chuckled. He said that although Swamiji was getting stronger, he would have to stay a few more days. He was by no means out of danger yet. He required careful medical surveillance. They needed to run another electroencephalogram.

Śrīla Prabhupāda still had pains around his heart, but he told the doctor his boys had a place for him to rest by the seaside. This was very good, the doctor said, but he couldn't let his patient go just yet.

But Prabhupāda had made up his mind. Brahmānanda and Gargamuni arranged for a rented car. They gathered Prabhupāda's things and helped him dress. As they escorted him out of his room and the hospital staff saw that the boys were actually taking the old man away, some of the doctors and nurses tried to stop them. Brahmānanda told them not to worry; Swamiji was very dear to them, and they would take good care of him. He would get regular massages and plenty of rest, and they would get him whatever medicines the doctors prescribed. After a rest by the seaside he could come back for a checkup.

Brahmānanda: *Then the doctors became fed up. They threatened us: "This man is going to die." They really scared us. They said, "This man is going to die, and it is going to be your fault." Even as we left they said, "This man is condemned to death." It was horrible.*

At ten A.M. on June 8 they left the hospital. Prabhupāda wanted to stop briefly at the temple at 26 Second Avenue before going to the house in Long Branch. Entering the storefront, walking shakily, he came before the portraits of his spiritual master, Bhaktisiddhānta Sarasvatī, and his spiritual master's father, Bhaktivinoda Ṭhākura. For the first time, Prabhupāda's disciples saw him offer fully prostrated obeisances. As he prostrated himself before his Guru Mahārāja, his disciples also paid obeisances and felt their devotion increase.

When Prabhupāda arrived at his cottage in Long Branch at one o'clock, he had Kīrtanānanda immediately begin cooking lunch. It would be Prabhupāda's first regular hot meal—rice, *dāl*, *capātīs*, *sabjī*—since his stroke nine days ago.

Prabhupāda went to bed but soon got up and came into the kitchen, asking, "Is it ready?" Kīrtanānanda made a few excuses and said he would hurry. After a few minutes, Prabhupāda returned. He seemed furious: "Why are you taking so long?" Kīrtanānanda moved as quickly as he could, but he couldn't make the *dāl* boil any faster. "Whatever you have," Prabhupāda said, "let me eat it. I don't care if it is raw." Kīrtanānanda served lunch, and Prabhupāda ate with the relish of a person in good health. Kīrtanānanda telephoned his pal Hayagrīva in San Francisco: "He ate like anything. It was wonderful to see."

The small one-story cottage was situated in a quiet suburb a short walk from the beach. The back yard was enclosed by trees and shrubs, and the neighborhood bloomed with fragrant roses.

But the weather was often blustery and the sky gray. Prabhupāda spoke of returning to India to recuperate. In Delhi, Sri Krishna Pandit had refused Prabhupāda's urgent request for Āyur Vedic medicine: "You are in such a long place—if the medicine gives some bad reaction, then how to arrange for the good?" Prabhupāda had written back asking if an Āyur Vedic physician could be sent to America, but the proposal seemed impractical. It would be better for Prabhupāda to go to India. He received Swami Nārāyaṇa Mahārāja's reply that since no Āyur Vedic doctor would go to America, Swamiji should come and be treated in Calcutta. Nārāyaṇa Mahārāja also enclosed a letter to Prabhupāda's secretary, Rāya Rāma: "There is no need for anxiety. Always utter hari nama (Hare Krishna Hare Krishna Krishna Krishna Hare Hare, Hare Rama Hare Rama Rama Rama Hare Hare) near his ears. God will do for the best."

Śrīla Prabhupāda talked of going to India not only for his health; he told Kīrtanānanda and Gaurasundara he wanted to start in Vṛndāvana an "American House," a place where his American disciples could learn Vedic culture to help them preach all over the world. He also said he wanted to make some of his disciples—Kīrtanānanda, Brahmānanda, Hayagrīva—into *sannyāsīs*, and he would do that also in India. His real work, however, was in America—if he could just regain his health. But where was the sunshine?

Govinda dāsī had cherished the desire to serve Swamiji personally ever since she had first met him in San Francisco. She saw that he was selfless, and his love for his disciples was unlike anything she had ever known before. She didn't mention her cherished desire to anyone, even to

Gaurasundara. But now Kṛṣṇa was fulfilling her desire by allowing her and Gaurasundara to come to New Jersey to serve Swamiji. To the devotees in New York, having a married couple take care of Swamiji seemed the best arrangement, and Govinda dāsī and Gaurasundara had been available. These were external reasons, but Govinda dāsī understood that Kṛṣṇa was fulfilling her desire.

Serving Swamiji, Govinda dāsī felt completely satisfied. Now that she was actually dedicating herself to Swamiji as she had always wanted, nothing else was on her mind. Despite the problems of working with Kīrtanānanda—who seemed to think she was less intelligent because she was a woman and who sometimes corrected her—she was happy.

Govinda dāsī: *Swamiji would sit on a little couch with a table before him, and Gaurasundara and Kīrtanānanda and I would sit on the floor, and we would all eat together, like a family. We would talk, and one time the subject was rice. Kīrtanānanda said, "White rice is for human beings, and brown rice is for animals." So I said, "I must be an animal, then, because I really like brown rice better." And Swamiji just laughed and laughed and laughed. He thought it was so funny. I guess it did sound pretty simple. But he laughed and laughed.*

Prabhupāda was sitting in the back yard when Govinda dāsī saw a large slug climbing on a wall. She showed it to Prabhupāda. "Chant to the poor thing," he said, and she began to chant Hare Kṛṣṇa.

Govinda dāsī would take walks daily and, with the neighbors' permission, pick dozens of roses. On returning she would arrange them in vases and place them all around in Prabhupāda's room. One time when Prabhupāda heard her loudly singing Hare Kṛṣṇa as she returned from the neighborhood, he remarked to Gaurasundara, "She is very simplehearted."

Govinda dāsī: *Swamiji talked about Kṛṣṇa in such a way that Kṛṣṇa was present in the room. This was so striking to me. He would talk about Kṛṣṇa's activities—about how Kṛṣṇa is doing this and that and how Kṛṣṇa is so wonderful and mother Yaśodā is thinking like this. He would talk, and he would get into such a beautiful state that the whole room would glow golden. I would feel as if I were being transported to some other realm, and it was all very new to me. I didn't have any great understanding of what was going on, but it was all very new to me, and it was an actual transcendental experience of feeling Kṛṣṇa's presence and almost glimpsing within the heart the memory of His pastimes.*

Swamiji playing *karatālas*, Swamiji walking on the beach, Swamiji sitting in his room or taking a nap—everything he did seemed wonderful to Govinda dāsī. And everything he did or said seemed to endear him more and more to her..

Devotees would travel—no more than two at a time and only once a week—from Manhattan to Long Branch to visit Swamiji. Mostly they would see him sitting on his bed, but sometimes they would walk with him on the beach. The morning sunshine, he said, would help him. But the gray skies persisted.

As Prabhupāda sat one morning with Kīrtanānanda, Gaurasundara, Satsvarūpa, Govinda dāsī, and Jadurāṇī on a blanket spread on the sand, he noticed some boys with surfboards trying to ride the waves. "They think this is bliss, playing in the water," he said. "Actually there is some bliss there, but it is not *ānanda*, the bliss of the spiritual world. On Kṛṣṇaloka everything is conscious. The water is conscious, the land is conscious. And everything is blissful. Here that is not so." Devotees looked with him at the surfers bobbing in the sea. "Yes," Kīrtanānanda said, "and also here it is dangerous. At any moment one of the surfboards could jump up and hit them on the head."

"Yes," Śrīla Prabhupāda said, "this is not real *ānanda*. Prahlāda Mahārāja has said that this material world is crushing him like a grinding wheel of repeated birth and death. He says that in material life he experiences either separation from what is beloved to him or meeting up with an obstacle he doesn't want. And in order to combat this condition, the remedy he takes is even worse than the disease. LSD is like that, a remedy worse than the disease."

Except that Prabhupāda's face looked thin, his appearance was the same as before his illness. He sat among them, wrapped in a gray wool *cādar*. They knew he must be very careful about how much he did. They would never forget, as they had forgotten before, that he was seventy-two years old. Perhaps never again would they be able to enjoy spending as much time with him as before. Certainly for now his intimate association had become a rare treasure.

Sitting inches away from Prabhupāda on the beach blanket, Satsvarūpa asked a question on behalf of the devotees in New York. "Swamiji, is wearing of leather shoes permissible?"

"No."

"What if someone has given us some leather shoes?"

"Leather means violence," Prabhupāda said. He pointed to Satsvarūpa's shoes of inexpensive man-made material. "Your country is very nice. By your technology you can get these shoes easily without wearing leather." For Satsvarūpa and the others the question was answered for a lifetime; and the time and place became a reference, like a chapter and verse number in the scriptures.

As Jadurāṇī helped Govinda dāsī gather flowers, the two girls talked together. Both had heard the men say that women were less intelligent, and they felt discouraged. Later Govinda dāsī told Prabhupāda about the problem. "Is it true," she asked, "that because we are women we won't make advancement as quickly as the *brahmacārīs*?"

"Yes," Prabhupāda answered. "If you think of yourselves as women, how will you make any advancement? You must see yourself as spirit soul, eternal servant of Kṛṣṇa."

Śrīla Prabhupāda gave Jadurāṇī a photograph of himself to paint from. Taken in India, before he had come to America, it showed him grave and standing very straight against a blank white wall. "Oh, Swamiji," Jadurāṇī remarked, "you look so unhappy here."

"*Noooo*," he said thoughtfully, stretching out the sound of the word. "No. That is not unhappy. That was a moment of ecstasy."

Prabhupāda drew Jadurāṇī's attention to a picture on his wall. Mother Yaśodā was rebuking her son, Kṛṣṇa, for stealing butter, while in the distance two of Kṛṣṇa's friends were hiding behind a tree, laughing. Prabhupāda asked, "Do you think that Kṛṣṇa would let Himself get caught and His friends get away?" She looked at the picture again. By the light of Swamiji's words she could see that Kṛṣṇa's friends would also soon be caught. She suddenly felt she was there in Vṛndāvana. They both laughed.

After staying with Prabhupāda for two days, Satsvarūpa and Jadurāṇī, the devotees visiting from New York, had to return to their duties. Although Prabhupāda had been resting, he awoke just as they were about to depart, so they came into his room. In a faint voice Prabhupāda spoke a few words from his bed. Then he sat up and Gaurasundara began to massage him. People who think God is dead are crazy, Prabhupāda said. Although no one had introduced the subject, for Prabhupāda, preaching about Kṛṣṇa was always apropos. His voice picked up volume as he denounced the atheists: "Just like if I go to the doctor. If he checks my heart and it is beating well and if he checks my blood pressure and it is going on and my breathing is there and after observing all these symptoms of life if I ask him, 'So, doctor, what is the condition?' if the doctor says, 'My dear sir, you are dead'—is this not a crazy diagnosis?"

Gaurasundara, still massaging, glanced wide-eyed at the others. Prabhupāda was now speaking in a loud, forceful voice, as if addressing a large audience instead of a few visitors in his sickroom. "Similarly, just see the signs of life in this universe! The sun is rising just on time, the planets are all moving in their orbits, there are so many signs of life. And the universe is God's body. And yet they are seeing all these symptoms and declaring God is dead? Is it not foolishness? They are rascals! I challenge them. Simply rascals!"

A few soft words had become half an hour of strong, emphatic speech meant to move the audience against all kinds of atheistic theorists. Although Kīrtanānanda had at first cautioned Swamiji, reminding him about his health, Swamiji had dismissed the caution by saying, "That's all right." But now he was exhausted and had to lie back down.

The devotees had just seen Swamiji immediately use up whatever energy he had gained from his afternoon's rest. Although they admired how he was using everything for Kṛṣṇa, they were also fearful. But they were helpless to restrain him. They were even implicated—they wanted to hear him.

When Satsvarūpa and Jadurāṇī returned to New York, Brahmānanda had them tell the others about Swamiji. Satsvarūpa told how he had slept in the room with Swamiji and had felt that this nearness to Swamiji was very auspicious. He had felt light and peaceful and close to Kṛṣṇa all night. Satsvarūpa and Jadurāṇī told about sitting on the beach with Swamiji and his talking about everything's being conscious in Kṛṣṇaloka. And they told how Swamiji had sat up in bed and had used his energy preaching, showing them that they should also use everything in the service of Kṛṣṇa. Brahmānanda beamed at the other devotees. "Just look! By your *talking* about Swamiji, everyone is feeling blissful."

Prabhupāda stayed in Long Branch for three weeks. But when Sri Krishna Pandit wrote saying that he couldn't arrange for an Āyur Vedic doctor to come to America, Prabhupāda began to think more seriously about going back to India. In India he could get sunshine and Āyur Vedic treatment. But his plans would vary from one day to another—San Francisco, Montreal, India, New York. He told Kīrtanānanda to inform the devotees in San Francisco that if they held a Ratha-yātrā festival he would come.

At the end of June, he returned to 26 Second Avenue and to the hospital for a checkup. The doctor was surprised at Swamiji's recovery and had no objection to his flying to San Francisco. So in search of sunny skies, and eager to guide his followers in performing the first Ratha-yātrā, Prabhupāda had airline tickets booked for himself and Kīrtanānanda to San Francisco, New Jagannātha Purī.

CHAPTER FIVE

Swamiji's Departure

At the San Francisco airport Prabhupāda smiled but said little as the devotees greeted him with flowers and *kīrtana.* It was different this time. He walked straight ahead, with the aid of a cane.

Jayānanda was waiting with his station wagon to drive Prabhupāda to the private house they had rented north of the city, at Stinson Beach. But first, Prabhupāda said, he wanted to visit the San Francisco Rādhā-Kṛṣṇa temple. Jayānanda drove to 518 Frederick Street. Prabhupāda got out of the car and entered the small storefront, which was filled with waiting devotees and guests. He bowed before the smiling Jagannātha deities and, without speaking a word, left the room, returned to the car, and departed for Stinson Beach.

The ride up through the seaside cliffs was so winding and climbing that Prabhupāda became nauseated. And even lying down in the back seat and having Jayānanda drive slower didn't help much. Kīrtanānanda realized that it would be too difficult for Prabhupāda to visit the San Francisco temple from Stinson Beach. But maybe that would be just as well; he could spend all of his time recuperating.

It was a modern single-story six-room house with a Japanese roof. A sign out front read Paradisio. Śrīla Prabhupāda noticed in the front yard, amidst fashionable lawn furniture, a statue of Lord Buddha—a garden ornament. When Prabhupāda entered the house, he found Mukunda and his wife, Jānakī, waiting for him. They bowed down, and Jānakī wept in happiness. Prabhupāda smiled but kept walking, slowly and silently, through the house. The large living room overlooking the Pacific Ocean was decorated with some of Jadurāṇī's paintings of Lord Viṣṇu, Rādhā and Kṛṣṇa, and Lord Caitanya, as well as with Indian prints of Jagannātha Purī. Prabhupāda's bedroom, also facing the ocean, had sliding windows. On the wall was a portrait of Śrīla Bhaktisiddhānta Sarasvatī and a painting of Rādhā and Kṛṣṇa. Prabhupāda smiled and said the paintings were very nice.

The devotees agreed that only Kīrtanānanda and Upendra would stay and serve Swamiji. They wanted Swamiji's stay to be peaceful, so that his health could improve.

That night Śrīla Prabhupāda felt pain in his heart and couldn't sleep. And he didn't rise early for translating. At five A.M. Kīrtanānanda came in and opened the window slightly so that Prabhupāda could receive the soft ocean breeze. Prabhupāda sat up in his bed chanting his *japa* and gazing at the feet of Lord Kṛṣṇa and Śrīmatī Rādhārāṇī. A mountain range to the east blocked the morning sun.

Ever since Prabhupāda's stroke, Kīrtanānanda had been regularly massaging Prabhupāda morning and evening. Kīrtanānanda would rub Prabhupāda's head vigorously and then sit behind him and massage his back; next he would massage Prabhupāda's chest, his arms, and his legs, the complete massage lasting sometimes more than an hour. Since leaving the hospital, Prabhupāda had also been taking daily morning walks, even while on the Lower East Side. And this morning he went down for a walk on the beach, accompanied by Kīrtanānanda and Upendra.

As Prabhupāda walked on the beach, he pointed his cane towards some bubbles in the sand. "Just see," he said. "There are living entities everywhere. There is no place without living entities. And yet they say there is no life on the moon!" The beach was rocky, and there were cliffs where the waves crashed powerfully like thunder. "You hear this sound?" Śrīla Prabhupāda asked. "This is an echo of the *gopīs'* heartbeats when they are feeling separation from Kṛṣṇa."

He walked for an hour, until his two young servants were both tired. "Do I tire you walking?" he laughed. "This walking and massaging are saving my life from day to day." Then he continued walking.

By eleven o'clock the sun finally appeared over the mountains and through the clouds. Śrīla Prabhupāda, his head wrapped with a towel, sat in a folding chair on the beach, taking in the sunshine. He kept saying he needed more sun. After lunch the sky was again overcast.

In the evening Prabhupāda called Kīrtanānanda and Upendra into the large living room and led them in a subdued *kīrtana*, singing Hare Kṛṣṇa and Govinda Jaya Jaya. He stood and led them in a large circle around the room. He would stop before the picture of Kṛṣṇa, bow slightly with folded palms, turn around, and then continue in the circle.

On July 8, after Prabhupāda had been at Paradisio for two days, Śyāmasundara and Mukunda drove up from San Francisco. The next day was to be Ratha-yātrā, and Śyāmasundara and Mukunda, the first devotees to visit Prabhupāda since his arrival at Stinson Beach, told Prabhupāda all about the festival preparations. Of course, the whole festival had been Prabhupāda's idea, but the devotees in San Francisco were trying to do exactly as he had asked.

Śrīla Prabhupāda had first gotten the idea for the festival while looking out the window of his room above Frederick Street. Noticing flatbed trucks passing below, he thought of putting Jagannātha deities on the back of such a truck and conducting an American-style Ratha-yātrā festival. He had even sketched a truck with a four-pillared canopy on the back and decorated with flags, bells, and flower garlands. And he had called in Śyāmasundara: "Make me this cart for Ratha-yātrā." Now, ready and sitting outside the temple on Frederick Street was the cart—a yellow Hertz rental truck, compliments of the Diggers and complete with five-foot columns and a pyramidal cloth canopy.

Sitting with Prabhupāda on the beach, Mukunda told how all the devotees were working with great enthusiasm and how the hippies in Haight-Ashbury were talking about the Jagannātha parade that would take place the next day. The devotees had tried to route the parade through Golden Gate Park, but the police department would only give permission for them to go south down Frederick Street to the sea. Mukunda said the devotees planned to have Jagannātha under the canopy, facing the right side of the truck, Subhadrā facing the rear, and Balarāma facing the left side; he wanted to know if that was all right. Actually, Prabhupāda said, the deities should ride in separate carts, pulled with ropes by the crowd through the streets; maybe that could happen in future years.

"Do it nicely," he cautioned them. "And don't hurry it up." The devotees should drive the truck slowly through the streets down to the beach, and there should be constant *kīrtana.*

Mukunda and Śyāmasundara glorified Jayānanda: he drove all around San Francisco getting donations of fruits and flowers, found people to help decorate the cart, installed the sound system on the truck, and distributed posters in the stores. He was tireless, and his enthusiasm was inspiring everyone else to take part. The women had been cooking *capātīs* all day, so there should be thousands to give away to the crowd. The devotees had prepared hundreds of Hare Kṛṣṇa Ratha-yātrā festival balloons to release on the streets as the parade began.

When the devotees asked what else they should do, Prabhupāda said that this was all—a procession, *prasādam* distribution, *kīrtana.* The people should get a chance to see Lord Jagannātha and chant Hare Kṛṣṇa. There should be chanting and dancing in front of the cart throughout the procession. "But do everything nicely," Prabhupāda said. "Do it as well as you can, and Lord Jagannātha will be satisfied."

The next day, in the quiet afternoon, Prabhupāda was sitting in the living room, chanting on his beads. Upendra was with him, and Kīrtanānanda was in the kitchen cooking a feast. Suddenly Prabhupāda heard the familiar ringing of cymbals, and he became very happy, his eyes widening. Looking outside he saw the Ratha-yātrā truck, with Lord Jagannātha, Subhadrā, and Balarāma and dozens of devotees and hippies eager to see him. He went out to greet them and had them bring the deities inside and set them on top of the upright piano. Devotees and guests followed, filling the large living room. Smiling, Prabhupāda embraced some of the men while others made obeisances at his feet. Some devotees helped Kīrtanānanda in the kitchen get ready to distribute the large feast he had prepared. Others reported on the success of the Ratha-yātrā festival.

It was great! It was wonderful! It was a beautiful day, they said. And Prabhupāda listened, moved by his disciples' description of the celebration. Many hippies had joined the large procession. Mukunda, Haridāsa, Hayagrīva, and some of the women had been on the cart, and the instruments, including Yamunā's playing on the harmonium, had all been amplified. Everyone in the streets had liked it. The police motor escorts had tried to hurry the devotees, but so many people had crowded in front that the parade had been obliged to go slowly, just as Swamiji had asked. Subala had danced wildly the whole time, and Jayānanda had been jumping up and down, playing *karatālas*. From the truck some of the women had handed out cut oranges, apples, and bananas, and others had thrown flowers. The crowds had loved it.

Śyāmasundara told how they had been going up a steep hill—Śyāmasundara had been driving, with his dog Ralph beside him on the front seat—when the truck had stalled. He had tried to start the engine but couldn't. Then the brakes wouldn't hold. The truck began rolling backward downhill! Finally he had managed to stop. But when he had tried to go forward the engine had stalled and the truck had rolled backwards again! He would get it started, the truck would go forward, then stall, then roll backwards. Everyone had been in anxiety. At last the truck had started forward, and the procession had continued all the way to the beach.

Śrīla Prabhupāda smiled. It was a pastime of Lord Jagannātha's, he said. The same thing had happened when Lord Caitanya had attended Ratha-yātrā in Jagannātha Purī. Then also the cart had gotten stuck, and no one had been able to move it. The king of Orissa had brought forward the most powerful wrestlers to push the cart and pull on the ropes. But it wouldn't go. Even the elephants couldn't move it. Lord Caitanya Mahāprabhu had then put His head against the cart and pushed, and only then did the cart begin to move. Now Ratha-yātrā had come to the West, and with it this pastime of Lord Jagannātha's.

Prabhupāda noticed some devotees were missing. "Where are Yamunā and Jānakī?" he asked. The devotees told him that some hippies had handed out candy spiked with LSD and that a few of the devotees had unwittingly accepted it and were just now recovering.

Subala related how, after the festival, they had traveled out on the freeway in their flower-bedecked, canopy-covered truck carrying thirty devotees and the deities of Jagannātha, Subhadrā, and Balarāma. They had driven up through the mountains in what must have been one of the most unusual vehicles ever seen.

After all the visitors departed, the deities remained in the house with Prabhupāda and his servants. Prabhupāda felt satisfied that his disciples had successfully held a Ratha-yātrā festival. Although untrained, they were sincere. Bhaktisiddhānta Sarasvatī and Bhaktivinoda Ṭhākura would have been pleased to see the first American Ratha-yātrā.

The whole world was in anxiety, Prabhupāda explained to the devotees gathered in his room that evening. Only in the spiritual world was there freedom from anxiety. Becoming free from all anxiety and returning to the spiritual world was the purpose of Kṛṣṇa consciousness. And festivals like Ratha-yātrā made people Kṛṣṇa conscious. Prabhupāda had many, many ideas for festivals. If he had the money and the manpower, he said, he could have a festival every day. There was no limit to Kṛṣṇa consciousness. This Ratha-yātrā festival was another sign of the good reception for Kṛṣṇa consciousness in the West.

He wrote Brahmānanda in New York:

> The house is situated in an exceptionally nice spot and the house itself is aristocratic. So there is nothing to complain about the house and place. The only difficulty is that I cannot go to the temple on account of the zigzag course of the road and crossing the mountains. Anyway, the devotees are coming here, and the Ratha-yatra festival was just performed with great pomp. More than five hundred people followed the procession to the beach, and there were about two dozen cars. They distributed thousands of chopaties, and at last Sri Jagannatha, Subhadra and Baladeva kindly came here in our house and will stay here for one week and then return.

* * *

Śrīla Prabhupāda still talked of going to India. He had virtually made up his mind to go; the question now was when, and whether by the western route, via Japan, or the eastern route, via New York. The gray skies and unseasonably cool temperatures of Stinson Beach were a disappointment. His health was still poor. He even spoke of dying. It didn't matter whether he died in America or in Vṛndāvana, he said. If a Vaiṣṇava dies in Vṛndāvana, the land where Kṛṣṇa appeared, he is assured of joining Kṛṣṇa in the spiritual world. Yet when Lord Caitanya had traveled outside Vṛndāvana, His devotee Advaita had assured Him, "Wherever You are is Vṛndāvana." To be always absorbed in thinking of

Kṛṣṇa was also Vṛndāvana. So if he were to pass away while preaching Kṛṣṇa consciousness—anywhere in the world—certainly he would still attain to the eternal Vṛndāvana in the spiritual sky.

Nevertheless, Prabhupāda wanted to go to Vṛndāvana. It was the best place—to die or to recuperate. Besides, he had a plan for bringing his disciples to Vṛndāvana for training. He expressed this plan in a letter to Sumati Morarji, the owner of the Scindia Steamship Company.

> I am thinking of going back to India as soon as I get sufficient strength. I am now considerably old; I will be 72 years next September. But the work which I have begun in the western world is not yet finished, and I require to train some of the American boys to preach this cult all over the western world. So if I return to India I will have to take with me some of the boys for training. They are all nice boys to take up the training. So your cooperation in this connection is greatly needed. You have already allowed my men from India free passage; similarly if you allow free passage for some of my American disciples they can come to India and taking training from me at Vrindaban. The idea is that in this old age I do not know when death will overcome me. And I wish to die in the last days of my life at Vrindaban.

Prabhupāda told Kīrtanānanda, Hayagrīva, and others that he would take them with him and show them the sacred places of Kṛṣṇa's pastimes. With the New York temple's building fund, he would start his American House in Vṛndāvana.

> I may come to Montreal, perform the opening ceremony of installation of Radha-Krishna Vigraha. Then I may go back to India for six months, as there is a program for construction of an American house for training preachers at Vrindaban. Vrindaban is the only solitary transcendental abode within this universe where Krishna consciousness automatically reveals. Therefore I have a great hope to train some of my disciples for preaching work, even in my absence. I am now old man, and attacked with serious disease; I may be overcome by death at any moment. Therefore I wish to leave some trained preachers so that they can do the work of Krishna consciousness in the Western world. That is my ambition. I hope you all pray to Krishna so that I may be able to execute my duty properly.

When Govinda dāsī wrote Prabhupāda that she was anxious to serve him again as she had in New Jersey, he replied that he would be going to India to try to construct an American House "where you will be invited to come and live for all the days. Both your husband and yourself, you will find a very peaceful atmosphere in Vrindaban to worship Krishna."

Waiting for sufficient strength to travel, Prabhupāda continued his daily routine at Stinson Beach. One or two at a time, devotees would visit him from San Francisco. His morning walks on the beach, his sitting to take in the sunshine whenever it peeked through the clouds, and his evenings of *kīrtana* or reading in the living room remained undisturbed and peaceful.

Upendra: *He would sit in his chair on the beach side of the house. He liked to see us go in the water and play. At first I felt a bit strange going in the water and knowing that Swamiji was watching me. But I went in and began washing my body. When I looked back at Swamiji he was motioning from his chair, throwing his arms up like he was splashing in the water. He kept doing it until finally I understood that he wanted me to splash and play in the water. As I began to splash and jump around in the water, he nodded his head and smiled broadly.*

Mukunda: *I went on a walk on the beach with Swamiji, and when he sat down, I sat down opposite him. Then he asked me, "What is your definition of Kṛṣṇa?" I said, "Kṛṣṇa is God. He is the Supreme Being. Our duty is to worship and serve Him." Swamiji seemed fairly satisfied, and then he said, "You must chant sixty-four rounds per day on your beads." I was shocked at this and could not answer. I did not know if there were any need to answer. I just kept looking at Swamiji, and he looked at me. After some time he said, "Or at least you can chant thirty-two rounds a day." Still silence. I considered it to be very difficult to chant even sixteen rounds. I was wondering how I could possibly chant thirty-two rounds. After some time, Swamiji said, "At the very least you must chant sixteen rounds every day." I said, "Yes, Swamiji." I knew that I could at least try to handle that much.*

Prabhupāda told Kīrtanānanda that he wanted to play the piano. (The Jagannātha deities, who had sat atop the piano for a week, were now back in San Francisco at the temple.) But when Kīrtanānanda and Upendra moved the piano away from the wall, they heard the thud of a falling object. "What is that?" Prabhupāda asked. Kīrtanānanda reached behind the piano and produced a framed canvas wrapped in a madras. He uncovered it and revealed a painting of Lord Nṛsiṁhadeva. "Why is this being hidden behind the piano?" Prabhupāda asked. Jānakī happened to be visiting at the time, and she confessed. While she had been arranging the house for Prabhupāda's arrival, someone had sent the painting out to the house. She had found it and hidden it. It was ghastly, she explained. Lord Nṛsiṁha was tearing open Hiraṇyakaśipu's abdomen, and there was blood everywhere.

Patiently Prabhupāda explained that although materialistic people feel sorry for Hiraṇyakaśipu, devotees become ecstatic when they see Nṛsiṁhadeva tearing him apart. Hiraṇyakaśipu, he said, had terrorized the whole universe and had usurped the throne of Indra, the king of heaven. Hiraṇyakaśipu had even tortured his own five-year-old son, Prahlāda, a pure devotee of Lord Kṛṣṇa. So there was nothing wrong in Lord Nṛsiṁha's pastime. In fact, Hiraṇyakaśipu, having been killed by the Lord, had been liberated.

After directing the devotees to hang the picture on the wall, Śrīla Prabhupāda sat down and played the piano. The devotees had seen Prabhupāda beautifully play the Indian harmonium—his left hand pumping the bellows, his right hand fingering the keyboard—but never a piano. They weren't aware he knew how. But he expertly played the melodies of Indian *bhajanas*. After about five minutes he stopped.

Some evenings Prabhupāda would speak or arrange debates, although Kīrtanānanda was constantly cautioning. When Prabhupāda wanted to speak, it was impossible for any of his disciples to stop him. Sometimes he would ask Kīrtanānanda to debate with one of the visiting devotees. One devotee would argue for the impersonalist's or atheist's position, and the other would argue for the Kṛṣṇa conscious position. Prabhupāda would judge. But no sooner would the argument begin than Prabhupāda would interrupt, take the position of the devotee, and defeat the atheistic or impersonalistic argument. The devotees loved it. Prabhupāda was unable to confine himself either to the role of a silent judge or to that of a recuperating patient.

"Why do we concentrate on the impersonalists?" Kīrtanānanda asked. "Why do we attack them so much? Why don't we concentrate our attack on the atheists?"

"You say that because you are an impersonalist," Prabhupāda answered angrily.

On another occasion, Prabhupāda explained that nondevotees who mislead the innocent public are demons and should be exposed. Kīrtanānanda objected, "If we call them demons, they'll never come around."

"But they are demons," Prabhupāda replied.

"But we can't call them demons, Swamiji."

"Yes, they are demons! Unless you understand this point, you will not make advancement in Kṛṣṇa consciousness."

"Can demons become devotees?" Kīrtanānanda asked.

"Oh, yes," Prabhupāda answered. "If they chant Hare Kṛṣṇa and render service, even demons become devotees."

Most of the devotees had to remain in San Francisco, hoping for a chance to visit Swamiji. From the few who knew firsthand, they heard about Swamiji's plans to leave for India, perhaps never to return. It was painful to hear. His going almost to death but then returning by Kṛṣṇa's grace and rejoining them in San Francisco, yet being unable to stay with them as before, and now his plans of going to India, maybe forever—these activities intensified their concern and love for him.

Devotees worried, speculating on whether they could carry on without Swamiji. One devotee suggested that perhaps one of Swamiji's Godbrothers should come to America and fill in for Swamiji and, if the worst happened, take over the leadership of the International Society for Krishna Consciousness. When the suggestion reached Prabhupāda, he considered it without immediately replying.

Mukunda: *I was sitting alone with Swamiji in his room, and he was very grave and silent. His eyes were closed. Then, suddenly, tears began flowing from his eyes. And he said in a choked voice, "My spiritual master was no ordinary spiritual master." Then he paused for some time, and wiping the tears from his cheeks, he said in an even more choked voice, "He saved me." At that point I began to understand the meaning of "spiritual master" and dropped all consideration of ever replacing Swamiji.*

After two days Prabhupāda said he would not call any of his

Godbrothers to come and take care of his disciples. He said, "If this person speaks just one word different from what I am speaking, there will be great confusion among you." Actually, he said, the idea was an insult to the spiritual master.

Prabhupāda said that he would initiate the new followers in San Francisco and asked that they come one at a time and stay overnight. Without performing any fire ceremonies, he simply talked with each new person, asking him to follow the four rules and chant sixteen rounds a day. When the follower promised, Prabhupāda initiated him, sitting on the bed while the disciple sat before him on the floor. Prabhupāda would chant quietly on the disciple's beads and then give him or her a spiritual name.

One day one of the new candidates for initiation came in very nervously and bowed down before Prabhupāda. The boy didn't get up. "You can get up now," Prabhupāda said. "So you want to be initiated?" The boy said yes and began chanting, not knowing what else to say. "I'll chant on your beads," Prabhupāda said. After chanting for ten minutes he returned them, saying, "Your name is Aniruddha."

"What does that mean?" the boy asked.

"He's the grandson of Kṛṣṇa. Do you have any questions?" Aniruddha couldn't think of anything—he had already forgotten his name—and Prabhupāda said he could go

Later, Prabhupāda called for Aniruddha, but Aniruddha didn't know that it was his name being called. "Aniruddha," Kīrtanānanda said and looked at him. "Swamiji is calling you."

Another boy who came out received the name Uddhava. The next day, as Prabhupāda was sitting in the yard, he called, "Kīrtanānanda, Upendra, Uddhava." He wanted to read them a verse he had encountered while studying *Śrīmad-Bhāgavatam.* Kīrtanānanda and Upendra came and sat at Prabhupāda's feet. "Oh, where is Uddhava?" Prabhupāda asked. Upendra told him that Uddhava had gone up to the hills to look at the cows and chant to them. Upendra thought that Swamiji would be pleased to hear that his new disciple had climbed the hills just to chant to the cows. But Prabhupāda shook his head unhappily: "Restlessness!" He had wanted the new boy to hear the verse.

jayati jayati devo devakī-nandano 'sau
jayati jayati kṛṣṇo vṛṣṇi-vaṁśa-pradīpaḥ
jayati jayati megha-śyāmalaḥ komalāṅgo
jayati jayati pṛthvī-bhāra-nāśo mukundaḥ

Prabhupāda gave the translation: "All glories to the Supreme Personality of Godhead, who is known as the son of Devakī. All glories to the Supreme Personality of Godhead, the light of the Vṛṣṇi dynasty. All glories to the Supreme Personality of Godhead, whose bodily luster is like that of a new cloud and whose body is as soft as lotus flowers. All glories to the Supreme Personality of Godhead, who walks on the planet earth to deliver the world from the scorn of demons and who can offer liberation to everyone." After repeating the Sanskrit and the translation, he told them they could return to their duties.

* * *

Prabhupāda told Kīrtanānanda he had definitely decided to go to India, via New York, as soon as possible. Kīrtanānanda packed Swamiji's things and drove Swamiji down to San Francisco to spend the night at the temple. They would leave the next morning.

The temple and even Prabhupāda's apartment were very hectic that night, with many devotees and guests wanting to see Prabhupāda and dozens of people wanting initiation. When Kīrtanānanda advised Prabhupāda not to exert himself by going down for the evening program, Prabhupāda insisted on at least going and sitting during the *kīrtana.*

When he entered the storefront, the devotees immediately stopped their *kīrtana,* dropping down to offer obeisances. There was a hush. He commanded a new reverence. This might be the last time they would see him. They watched him during the *kīrtana* as he played his *karatālas,* singing with them for the last time. The uninitiated wanted to accept him as their spiritual master—tonight, before it was too late.

Śrīla Prabhupāda asked for the microphone. No one had expected him to speak. Kīrtanānanda, the only person in a position to restrain him, said nothing and sat before him like the others, submissive and expectant. Prabhupāda spoke quietly about his mission: under the order of his spiritual master he was bringing Lord Caitanya's movement to America, and Kṛṣṇa had kindly sent him so many sincere souls. "I have a few children in India from my family days," he said, "but you are my real children. Now I am going to India for a little while."

Everyone fixed his attention on Swamiji as he sat before them, leaning against the madras-covered wall, speaking softly. Suddenly the door opened, and Ravīndra-svarūpa unhappily entered. Everyone knew that Ravīndra-svarūpa wanted to leave Kṛṣṇa consciousness. He hadn't taken his initiation vows seriously. He wanted to move on. He didn't want a spiritual master any more. The other devotees had discouraged him, but he had persisted. They were incredulous. How could he do such a thing on the night before Swamiji's departure!

Ravīndra-svarūpa fell to the floor to offer obeisances. But he didn't rise up. Instead, he began crawling on his hands and knees towards Prabhupāda. Ravīndra usually had a cavalier manner, enhanced by a handsome face, long tousled hair, and a beard. But now he was wretched and sobbing and crazy. He crawled towards Prabhupāda, who sat but two steps off the floor on the simple redwood dais. Prabhupāda looked at him with compassion: "Come here, my boy." Ravīndra crawled up the steps and placed his bushy head on Prabhupāda's lap. Moved, the devotees watched as Prabhupāda stroked Ravīndra's head and the boy cried and cried.

"What's wrong, my son? You don't have to be so unhappy."

Ravīndra bawled out, "I want . . ." He sobbed, "*Aah* . . . to . . . *aah* . . . reach God directly! Without anyone in between!"

Prabhupāda continued to pat and stroke the boy's head: "No, you continue to stay with us if possible. Don't be a crazy fellow." Ravīndra's weeping subsided, and Prabhupāda continued, speaking both to Ravīndra and to the emotion-struck group in the room. "I am an old man," he said. "I may die at any moment. But please, you all carry on this *saṅkīrtana* movement. You have to become humble and tolerant. As Lord Caitanya says, be as humble as a blade of grass and more tolerant than a tree. You must have enthusiasm and patience to push on this Kṛṣṇa conscious philosophy."

Suddenly Ravīndra's tears were gone. He jumped up, dejectedly stood, hesitating for a moment, and then hurried out the door, banging it behind him.

Ravīndra-svarūpa's dramatic exit from Kṛṣṇa consciousness shocked the devotees. Prabhupāda sat still and continued speaking to them gravely, asking them to stick together and push on the movement, for their own benefit and for others. Whatever they had learned, he said, they should repeat.

They realized, perhaps for the first time, that they were part of a preaching mission, a movement. They were together not just for good times and good vibrations; they had a loving obligation to Swamiji and Kṛṣṇa.

Prabhupāda returned to his apartment, which soon became chaotic. It was late. Many people wanted initiation. Mukunda, Jayānanda, and other temple leaders tried to determine which candidates were sincere. They selected candidates, half a dozen at a time, and allowed them into Prabhupāda's room.

Prabhupāda sat behind his little desk, chanted on each person's beads, and returned them, giving each person a spiritual name. Kīrtanānanda requested him to stop; further initiations could be done through the mail. But Prabhupāda said he would continue initiating whoever was present.

Mukunda and Jayānanda set priorities. Some persons had been waiting months to be initiated and were obviously sincere. Others would have to be turned away.

John Carter: *At the end of the lecture I was sure that I wanted to be initiated. And even though there was some talk of being initiated by mail, I knew I wanted to have that personal connection with my spiritual master and be personally initiated by him, personally accepted. I ran up to Mukunda and said, "How many are on the list? I would like to get on the list."*

He said, "Well, Swamiji isn't really taking them in any particular order. We are just going to try to pick out the most sincere people."

"Please put my name on the list," I said. "I am really sincere, I really want to get initiated."

So he put me down and took the list up to Swamiji, and Swamiji began calling for people one by one. After the third person, when my name wasn't called, I became a little worried. Then after the fourth person, I was really sitting on edge. Then when they called the fifth person and it wasn't me, I was totally destroyed. I felt, "Oh, he's going to India, and then he's going back to Kṛṣṇa. I just lost my chance. This is it. There's no use in me living anymore."

I was trying to make it to the coat rack and get my coat and get out before anybody could see me crying. I hadn't started crying, but I could tell it was coming. A couple of people patted me on the back and said, "It's all right. He can write you a letter and tell you your name." All I could think was, "Yeah, the way he was talking tonight, it may never happen." I could barely stand up. I went outside and started walking across the parking lot towards Golden Gate Park. I was kind of heading towards the Golden Gate Bridge. I thought, "I'll just jump off." I hadn't been there long enough to understand that if you commit suicide you have to become a ghost. I just figured my life was useless.

I got about halfway across the parking lot when the idea struck me: "What if he decided to take one more and I was out here somewhere?" The thought filled me with so much hope that I turned around and ran back to the temple. And just as I walked in the front of the temple Jānakī ran down and said, "He will take one more." And she grabbed somebody else and ran up the stairs. I felt my knees start to collapse and tears came jutting out of my eyes. Harṣarāṇī was standing there, and she grabbed me by the arm and said, "Come with me." She raced up the stairs, pulling me to the top, and burst into Swamiji's room without even knocking.

Swamiji looked up with amazement. She said, "Swamiji, you have to initiate this boy." I was just bawling, and Swamiji began to laugh. He said, "It's all right. Don't cry. Everything will be all right." He chanted on my beads and gave me the name Jīvānanda.

* * *

The next morning, Prabhupāda had to leave his affectionate followers. Several cars filled with devotees accompanied him to the San Francisco airport.

Nandarāṇī: *Some were sincere, and some were crying because it was appropriate to cry when the spiritual master leaves. Actually, none of us really knew much about what the spiritual master was.*

Jānakī mischievously stole the ticket and passport from Prabhupāda's hand. "Now you can't go," she said.

"That's all right," he smiled. "I already have my boarding ticket. I am

Indian. They will let me into my own country."

Prabhupāda turned to his adoring followers gathered close around him at the boarding gate: "Actually I have only one desire, and whoever does this will please me very much. Now I have a temple in New York, in Montreal, and a temple in San Francisco. But I do not have any temple in Los Angeles." He told them to remain in Kṛṣṇa consciousness and to please preach.

They watched as he turned and walked through the gate, his cane in one hand, boarding pass in the other.

* * *

In New York there was hardly time for sadness. Śrīla Prabhupāda telegraphed Sri Krishna Pandit that his arrival in Delhi would be on July 24 at 7:30 A.M. and that Sri Krishna Pandit should prepare Prabhupāda's quarters at the Chippiwada temple. In the telegram Prabhupāda mentioned his intention to consult a physician in Delhi and then go to Vṛndāvana. He was anxious to return to Vṛndāvana.

The day before his departure, Prabhupāda wrote to Sumati Morarji. In reply to his last letter she had agreed to provide free steamship passage to India for him, but not for his disciples. "As I had arranged for your passage to America," she had written, "I think it is my duty to see that you return back to India safely, more so due to your indifferent health." But she would not allow free passage for any disciples.

On July 20, Prabhupāda wrote:

> I am feeling too much to return to Vrindabana to the lotus feet of Vrindabana Behary Lord Krishna; and therefore I have decided to return to India immediately. I would have liked to return via sea, as you have so kindly offered me passage in your letter, but in my precarious state of health that is not possible. So by the mercy of Krishna and through one friend here, somehow or other, I have received air passage, and I am expecting to leave here for New Delhi on Saturday next, reaching the Palam airport on the 24th instant at 7:30 a.m. From there I shall proceed to Vrindabana after a few days rest in Delhi.
>
> I can understand that at present you cannot allow free passage to my disciples. But if you don't do so, at least in the near future, then my mission will be half finished or failure. I am just enclosing one letter of apprecia-

> tion for one of my principal students (Bruce Scharf) from Professor Davis Herron, and another from Professor Roberts of New York University. I think these letters will convince you how much my movement of Krishna consciousness is taking ground in the western world. The holy name of Hare Krishna is now being chanted not only in this country but also in England, Holland, and Mexico, that I know of. It may be even more widespread. I have sent you one gramophone record which I hope you may have received by this time. You will enjoy to learn how Krishna's Holy Name is being appreciated by the Western World.

Acyutānanda told Prabhupāda he wanted to go to India to study intensively, gather experiences, and become attached to Kṛṣṇa. He had heard Prabhupāda say that one could become more Kṛṣṇa conscious in two days in Vṛndāvana than in ten years in America. "Do you think I'll be able to go?" Acyutānanda asked.

"Rest assured," Prabhupāda told him, "we will meet again in Vraja."

Devotees had been asking Satsvarūpa to transfer his civil service job to Boston and open a Kṛṣṇa conscious center there. They had also asked Rūpānuga to do the same in Buffalo. Satsvarūpa and Rūpānuga approached Prabhupāda to find out what he wanted. He became very pleased. Subala was going to open a center in Santa Fe, he said, and Dayānanda was going to Los Angeles. "Hare Kṛṣṇa *mantra* is like a big cannon," he told them. "Go and sound this cannon so everyone can hear it, and it will drive away *māyā*."

The devotees wanted to ask, "But what if you don't return?" They were fearful. What if Kṛṣṇa kept Swamiji in Vṛndāvana? What if Swamiji never returned? How could they survive against *māyā*? But Swamiji had already assured them that whatever Kṛṣṇa consciousness he had given them would be enough, even if he never returned.

Just thirty minutes before he had to leave for the airport, Prabhupāda sat in his room chanting on the beads of a girl who had asked to be initiated. Then, as he had done many times before, he left his apartment, went downstairs, crossed the courtyard, and entered the storefront.

Sitting on the old carpet, he spoke quietly and personally. "I may be going, but Guru Mahārāja and Bhaktivinoda are here." He looked toward the paintings of his spiritual master and Bhaktivinoda Ṭhākura. "I have asked them to kindly take care of all of you, my spiritual children. The grandfather always takes care of the children much better than the father. So do not fear. There is no question of separation. The sound vibration fixes us up together, even though the material body may not be there. What do we care for this material body? Just go on chanting Hare Kṛṣṇa, and we will be packed up together. You will be chanting here, and I will be chanting there, and this vibration will circulate around this planet."

Several devotees rode with Prabhupāda in the taxi—Brahmānanda in the front with the driver, Rāya Rāma and Kīrtanānanda in the back beside their spiritual master. "When Kīrtanānanda sees Vṛndāvana," Prabhupāda said, "he will not be able to understand how I could have left that place and come to this place. It is so nice. There are no motorcars there like here, rushing whoosh! whoosh! and smelling. Only there is Hare Kṛṣṇa. Everybody always chanting. Thousands and thousands of temples. I will show you, Kīrtanānanda. We will walk all about there, and I will show you."

Brahmānanda began to cry, and Prabhupāda patted him on the back. "I can understand that you are feeling separation," he said. "I am feeling for my Guru Mahārāja. I think this is what Kṛṣṇa desires. You may be coming there to me and be training up, and we will spread this movement all over the world. Rāya Rāma—you will go to England. Brahmānanda—you want to go to Japan or Russia? That's all right."

The devotees converged on the Air-India waiting room, near a crowded cocktail lounge. Wearing a sweater, his *cādar* folded neatly over one shoulder, Prabhupāda sat in a chair. His disciples sat as closely as possible around his feet. He held an umbrella, just as when he had first come alone to New York, almost two years ago. Although exhausted, he was smiling.

Prabhupāda noted a mural of Indian women carrying large jars on their heads, and he called the name of a young girl who had recently gone with her husband, Haṁsadūta, to join the ISKCON center in Montreal. "Himāvatī, would you like to go to India and learn to carry this waterpot like the Indian women?"

"Yes, yes," she said. "I'll go."

"Yes," Śrīla Prabhupāda said, "some day we will all go."

Kīrtanānanda was carrying a portable battery-operated phonograph and two copies of the Hare Kṛṣṇa *mantra* record. "Kīrtanānanda," Prabhupāda asked, "why not play the record? They will enjoy." Kīrtanānanda played the record very softly, its sound catching the attention of people in the cocktail lounge. "Make it a little louder," Prabhupāda asked, and Kīrtanānanda increased the volume. Prabhupāda began nodding his head, keeping time.

Soon the devotees began humming along with the record, and then quietly singing, until gradually they were singing loudly. Kīrtanānanda, Brahmānanda, and other devotees began to cry.

Haṁsadūta: *I was sitting right next to Swamiji, and all the time I was thinking, "Oh, my spiritual master is going to India." And he said, "I want to die in Vṛndāvana." We all* knew *Swamiji was going, but now it was the last moment. I was also seeing that I hadn't done anything for my spiritual master. "He doesn't even know who I am," I thought. "There's no relationship. I must do something. I must do something* now. *I must serve him in some way which will establish some place in his heart. Something." I was thinking, "What can I do?" I was crying, and he didn't even look at me. It was like I wasn't even there, just like a chair or something. He was just always looking around and everything, and I was trying to catch his eye: if all of a sudden he would say something.*

The kīrtana *was getting heavier and heavier, and so was the crying. And the people in the waiting room were just looking at Swamiji like he was someone very special. And in the middle of it all, Swamiji was completely relaxed, as if this were his place and this was just a normal thing to do.*

When the record ended, Haṁsadūta asked, "Swamiji, can I take a collection?" Prabhupāda nodded. Haṁsadūta stood and made a little speech: "Our mission is to spread Kṛṣṇa consciousness. We have a temple in New York. We are always badly in need of money. Please help us." Borrowing a hat from a soldier, Haṁsadūta went around taking a collection.

"Our traveling is very auspiciously beginning," Prabhupāda said. "We had a nice *kīrtana*, and we had a nice collection. It is all Kṛṣṇa's mercy."

Then it was time to board the plane. Prabhupāda embraced each of his men. They stood in a line, and one after another approached him and embraced him. He patted a few of the women on the head.

Rūpānuga: *Swamiji was embracing the men: Kīrtanānanda, Brahmānanda, Gargamuni. I never expected that he would ask* me *to step forward. I didn't consider myself in the same category with the other devotees, so I was very much surprised when Swamiji motioned to me and spoke my name, "Rūpānuga." I got up and walked to Swamiji. It might have been ten feet, but it seemed like a long distance. I embraced him, and that embrace was the most memorable embrace of my life. Right away I noticed Śrīla Prabhupāda's strength. He was so strong it was like embracing a young man—a man my age. I was twenty-seven, and he seemed even stronger and younger than I. And he hugged me tightly, and I also embraced him very firmly. He was smaller than me in stature, so I instinctively buried my chin in the hollow of his left shoulder. While I was embracing him I felt very blissful, and I felt a light. I felt there was a light, something bright and pure, some kind of energy emanating from my face. I opened my eyes and I saw Kīrtanānanda watching. He was standing behind Swamiji, a few feet away, and I looked right into his eyes. And I was so happy and blissful that it reflected in him somehow. He broke into a big smile, smiled at me. And his eyes were very bright. It was as if some spiritual energy was actually emanating from me.*

That airport scene was a very important part of my life. Because for me, a person who always had difficulty in loving another person, Swamiji's leaving forced out a lot of love from my heart I didn't even know was there. It's like becoming a spiritual person when you feel love really developing for the spiritual master. I was becoming a spiritual person. It was a tremendous outpouring of feelings of separation and grief at his departure, because we all knew he was our life and soul. And to a person, none of us were sure we would ever see him again.

Accompanied by Kīrtanānanda, whose head was shaven and who wore an incongruous black woolen suit, Prabhupāda walked slowly toward the gate. As he disappeared from view, the devotees ran for the observation deck to get a last look at his departing plane.

A gentle rain was washing the airfield as the devotees raced across the wet observation deck. There below were Prabhupāda and Kīrtanānanda, walking towards their plane. Abandoning decorum, the devotees began to shout. Prabhupāda turned and waved. He climbed the movable stairway, turning again at the top and raising his arms, and then entered the plane. The devotees chanted wildly while the boarding steps moved away, the door closed, and the plane began to turn. The devotees had pressed close to the rail, but they pulled back as the jet exhaust blasted them with heat. With a great roar the Air-India jet, lights blinking, taxied out to the runway. The devotees continued to chant Hare Kṛṣṇa until the plane left the ground, became a speck in the sky, and then disappeared.

CHAPTER SIX

India Revisited: Part I

The plane flew during the night and arrived in London by morning. Śrīla Prabhupāda had planned a stopover. He checked into an airport hotel, took his massage, and rested. In the afternoon he rose and bathed, and then he and Kīrtanānanda boarded their plane, bound for New Delhi via Moscow. While the plane was still on the ground, however, a crew member announced "a short delay due to health regulations." A passenger who had disembarked earlier that day was now sick, apparently with smallpox, so the plane would have to be thoroughly fumigated. Prabhupāda and Kīrtanānanda stayed in a room at the Excelsior Hotel for the night.

Early the next morning, July 24, seated in his hotel room, complete with air conditioning and television, neither of which he had used, Śrīla Prabhupāda wrote a letter to Brahmānanda in New York.

> Accept my blessings. I am always thinking of your separation feelings. Please do your duty nicely and Krishna will help you in all respects. We were delayed here for 16 hours. Starting this morning at nine for Delhi. The attention of Mr. B. K. Nehru the Ambassador of India was drawn to me the other day. I have told him about my Permanent Visa and He has promised to help me when I come back. Please make an appointment with him informing that I wish to present him our set of Bhagavatam and our other literatures. Then go to him and personally present the books etc. at Washington D.C. It may be that as soon as I feel some strength I shall be coming back. Up to now there was no disturbance about my health and I

hope to reach Delhi this night. I shall write you again after reaching Vrindaban. Convey my ardent affection and blessings for all the boys and girls. I am very much hopeful of my movement. Please keep steady, follow all my instructions scrupulously, chant Hare Krishna and Krishna will give you all strength.

Prabhupāda and Kīrtanānanda flew to Moscow. There they walked around the terminal, observing what Prabhupāda called "propaganda pictures." After a one-hour stopover they reboarded and flew another eight hours, arriving in Delhi around midnight.

The wall of heat that greeted them felt good to Prabhupāda. He had come for this. Inside the airport terminal, overhead fans stirred the muggy air as Prabhupāda and Kīrtanānanda stood in slow-moving lines while uniformed clerks checked passports and customs forms, without Western-style computers or efficiency. Just beyond the areas for immigration and customs, people waiting for arriving passengers were waving, calling, and coming together with friends and family members.

After Prabhupāda and Kīrtanānanda claimed their luggage and cleared customs, they stood on the sidewalk outside the terminal. Although Prabhupāda had removed his sweater, Kīrtanānanda stood sweltering in his black wool suit. It was two A.M. All around, passengers were meeting loved ones, who embraced them—sometimes even garlanded them—and helped them into cars or taxis. But no one was there for Prabhupāda. It was certainly different from the recent tearful airport scenes, where Prabhupāda had been with *his* loved ones. Now, instead of being surrounded by loving disciples, Prabhupāda was besieged by taxi drivers and porters wanting to carry his luggage for a fee. In Hindi Prabhupāda asked one of the drivers to take them to Chippiwada, in Old Delhi. The driver put their luggage in the trunk, and Prabhupāda and his disciple climbed into the back seat.

The small Ambassador taxi drove through streets well known to Śrīla Prabhupāda. Nighttime traffic was light—an occasional taxi or motor ricksha. Mostly the streets were empty and quiet, the shops closed, an occasional person or cow sleeping outdoors.

Just a few years before, Prabhupāda had sold *Back to Godhead* magazines, solicited donations, and printed his *Śrīmad-Bhāgavatam*s here. In those days he had been alone, practically without money or residence. Yet he had been happy, completely dependent on Kṛṣṇa.

But India's leaders were rejecting Vedic culture and imitating the West. Although some Indians still professed to follow Vedic culture, mostly they were victims of hodgepodge teachers who didn't accept Kṛṣṇa as the Supreme Personality of Godhead. So he had felt obliged to leave—to go and transplant the Vedic culture in the West. He had held strictly to the vision of his predecessor spiritual masters, and he had been proven right: the West was a very good field for Kṛṣṇa consciousness.

As the taxi drove through Old Delhi and approached Chawri Bazaar, Prabhupāda saw the printing and paper shops, now closed for the night. And the usual dense traffic of human-hauled carts was now absent, though some laborers were sleeping on their carts till the morning, when they would bathe in an outdoor well and begin another day's hauling. When Śrīla Prabhupāda had been overseeing the publishing of his first volumes of *Śrīmad-Bhāgavatam,* he had daily walked these streets, buying paper, picking up proofs from the printer, returning with the corrected proofs. His First Canto had been a triumph.

Chawri Bazaar led to side streets that led to the narrow lanes of Chippiwada, where upright metal posts blocked autos and rickshas from entering. The driver stopped the taxi on an empty road and turned for his payment. Prabhupāda took from his billfold forty rupees (the same forty rupees he had carried with him on the boat to America in 1965). But the driver took the entire forty rupees and said he would keep it all as the just fare. Prabhupāda protested; the fare should not be even half that! Loudly they argued back and forth in Hindi. The driver had pocketed the money and would give no change. Prabhupāda knew that to get a policeman at this hour would be very difficult. Finally, although this had been nothing less than a robbery, Prabhupāda let the man go. "He cheated me," Prabhupāda said. He and Kīrtanānanda took their luggage and walked the last block, up to the door of the Chippiwada Rādhā-Kṛṣṇa temple.

It was locked. As they pounded loudly, Prabhupāda called out for Sri Krishna Pandit until a man came to the door, recognized Prabhupāda, and let them in. The man showed them upstairs and unlocked the door to Prabhupāda's room. Prabhupāda turned on the light.

The room was bare and dusty, and the bulb hanging from the ceiling created stark light and shadows. On the floor was the three-foot-high cement dome indicating that directly below were the altar and the Deities of Rādhā and Kṛṣṇa. (The dome prevented anyone from accidentally committing the offense of walking directly above the Deities.) The closet was stacked with printed *Śrīmad-Bhāgavatam* pages, *Śrīmad-Bhāgavatam* dust jackets, and form letters to prospective members of the League of Devotees. Everything was just as Prabhupāda had left it.

"This is the room where I compiled *Śrīmad-Bhāgavatam,*" Śrīla Prabhupāda told Kīrtanānanda. "I slept here. And over here was my cooker and my typewriter. I would sleep and type and cook and type and sleep and type." Kīrtanānanda was shocked to think of Swamiji living here in such a poor, humble place. It wasn't even clean.

Although Kīrtanānanda was uncomfortable in his suit and wondered when he would be able to get rid of it, he managed to get a thin mattress for Swamiji. Two Āyur Vedic doctors came. They both agreed that the trouble was Swamiji's heart but that the danger was now past. They gave him medicines and advised him to keep to a regulated schedule of eating, resting, and working. Sri Krishna Pandit came by to sit and converse, and Prabhupāda told him of his success in America and of all the young devotees in New York and San Francisco. Prabhupāda played his record for Sri Krishna Pandit, and this drew a crowd of curious persons from other rooms in the temple.

In the afternoon Prabhupāda developed a cough. It didn't seem serious, and he said he wanted to travel the next day to Vṛndāvana. But by evening the cough had become persistent; he couldn't rest. Kīrtanānanda tried massages and the pills the Āyur Vedic doctors had prescribed, but nothing worked; Prabhupāda remained awake all night, and when Kīrtanānanda touched him in the morning he was feverish.

The doctors came again. Prabhupāda's temperature was over 104. They gave teas and Āyur Vedic powders while Kīrtanānanda looked on skeptically. Because Prabhupāda was having a lot of difficulty breathing when he lay down, Kīrtanānanda thought it might be pneumonia. So Kīrtanānanda gave him penicillin, of which he had brought a supply. In the afternoon an elderly Sikh doctor who practiced Western medicine came by and gave Prabhupāda a penicillin injection. Prabhupāda then fell asleep and rested quietly for the first time in twenty-four hours.

While Prabhupāda slept, Kīrtanānanda wrote a letter to his Godbrothers in New York.

> I know you would like me to say straight out my opinion as to how He is, and that is not good. The outcome—as always, but now very apparently—is only in Krishna's hands. Please chant HARE KRISHNA for that is the only thing that can save Him. That is what saved Him before, and that can do it again. I know that His task is not yet complete, and by Krishna's Mercy He can again be spared.

Kīrtanānanda also asked the New York devotees to call the devotees in San Francisco, Santa Fe, and Boston and have them continue chanting for Swamiji's health. He reminded them to strictly follow all of Swamiji's instructions.

The next day Śrīla Prabhupāda's fever was down to 100.6. He was still sick, but he talked again of going to Vṛndāvana. He dictated a letter to his bookselling agents in Delhi, Atmarama & Sons, asking them for an up-to-date account of their sales of his *Śrīmad-Bhāgavatam.* Old acquaintances came by and were disappointed to find Swamiji unable to accept their invitations. Prabhupāda asked that they invite Kīrtanānanda in his stead.

For several days Kīrtanānanda visited the homes of these pious Hindus. He played the record on his portable phonograph, chanting along and dancing with his arms upraised. Then he would give a short speech. His hosts accepted him as a *sādhu,* fascinated that an American had taken so seriously to Kṛṣṇa consciousness.

* * *

On August 1, after six days in Delhi, Prabhupāda went to Vṛndāvana. Kīrtanānanda wrote back to New York:

> My dear brothers and sisters,
>
> Greetings in the NAME of KRISHNA from VRINDABAN.
>
> Obviously Swamiji is much better—especially after reaching Vrindaban—His eyes now have a special glow. We left Delhi yesterday (31st) morning on the Taj Express, and in two hours were at Mathura. We rode "special third class" and it was quite satisfactory, not at all crowded like

the usual third class. Anyway, we are now here and are in the process of settling down. Swamiji has two very nice rooms—quite cool—just off the porch where the Bhagavatam is read. How appropriate! The only difficulty on His behalf is that these Indians all want to see Him—and they are very persistent, and I am not very successful in keeping them out....

Vrindaban, seen materially, is a very beautiful place. The country is very flat, and there are many trees, monkeys, peacocks, and of course temples. It is also very poor. Both the people and the temples are in a bad state of disrepair. But spiritually considered there are many great devotees here, and it is wonderful to walk down the streets and see teeloks all over the place, and people chanting on their beads. If I can develop a fraction of their devotion for Krishna, my life will be successful. It is also thrilling to hear the temple bells ringing so many times throughout the day. Last night I played our record for Lord Damodar here in the temple and then performed kirtan with some of the local devotees. It was very nice. But you will be surprised, I think, when I say that I prefer your kirtan in N.Y.

After Prabhupāda had been in Vṛndāvana only one day and his health had only slightly improved, he began planning his return to America. "I am always thinking of you," he wrote to the devotees, whom he addressed as his "dear students."

I cannot stop my western world activities and I have taken leave from you only for six months; and it may be that on or before I will come to you again. Kirtanananda says from my bodily feature that I am improving. I am also feeling like that.

In Delhi Prabhupāda had received a letter from Brahmānanda saying that the Macmillan Company was definitely interested in publishing the *Bhagavad-gītā*. In Vṛndāvana Prabhupāda wrote Brahmānanda to sign a contract at once on his behalf. Prabhupāda had been considering whether to print privately in Japan or India or to wait for Macmillan. He wasn't concerned with the prestige and financial advantages of publishing through Macmillan; his first concern was to *print as quickly as possible*.

I shall be satisfied with the commission and shall only be glad to see that the books are being read by hundreds and thousands of men. Whatever profit may be derived from it will be utilized for the development of an American House here.

Prabhupāda stayed in his old rooms at the Rādhā-Dāmodara temple. Still incapacitated, he was being massaged and cared for by Kīrtanānanda, who himself was listless and tired from the heat. But Prabhupāda continued to range from one active and ambitious vision for his youthful Kṛṣṇa consciousness movement to another. He would think aloud about the volumes of *Śrīmad-Bhāgavatam* ready to be published—if Macmillan would take them and the boys could act on his behalf. There was so much to do. He wanted to return by October and oversee things personally.

Temperatures rose to more than 110 degrees, and Prabhupāda and Kīrtanānanda had to stay inside with the doors shut and the overhead fan on. Although Kīrtanānanda could barely perform his duties, Prabhupāda found the heat bracing and said that it was restoring his health. Then, after the first week, the monsoon rains began, and the heat broke.

On August 10 Kīrtanānanda wrote home again.

God is it a hot place! But at last the rains have started again and there is some relief—from the heat. You can believe me when I say it was hot. But now it is raining a great deal of the time, and that has made the weather quite comfortable for me—but unfortunately not for Swamiji. Also I have developed the inevitable case of dysentery, which has been persisting for about a week now.

Yesterday began the festival of Jhulan, in which Radha and Krishna come out and swing for about five days, so I made the rounds of about a half dozen temples here. Some of them are extremely beautiful inside, although most are small. Still I can say this with all truthfulness and sincerity that none are so transcendentally beautiful and spiritual as 3720 Park Avenue Montreal—and I think even Swamiji would agree with me there.

Kīrtanānanda's letter gave heart to the devotees back home and confirmed their suspicion: it was not Hinduism, not India—it was Swamiji and chanting Hare Kṛṣṇa that was sustaining their spiritual life.

As Prabhupāda's spiritual children wrote from the fledgling centers in half a dozen cities in North America, he would reply.

> Vrindaban is an inspiration only but our real field work is all over the world. Even if I die you are my future hopes & you will do it. I am feeling very much for you all. Please let the ball roll on just as it is set.

Brahmānanda wrote from New York asking for an explanation of why Swamiji, a pure devotee, was suffering serious illness. Swamiji had explained that conditioned souls and even beginning devotees are "attacked by *māyā*." But was Swamiji also being attacked by *māyā*? On August 14 Śrīla Prabhupāda replied.

> Don't be afraid of my being attacked by maya. When there is fight between two belligerent parties, it is always expected that there will sometimes be reverses. Your country and the western world is mostly under the grip of Maya and the modes of nature in passion and ignorance, and my declaration of war against the maya is certainly a great battle. Maya saw me very successful within one year, so that I got so many sincere young followers like yourself and others, so it was a great defeat to the activities of maya: western country youngsters giving up illicit sex, intoxication, meat-eating and gambling is certainly a great reverse in the activities of maya. Therefore she took advantage of my old age weakness and gave me a death dash. But Krishna saved me; therefore we should thank more Krishna than eulogize maya. So far as my present health is concerned I think I am improving; at least I am taking lunch better than in N.Y. So, as soon as I am a little fit to return to the field of battle I shall again be in your midst.

* * *

Śrīla Prabhupāda envisioned an American House, a place where resident disciples could study Sanskrit and Vaiṣṇava literature in Vṛndāvana. When he had suffered his stroke he had said that Rāya Rāma should finish the translation of the *Bhāgavatam*s. He had also requested Acyutānanda, Gaurasundara, and others to learn Sanskrit, Bengali, and Hindi so that if he did not recover they could carry on his work. And he hoped that some of his leading men, like Brahmānanda, Hayagrīva, and Rāya Rāma, would come to India, obtain property, and establish his American House. "Even if I am well," he wrote on September 9, "it is not possible for me to look after the affairs of the American House."

Prabhupāda decided to ask one of his Godbrothers, Swami B. H. Bon Maharaja, to accommodate some students from America at his Institute of Oriental Philosophy. Swami Bon Maharaja's institute was a provincial college of about three hundred students, located in Vṛndāvana and affiliated with Agra University. It was what is known in India as a "degree college," an institution geared toward improving the economic condition of its graduates by making them eligible for better jobs.

When Śrīla Prabhupāda and Kīrtanānanda visited Swami Bon Maharaja at the Institute of Oriental Philosophy, Swami Bon received them in a clean parlor furnished with chairs, couches, and a radio. Swami Bon, wearing leather slippers, shorts visible through his thin *dhotī*, and an ironed shirt with brass studs, appeared suave and sophisticated—an educated man with straight, neatly parted graying hair. Although a resident of Vṛndāvana, in the 1930s he had spent several years in England, where he had been received by members of the royal family and had lectured at a number of colleges. But he had aroused no lasting interest. When Prabhupāda had been struggling alone in New York in 1965, he had written to Swami Bon asking for help. But Swami Bon had not responded. Even now, as Prabhupāda told him of the work in America, Bon Maharaja didn't have much to say. But he *was* interested in the prospect of Americans' coming to live and study at his institute; foreign students would enhance the prestige of the institute in the eyes of the government. He said the students could possibly be accommodated free of charge.

Encouraged by the meeting with Bon Maharaja, Prabhupāda wrote several letters to his disciples, inviting them to come and study Sanskrit.

> If you want to learn Sanskrit, there is ample opportunity in this institute. We had some preliminary talks, and it is hopeful that Swami Bon can give us some land for our own building; but even so, arrangements can

> be made with the existing facilities so that there would be no difficulty for the students who come here to study Sanskrit and the Goswami literature. . . . It is a good opportunity for our students, and I shall be very glad to learn how many of you desire to come.

* * *

On Janmāṣṭamī day, August 28, Śrīla Prabhupāda awarded the order of *sannyāsa* to Kīrtanānanda in a ceremony in the Rādhā-Dāmodara temple. Kīrtanānanda thus became Śrīla Prabhupāda's first disciple to become a *sannyāsī:* Kīrtanānanda Swami. During the initiation hundreds of visitors were present observing the birthday of Lord Kṛṣṇa, and many of them came by to congratulate the young *sannyāsī.* Someone said he looked like Lord Caitanya. Śrīla Prabhupāda wrote,

> He will be going back to the States very soon to begin preaching work with greater vigor and success. In the meantime, I shall try to utilize this "white sannyasi" for recruiting some members in India.

Early in September, Acyutānanda arrived in Delhi. A Hindu lady gave him five rupees, and he took the train to Mathurā, where he got directions to the Keśavajī Gaudiya Math. Nārāyaṇa Mahārāja, a friend of Prabhupāda's, took Acyutānanda under his care and, after showing him the hall where Prabhupāda had taken *sannyāsa* in 1959, put him on a bus to Vṛndāvana with an old gentleman for an escort. Accompanied by this escort, Acyutānanda arrived by ricksha before the Rādhā-Dāmodara temple.

Acyutānanda walked into Prabhupāda's room and fell prostrate at his feet. "Oh," Prabhupāda said, "you are here." When Acyutānanda looked up he saw that Swamiji had a five-day beard and was wearing only one piece of cloth, wrapped around his waist from behind, crossed over his chest, and tied behind his neck. Prabhupāda smiled, apparently in good health.

Kīrtanānanda Swami also greeted Acyutānanda and showed him his new *daṇḍa.*

For Acyutānanda, the most wonderful thing about Swamiji in Vṛndāvana was the simplicity of his life. Although in New York Swamiji had worn simple robes, he had always been regal, a *guru.* But here he lived very simply and humbly. Once when he sat down on the veranda outside his room to wash his hands, his body instantly became covered with flies. Kīrtanānanda and Acyutānanda were always being bothered by the flies—this was the rainy season—but Prabhupāda scarcely noticed them and sat quietly washing his hands.

Kīrtanānanda and Acyutānanda agreed that Swamiji wasn't just another Vṛndāvana *bābājī.* There was no one else like him. Certainly Gaurachand Goswami, proprietor of the Rādhā-Dāmodara temple, wasn't like Swamiji. He wore thick glasses and could barely see, and when Kīrtanānanda and Acyutānanda went before the Deities in the temple, Gaurachand Goswami asked them loudly, "So how do you like 'em? Which one do you like the best?"

"I like them all," said Acyutānanda.

"I like that big one on the end there," said the priest, pointing in an offhand manner at the Deity of Kṛṣṇa. "It looks a bit like General Choudry." The Swami's boys exchanged looks—what kind of guys are these?—and went back to Swamiji for an explanation.

"They are caste *gosvāmīs,*" Prabhupāda explained. The original *gosvāmīs,* such as Jiva Gosvāmī, who established the Rādhā-Dāmodara temple, had engaged householders to worship the Deities. And these caste *gosvāmīs* were descendants of those first householder *pūjārīs.* Prabhupāda explained that the caste *gosvāmīs* were the proprietors of the temples and that they maintained the temples and ran the Deity worship as a business to support their families. Several years ago each of the Deities now on the altar had had His own temple, land, income, and priests. But for economy the *gosvāmīs* had sold the property, reduced the opulence of the worship, and amalgamated the Deities.

There were many other interesting characters: the old widow Sarajini, with bald head and *śikhā* and calloused bare feet, who slept in a room by the gate of the temple and swept Swamiji's kitchen and washed his clothes; Pancudas Goswami, the temple proprietor's son, who always chewed *pān* and went around sleepy-eyed in a silk *dhotī* with a red-embroidered border; the dark old *bābājī* who came at night, who was constantly laughing, and who made sandalwood paste for Swamiji; the local herbal doctor, Vanamali Kaviraja, who presided, brightly smiling, from behind a desk in a tiny chamber filled from ceiling to floor with little bottles; and a famous *paṇḍita* who visited Swamiji and wore a gold-linked *tulasī* necklace and diamond rings. All of these persons were devotees, residents of holy Vṛndāvana. But no one was like Swamiji.

Kīrtanānanda Swami even became disappointed that no one else in Vṛndāvana was like Swamiji. In the land where everyone was an Indian and everyone was a devotee, Swamiji was still unique. No one else was so simple, so grave, so able to penetrate through falsity, so attractive to the heart, or so absolutely attached to Kṛṣṇa. No one else could lead them.

If Kīrtanānanda Swami and Acyutānanda were doubtful about some of the residents of Vṛndāvana, some of the residents of Vṛndāvana were also doubtful of them. When a European hippie couple wandered into Vṛndāvana one day, Acyutānanda accompanied them to some of the temples. But at the Raṅganātha temple they were refused entry. Acyutānanda told Prabhupāda, who replied, "That's because you went with those fools." When Prabhupāda walked in the streets, people regularly nodded to him with respect, saying, "Daṇḍavat, Mahārāja." But they were cautious about accepting his American followers as Vaiṣṇavas.

* * *

Śrīla Prabhupāda, accompanied by his two disciples, again visited Swami Bon. Riding to Swami Bon's institute by ricksha, Prabhupāda told Acyutānanda that Swami Bon had started the institute as an academy of Vaiṣṇava studies but had affiliated with Agra University because the institute had not been bringing in any money. Now Swami Bon had money, but the institute had become an ordinary school, devoid of spiritual value.

As Śrīla Prabhupāda and his disciples sat in Swami Bon's parlor, Bon Maharaja made it clear that although he would not donate land for Prabhupāda's American House, Prabhupāda's students could come and study at his institution. Acyutānanda, he suggested, could be the first one.

Swami Bon then took them to the main building to visit a class in session. Instead of seeing *paṇḍitas* and *brahmacārīs* studying Sanskrit, as they had expected, Prabhupāda's disciples saw boys with thin mustaches and giggling girls. Prabhupāda lectured and then asked Kīrtanānanda to play the Hare Kṛṣṇa record. After a few minutes, Bon Maharaja told Kīrtanānanda to stop the record, but Kīrtanānanda, seeing Swamiji enjoying the record, let it play.

Acyutānanda: *We walked around the place, and I thought, "This is just a mundane school. I don't want to go here. If I could learn Sanskrit and live at the Rādhā-Dāmodara temple, then I could have a nice time in India."*

They continued their tour of the facilities, and after seeing the dormitory Prabhupāda doubted whether his American disciples could endure the austerity and the academic studies. It seemed that one of the two boys was always sick. First Kīrtanānanda Swami had gotten dysentery, then something had been wrong with Acyutānanda's stomach, then they had both been exhausted from the heat. "On the whole," Śrīla Prabhupāda wrote to Rūpānuga in New York, "the American boys who come here become first depressed, so I do not know how far our American House in Vrindaban will be successful." His boys were not particularly studious or austere. Besides, both Kīrtanānanda Swami and Acyutānanda had developed a definite dislike for the rector of the Institute of Oriental Philosophy. And Śrīla Prabhupāda obviously had reservations about the place. "You can go and study there," Prabhupāda told them, "but don't live there. Live at the Rādhā-Dāmodara temple and go. You can get a bicycle and go there."

Gradually, the idea of immediately acquiring an American House in Vṛndāvana began to dwindle. Prabhupāda needed his own place for his disciples, and that would take time.

* * *

With regular medication, massages, rest, and the heat of Vṛndāvana, Prabhupāda felt himself recovering. By mid-September he declared himself ninety percent fit to return to the United States. He predicted that he would be back there by the end of October.

B. R. Śrīdhara Mahārāja, Prabhupāda's Godbrother, whose *āśrama* was in Navadvīpa, West Bengal, wrote to invite Prabhupāda to spend the month of Kārttika with him at the *āśrama* and join him for his Vyāsa-pūjā celebration. Śrīla Prabhupāda liked the idea of going to the holy land of Navadvīpa, where Lord Caitanya had spent His early years, and seeing his Godbrother. He also wanted to visit Delhi again and inquire about printing his books.

"Swamiji," Acyutānanda asked, "when you go to Navadvīpa am I supposed to stay here in Vṛndāvana and study?"

"Don't you want to see the birthplace of Lord Caitanya?" Prabhupāda asked.

Acyutānanda did, and Prabhupāda, Kīrtanānanda Swami, and Acyutānanda left Vṛndāvana together and returned to the Chippiwada temple in Delhi.

For Prabhupāda's two disciples, life at the Chippiwada temple was hard. Delhi was blazing hot and lacked the charm of Vṛndāvana. There was water for only two hours a day, early in the morning, and that only a slow trickle. They would fill two clay jugs for Prabhupāda's room and several buckets for his bath and their own, and then there would be no more water for the rest of the day. A mongoose ran freely through the building.

"Do they eat snakes?" Acyutānanda asked.

"They eat snakes," said Śrīla Prabhupāda, "they eat garbage, they eat anything." Prabhupāda, who regarded the heat, the lack of water, and even the mongoose as normal, was undisturbed. Several young Indian musicians in the adjacent room regularly played cinema music on their electric organ, bongo drums, and electric guitars, rehearsing for a dance. Prabhupāda tolerated it.

Sri Krishna Pandit praised Prabhupāda's work in America and his English translation of *Śrīmad-Bhāgavatam.* As manager of the Chippiwada Rādhā-Kṛṣṇa temple and secretary of an active Hinduism society, Sri Krishna Pandit was interested in spreading Hindu *dharma*, and therefore he wanted Prabhupāda to speak at the nearby Gaurī-Śaṅkara temple, one of Delhi's most popular Hindu temples. Prabhupāda agreed to go and take with him Acyutānanda (Kīrtanānanda Swami had already left for the West on August 22).

The Gaurī-Śaṅkara temple was on Chandi Chowk. After a short walk through some of the busiest, most congested streets of Old Delhi, Prabhupāda and Acyutānanda removed their shoes at the door and entered the temple. The main deity was Lord Śiva, but there were many others: Rāma, Durgā, Kālī, Rādhā-Kṛṣṇa, Hanumān. The crowds stood before the elaborate altars, viewing and petitioning the various deities.

Acyutānanda had learned about demigod worship from Prabhupāda at 26 Second Avenue. According to *Bhagavad-gītā*, demigods fulfill only material desires and are therefore worshiped by the less intelligent. A Vaiṣṇava, Prabhupāda had said, respects the demigods—in fact, he respects all living beings, even the ant—but he worships only the Supreme Personality of Godhead, Kṛṣṇa, or Viṣṇu.

Acyutānanda had already seen firsthand that impersonalists were misleading Indians to disavow the personal form of God and accept all methods of worship as equal. Most Indians had no clear understanding of *Bhagavad-gītā* or Kṛṣṇa. Acyutānanda kept this in mind as Prabhupāda led him in bowing down before a few of the demigods' altars. Then Prabhupāda brought him before the Deity of Rādhā-Kṛṣṇa. "Just see," Prabhupāda said, "Kṛṣṇa is just playing His flute. As for the demigods, someone is holding bows and arrows, someone is holding clubs, someone is holding weapons, but Rādhā and Kṛṣṇa are just dancing, and Kṛṣṇa is holding a flute. So He is the Supreme Lord."

In one large room a heavyset man with a great, white beard and wearing flower garlands sat on several pillows. Many people stood staring at him. He reminded Acyutānanda of Santa Claus. "Swamiji, who is that?" Acyutānanda asked.

"Some *yogī*," Prabhupāda replied indifferently.

The main lecture hall had a large painting of Lord Śiva on the wall and was crowded with people—women in colored *sārīs* and many of the men in bright turbans. Amid such a welter of rituals and worshipers, Acyutānanda felt protected by Swamiji. They sat on the dais, and Sri Krishna Pandit introduced his friend Bhaktivedanta Swami to the crowd. Śrīla Prabhupāda spoke in Hindi for about an hour.

Walking back to Chippiwada, Acyutānanda wondered why Swamiji had gone to speak at a place with such hodgepodge worship. But without his asking, it occurred to him that Swamiji was willing to speak about

Kṛṣṇa *anywhere* to *anyone*. Hadn't he come to New York City? And what could be a more hodgepodge place than New York's Lower East Side?

Sitting on the veranda outside his room, Prabhupāda could see the huge domes of the Jama Mosque in the early evening sky. One evening, as Prabhupāda sat softly chanting *japa* and as Acyutānanda, who had not yet memorized the Gāyatrī *mantra*, sat nearby reading it to himself, a Hindu gentleman came and conversed with Prabhupāda. Acyutānanda soon finished the Gāyatrī *mantra* and sat listening to his spiritual master talk in Hindi to the unknown gentleman. Acyutānanda could catch only a word here or there—some mention of Āyur Vedic medicine, addresses, Indian names, cities. They talked for hours, and Acyutānanda wondered who this man was who could speak so long with Swamiji. When the man left, Acyutānanda asked, "Swamiji, was he your Godbrother?"

Prabhupāda said, "No."

"Is he a *swami*?"

Prabhupāda said, "No."

"Is he one of your relatives?"

"No."

"Well, who was he?"

"He's my friend!" Prabhupāda answered emphatically.

Sometimes Prabhupāda's visitors would bring donations of cloth or fruits or even complete cooked meals in metal *tiffins*. One visitor—a middle-aged woman who had heard Prabhupāda speak at the Gaurī-Śaṅkara temple—came to Prabhupāda's office in Chippiwada requesting initiation. Prabhupāda spoke with her, agreed, and had Acyutānanda prepare a small fire sacrifice. At her initiation he gave her the name Mukunda dāsī. She came daily to clean Prabhupāda's room, and when she saw that his wooden-peg sandals were broken, she bought him new ones.

Chandrashekhar had known Prabhupāda for several years and was supposed to have been his secretary. But he was a drunkard. Prabhupāda suspected him of having stolen from his mailbox more than two thousand rupees during the past two years. Prabhupāda's Chippiwada address was listed in his magazines and books, and people had been sending money for books and *Back to Godhead* subscriptions. Even in the past two months, Prabhupāda's disciples had written that they were enclosing money in their letters, but Prabhupāda never found any. One day he caught sight of Chandrashekhar in the building and asked him, "Where is my mailbox key?"

"I believe you have it," Chandrashekhar replied. "Or maybe Sri Krishna Pandit has it." Chandrashekhar was drunk.

"Swamiji," Acyutānanda said angrily, "maybe we should make a police case."

Prabhupāda shook his head, "No."

"Well," Acyutānanda said, "if he's not punished by the law, then in his next birth Kṛṣṇa will punish him."

"That's true," Prabhupāda agreed. Chandrashekhar looked fearfully from Prabhupāda to his American disciple.

"Then there's only one thing to do," Acyutānanda said. "Shall I call the police?"

"No," said Prabhupāda, "I forgive him." Yet only a few days later Prabhupāda's record player disappeared, and Prabhupāda suspected the drunkard, Chandrashekhar.

Prabhupāda brought Acyutānanda with him to his bank, the Bank of Baroda, to exchange some American currency. As they were about to enter the door, the guard refused them entry, thinking they were *sādhus* come to beg. Prabhupāda was angry. He spoke loudly in Hindi to the guard, an old man with a shotgun, a big strap of bullets, and a shabby semi-official uniform. "I have an account here," Prabhupāda protested. Finally the guard allowed them to enter.

Prabhupāda went straight to the manager and complained. "Do you think," Prabhupāda said, "because I am a *sādhu* I am to be regarded as a beggar?" Prabhupāda told the man of his organization in America and his account in the Bank of Baroda. The manager apologized and reprimanded the guard.

One day Prabhupāda sent Acyutānanda to a certain restaurant. "If you want to see varieties of Indian food," Prabhupāda said, "tell the man you want ten rupees of sweets and ten rupees of salty preparations—that is called *miṣṭi* and *nimaka*. And just see the varieties." Acyutānanda was sick and couldn't imagine eating a lot of sweets. But he stopped by the restaurant and looked. When he returned to the temple at Chippiwada he told Prabhupāda that he had seen the food, although he couldn't eat it. "Yes, but just see the varieties," Prabhupāda concluded. And he explained how Kṛṣṇa consciousness was personal and full of varieties, not dry.

Another American disciple joined Prabhupāda—Rāmānuja, from Haight-Ashbury. He had been initiated just before Swamiji had left San Francisco, and he sported a full black beard. Prabhupāda didn't like the beard. Cautiously and indirectly he mentioned it; but Rāmānuja's beard stayed. Rāmānuja carried a book about Tibetan Buddhism, and he didn't seem fixed in Kṛṣṇa consciousness philosophy. But here he was, one of the looser, sentimental San Francisco devotees, ready for Indian adventures with Swamiji.

* * *

Śrīla Prabhupāda visited the wealthy Delhi industrialist Mr. Seth Dalmia to discuss plans for printing some of his books in India. Mr. Dalmia received him well but gave only vague promises of help. Prabhupāda also met with Hitsaran Sharma, Mr. Dalmia's secretary, who worked closely with Hanuman Prasad Poddar of the popular religious publishing company Gita Press. Śrīla Prabhupāda was already acquainted with all three gentlemen, since they had all donated toward his first volume of *Śrīmad-Bhāgavatam*. Prabhupāda wanted Gita Press to publish his *Gītopaniṣad* and *Śrīmad-Bhāgavatam*. Hitsaran Sharma showed him an illustrated *Gītā* in Hindi poetry that he had recently published. "But my *Gītā*, my *Bhāgavatam*," said Śrīla Prabhupāda, appearing disgusted, "is the description of God. It is the description of Kṛṣṇa." Mr. Sharma said he couldn't see how Gita Press could print Prabhupāda's voluminous writings. Nevertheless, Prabhupāda still considered privately printing *Gītopaniṣad*, with Mr. Sharma as his agent.

On October 11, Prabhupāda wrote to Brahmānanda,

We must have our books printed; we have wasted much time in the matter of editing and finding out a suitable publisher. When I was alone there was three volumes published but during the last two years I could not publish a single volume more. It is a great defeat. If I have one or two sincere souls like you and if we can make more publications, then our mission will be a great success. I am prepared to sit down underneath a tree with one sincere soul and in such activity I shall be freed of all diseases.

* * *

Devotees from America were regularly writing Swamiji, anxious to see him again in good health. But he didn't want to leave India, he explained, until he personally saw that the printing of his *Gītopaniṣad* was under way. Printing *Gītopaniṣad* and obtaining approval for permanent residency in the U.S. were the two short-term goals he wished to achieve before returning. But he thought often of his return to America.

As you are all feeling my separation, similarly I'm also anxious to return as soon as possible. I think I'm fit to go back to your country at present and as scheduled previously I'm sure by the end of October. I must be fit to return, but before this there are many things to be done. I'm not yet assured of the permanent visa. The best thing will be that from each center an invitation should be sent that my presence is urgently required.... Presently I'm very much anxious to begin printing here if Macmillan company does not take up the work. Please, therefore, let me know yes or no from Macmillan. If he is not serious, then immediately send the manuscripts finished or not to the following address: Pundit Hitsaran Sharma c/o Dalmia Enterprises, Scindia House, New Delhi. After dispatching let me know and I shall do the needful.

Indian friends who visited Prabhupāda's room listened eagerly as he told them about America—the millions of cars and the superhighways and thousands of young people rejecting their fathers' wealth. But Prabhupāda's visitors weren't fully able to understand his visit to

America. Not that they were too simple to understand and not just that they had never traveled in the West. Prabhupāda's experience in America consisted of intimate spiritual relationships with his disciples. How could an outsider understand the dynamics of his temples and his disciples in the West? How could anyone except Prabhupāda and his disciples understand these things?

> My mind is always with you. Practically your country is my home now. India is a foreign country for me. The reason is that my spiritual family is there and my material relationships are in India; therefore factually where my spiritual family exists, there is my home.

Śrīla Prabhupāda's vision of a worldwide society of devotees preaching in temples and publishing books—a vision he had had even before he had gone to America—was now becoming manifest. But it was dependent on him. In his absence his disciples were sustained only by carrying out his orders and receiving his letters. When Dayānanda and Nandarāṇī had gone from the San Francisco temple to start a temple in Los Angeles, it had been Swamiji's instructions that had sustained and guided them: "Wherever there is a new branch of our society for Krishna Consciousness I become very very happy. And my blessings in heart and soul are with you." On receipt of Swamiji's letter, they knew they had done the right thing. No matter that husband and wife sometimes quarreled and that there wasn't enough money—the main thing was that Swamiji was pleased.

From Boston, Satsvarūpa wrote that he and the other devotees there were moving from an apartment to a rented storefront near Boston University. The first time Satsvarūpa entered the new storefront, he found on the floor an aerogram from Swamiji, dated October 6 from Delhi.

> I can understand that you have secured a very nice place in Boston and there is a very good possibility of pushing our movement amongst the student community there. Our movement is certainly very much appealing to the younger section of your country and if we are successful in the matter of attracting the student community in your country certainly this movement will scatter all over the world and fullfill the foretelling of Lord Caitanya that in every village and every town of the world the Lord will be famous for His glorious sankirtana movement. Please try for this with your heart and soul and your life will be a successful mission.

The letter was as good as Swamiji coming personally to open the storefront and begin the preaching. It gave Satsvarūpa full direction and inspiration. And it was personal. In that same letter, Prabhupāda had written,

> I am always aspiring after returning to your care and overload you with typewriting tasks. . . . I hope we shall very soon meet again and help each other in the matter of discharging Krishna conscious engagements. I am now 90% alright and I think I can return safely. This typewriting work is done by me. For two days I am alone and doing everything myself as experiment. This proves that I am now well. Please offer my blessings to all the boys and girls there.

In New Mexico, Subala was trying to arrange public speaking engagements for Prabhupāda's return, and Prabhupāda was encouraging him: "If you think I can be on television by the first week in December, then you can arrange for it because I must be in your country by the middle of November."

Śrīla Prabhupāda wrote to Janārdana in Montreal answering his philosophical doubts and encouraging him to be patient with his spiritually reluctant wife. And to Rāya Rāma, who was editing *Back to Godhead* magazine in New York, he gave another kind of thoughtful assurance.

> I am very happy that since it [BTG] is entrusted to you the things are improving. This means that Krishna is giving you more & more facilities. Krishna is such a nice boss that he gives more facilities & improvement to the sincere servant.

On October 9, the day Prabhupāda started for Calcutta, he left behind a different kind of letter for Sri Krishna Pandit. Prabhupāda had been negotiating with Sri Krishna Pandit to purchase the Chippiwada temple for ISKCON or at least to rent the single room through a formal contract. Prabhupāda wanted the room as a Delhi headquarters for printing his books. On the day of his departure, however, Sri Krishna Pandit was unavailable, and Prabhupāda left him a short handwritten note.

> If you are not settling anything with the room, then I may not come back to Delhi any more. I will go to U.S.A. directly from Calcutta via the Pacific route for which Sri Dalmia Seth has already promised for the ticket.

CHAPTER SEVEN

India Revisited: Part 2

Prabhupāda's train, the Kalka Mail, pulled into Delhi Station. Prabhupāda and his two disciples had tickets with reserved seat numbers—but no car number. So while Prabhupāda waited with the baggage, Acyutānanda and Rāmānuja ran from one end of the train to the other looking for their car.

After they had found their seats and boarded, Acyutānanda untied Prabhupāda's bedding and spread it open on the upper tier. Prabhupāda climbed the little ladder, sat comfortably on his cotton-stuffed quilt, and opened his Sanskrit *Śrīmad-Bhāgavatam,* while Acyutānanda and Rāmānuja took their seats. It would take around twenty-four hours to reach Calcutta.

Near the end of the journey, a group of educated Bengali gentlemen struck up a philosophical conversation with the Swami. "We do not worship any form," said one, speaking fluent English in a loud, deep voice. "We have a marble *oṁkāra* that we worship, and we sit and pray to that."

"That is also a form," said Prabhupāda. He was reluctant to attack their philosophical position directly.

"We practice *karma-yoga,*" the gentleman went on, not heeding Prabhupāda's previous point. "Because in *karma-yoga* you can stay within your position."

"But *karma-yoga* is not full surrender of the soul," said Prabhupāda. "One must come to the stage of *bhakti.*"

"Oh, no," the man protested, "emotionalism is very harmful. *Karma-yoga*—"

Śrīla Prabhupāda exploded: "*Karma-yoga* is for the fools!" Silence.

Another man, not with the Bengalis but seated beside them, spoke up. "Obviously Swamiji is a learned scholar," he said. "You shouldn't argue like that." The Bengali that Prabhupāda had shouted at got up and moved to another seat. Later, he came back.

"Are you insulted?" Prabhupāda asked him.

"No, no, no," he replied. "But I have never heard anyone say that about the teachings of the *Gītā*."

The Bengalis then talked with Acyutānanda, lighting their cigarettes and smoking freely before him, although they had not dared to do so before Prabhupāda (it wasn't proper to smoke in front of a *sādhu*). Bengalis, Acyutānanda told them, citing one of Prabhupāda's examples, were very sorry that East Pakistan had been cut off from the rest of Bengal. But Kṛṣṇa consciousness could elevate people to international, universal consciousness. Then there wouldn't be any such division. The Bengalis appreciated Acyutānanda's remark, though they continued to blow smoke in his face as the train rattled over the last miles to Calcutta.

Prabhupāda was greeted at Calcutta's Howrah Station by relatives, mostly from his sister's family, and by devotees of the Goswami Math. About fifty people were on hand. They offered Prabhupāda flower garlands and sandalwood paste and then escorted him and his disciples into a car. Acyutānanda and Rāmānuja noticed that although Swamiji's sister was shorter and more rotund than Prabhupāda, her facial features were strikingly similar. Her name was Bhavatarini, but Prabhupāda told them to call her Pisīmā, "aunt."

As Prabhupāda rode through the streets he saw many images of goddess Kālī, ten-armed, riding a lion. Calcutta was observing the biggest religious celebration in Bengal, Kālī-pūjā, a month of festivities in honor of the goddess Kālī. Throughout the city, brass bands and radio music blared, and there were decorative lights, stages, and tents.

When Prabhupāda arrived at Pisīmā's house in south Calcutta, his relatives seated him and performed an *ārati* ceremony in his honor, reverently offering him the traditional items: incense, a flaming lamp, flowers. They also bathed his feet. He sat smiling within the crowded room of relatives, who were proud of his having journeyed to America on behalf of Lord Kṛṣṇa.

As Prabhupāda's family members sang Hare Kṛṣṇa *kīrtana*, from outside the room the ladies of the house began singing a high, shrill whooping sound. Acyutānanda and Rāmānuja were startled.

Pisīmā had prepared a large feast, much of it cooked in mustard seed oil, for the homecoming celebration. And Prabhupāda satisfied her by honoring the *prasādam*, even though he wasn't feeling well and was tired from the train ride.

Soon after the festivities Prabhupāda and his disciples retired. Again his health wavered—this time because of his sister's heavy cooking—and he felt a strain on his heart. He sent for an Āyur Vedic doctor, who taught Acyutānanda how to do a very gentle massage to help circulation and restricted Prabhupāda from sweets.

As Prabhupāda recovered he began regularly lecturing in his room during the evening. Although he spoke in English (for his disciples), the room would soon fill to capacity with relatives and friends. There were generally disturbances from outside due to the noises of Kālī-pūjā. Nearby Pisīmā's house was a large tent, a center for evening street parties, which included a sweets counter, fireworks, and an excessively loud public address system that incongruously blared Julie Andrews singing songs from *The Sound of Music.*

One evening as Prabhupāda spoke—"My only qualification is that I have unflinching faith in my spiritual master"—a large firecracker exploded right outside the door. The audience smiled tolerantly. "Yes," Prabhupāda said, taking the explosion as confirmation of his words, "it is glorious."

One night Prabhupāda explained that according to *Bhagavad-gītā* demigod worshipers are less intelligent. People worship Kālī for material rewards, he said, but since all material things are temporary, such worship is inferior to the worship of Kṛṣṇa. Kālī is not able to grant the worshiper liberation from birth and death.

"Which is better?" Acyutānanda asked, "the worship of the Christians and Jews, which is mostly impersonal, or the worship of the non-Absolute by the worshipers of Kālī?"

"Worship of Kālī is better," Prabhupāda said, "because the worshipers are in the Vedic system. They are more likely to bow down to Rādhā-Kṛṣṇa or chant Hare Kṛṣṇa than a Christian or Jew. There is a chance that they will become Kṛṣṇa devotees in the future, if they lose their material attachments."

Prabhupāda regularly invited his Godbrothers and their disciples to join him in America. Sometimes he seemed to do it just to get them at least to think more of preaching. Bhaktisiddhānta Sarasvatī had once chided that the Gaudiya Math *āśrama* was no more than a "joint mess," the members going out each day and collecting enough alms so that they could eat together, but with no dynamic vision for preaching. So Prabhupāda's frequent invitations—"You should go to America. Come back with me"—would stir them, even if they couldn't actually come. On visiting the *āśrama* of Bhaktisāraṅga Goswami, Prabhupāda saw that the audience consisted almost entirely of old widows. But he spoke as usual.

One day, Prabhupāda's Godbrother Haridāsa Swami came by. He was heavyset and loud, and he spoke very rapidly: "Very happy to see you coming here from America. This is wonderful—Kṛṣṇa is the summum bonum, the cause of all causes—I want you to come to my temple. . . ."

When Haridāsa Mahārāja went into a separate room, Prabhupāda turned to Acyutānanda: "He wants us to go to his temple. But to go there I will have to go onto a ricksha and then onto a tramcar and then onto a train and then another ricksha." Aware of Prabhupāda's weak condition, Acyutānanda began shaking his head negatively.

When Haridāsa Mahārāja returned, Acyutānanda said that Swamiji couldn't come to his *maṭha*. "Who are you?" Haridāsa Mahārāja said angrily. "You are just a *brahmacārī*! You should risk your life!"

Acyutānanda replied, "I will risk *my* life, but I can't risk my spiritual master's life."

Haridāsa Mahārāja left insulted. "Don't worry," Prabhupāda said. "He is just very talkative."

Prabhupāda paid a visit to B. P. Keśava Mahārāja, the Godbrother who had awarded him the *sannyāsa* order in 1959. Prabhupāda sat on the floor and spoke in Bengali to his Godbrother, who was very old and apparently on his deathbed. Prabhupāda had Acyutānanda sing for Keśava Mahārāja. Keśava Mahārāja requested Prabhupāda to visit his *āśrama*, Devānanda Math, in Navadvīpa.

* * *

Śrīla Prabhupāda had wanted to return to the U.S. as a permanent resident, but his students in America hadn't been able to get the necessary clearance from the U.S. immigration department. The devotees in Boston had gotten in touch with a few Harvard Indology professors but had obtained no signed statements about Prabhupāda's importance. All the ISKCON centers had written formal letters inviting A. C. Bhaktivedanta Swami and had presented copies to the U.S. immigration office. But unless the devotees could produce something more impressive, like a government recommendation or a university's offer for him to join their faculty, Prabhupāda could not become a U.S. resident.

On October 13 Prabhupāda wrote to his disciples in Montreal:

> I am very anxious to go to Montreal. Therefore you must try your best to get my immigration visa on the basis of my being an authorized Vaishnava minister, based on Srimad Bhagawatam and Srimad Bhagavad Gita.

Rather than wait indefinitely for permanent residency, Prabhupāda decided to apply for a visitor's visa. He went with Acyutānanda to the U.S. Consulate on Harrington Road. There, in the middle of Calcutta, they entered a small piece of America, with everything shiny, new, and efficient: air conditioners, stainless steel water coolers, electric security doors, U.S. Marines, and American flags. Sitting before the secretary of the Consulate, Prabhupāda looked small and humble. "I want a visa to see my students in America," he said softly.

"Do you have any letters?" the secretary asked. Acyutānanda handed over the letters from the temples. The secretary reviewed them and quickly gave Prabhupāda a four-month visa. While leaving the building

Prabhupāda remarked, "I will just get anything, and then it can be extended."

On October 19, Prabhupāda wrote Hayagrīva regarding his imminent return.

> I am already preparing for returning to U.S.A. & I have obtained a visitor's visa the day before yesterday. Most probably I shall take the first chance to return to U.S.A. upon my return from Navadwipa.

And on October 22 he wrote Umāpati.

> You will be glad to know that I have already secured a visitor's visa to your country and have asked my travel agent to book my seat on the earliest possible date. I think I shall be in your midst by the middle of Nov.

* * *

On October 24 Prabhupāda traveled with Acyutānanda and Rāmānuja to Navadvīpa. Although the local train took four hours, the lush Bengal countryside gradually revealed its heavenly beauty, and Prabhupāda's health seemed to improve just from the pleasant journey. By the time they arrived at Navadvīpa, Acyutānanda and Rāmānuja were also feeling relief from the rigors of Calcutta; for the first time in weeks they could open their eyes without blinking through drops of perspiration.

A large *kīrtana* party of *brahmacārīs*, mostly members of Keśava Mahārāja's Devānanda Gaudiya Math, met Śrīla Prabhupāda at the Navadvīpa train station. The *brahmacārīs* were meticulously neat, with their robes all dyed the same shade of saffron, their Vaiṣṇava *tilaka* markings bold and distinct, their heads smoothly shaved, their *śikhās* precise. They offered Prabhupāda and his party aromatic garlands made from flowers resembling lotuses and gathered around Śrīla Prabhupāda with worshipful enthusiasm. Also present were a few of Śrīdhara Mahārāja's disciples, waiting with rickshas to take Prabhupāda and his disciples to their *guru's āśrama.* Although between the two groups there was an unspoken competition for Prabhupāda's presence, he had previously agreed to go to Śrīdhara Mahārāja's place. He promised the members of Devānanda Math that he would visit them next.

Soon after leaving the station the rickshas turned onto a road lined with lush tropical vegetation: banana trees, tall bamboos, exotic blossoming flowers. Prabhupāda saw simple villagers working near their straw-and-mud huts and, in the distance, the spire of Śrīdhara Mahārāja's temple.

A *kīrtana* party greeted Prabhupāda at the outer gates of Śrīdhara Mahārāja's *āśrama*, chanting Hare Kṛṣṇa and playing *karatālas* and clay *mṛdaṅgas*. Prabhupāda entered the temple, offered obeisances before the Deities of Rādhā and Kṛṣṇa, and then went to see his Godbrother.

Śrīdhara Mahārāja was very old, his sight failing, his joints stiff with arthritis. He stayed mostly in his room or sometimes on his veranda and moved only with slow, rickety motions. He was an austere and kindly Vaiṣṇava and smiled heartily on seeing Prabhupāda and his disciples. In fluent English he began praising Prabhupāda's preaching in America, repeatedly using Prabhupāda's phrase "Kṛṣṇa consciousness." Swamiji's work, he said, was the fulfillment of Lord Caitanya's prophecy that Kṛṣṇa consciousness would one day spread all over the world. He laughed and smiled and praised the Kṛṣṇa consciousness movement with no trace of jealousy.

"So you appreciate this phrase, 'Kṛṣṇa consciousness.'" Prabhupāda smiled.

"Yes," Śrīdhara Mahārāja replied, "and the disciples of Swami Mahārāja also." And he turned towards Acyutānanda and Rāmānuja. "With very little effort your preaching will go far."

The boys were astonished. This was really something to write home about: sitting on the roof of a temple in this jungle paradise with old Śrīdhara Mahārāja appreciating Swamiji's work as the greatest work on behalf of Lord Caitanya, and Swamiji sitting relaxed, grinning, and making humble replies! It was the high point of the trip.

My dear Satsvarupa,

Please accept my blessings. I have already duly received the invitation from Harvard University. It is understood that they are scheduling me for 20 Nov. between 6 and 10 p.m. I can start immediately on the strength of my visitor's visa, but I am awaiting for Mukunda's reply for his trying for my permanent visa. Yesterday we have all come to Navadvipa. This place is

> another establishment of one of my Godbrothers. It is very nice and extensive place and my Godbrother, B. R. Sridhar Maharaj, has spared one entire nice house for our stay. He has also agreed to cooperate with our society. We shall observe his birthday ceremony tomorrow and the brahmacaris shall learn how to celebrate the spiritual master's birthday.

Vyāsa-pūjā day, the observance of B. R. Śrīdhara Mahārāja's birthday, was October 27. His disciples had erected a *paṇḍāl* on the temple road, and about a hundred people attended. Śrīdhara Mahārāja sat on his *vyāsāsana*, and Prabhupāda and other *sannyāsīs*, all wearing flower garlands, sat in chairs next to Śrīdhara Mahārāja. Prabhupāda spoke in Bengali. Some of Śrīdhara Mahārāja's disciples, inspired by Prabhupāda's preaching about the glories of spreading Kṛṣṇa consciousness in the West, delivered speeches in English as Vyāsa-pūjā homages to their spiritual master. Śrīdhara Mahārāja, also speaking in English, gave a very scientific lecture on Kṛṣṇa consciousness and the senses. Afterwards Prabhupāda told his disciples, "He has very high realizations, but he is keeping them to himself."

Every morning before dawn Śrīdhara Mahārāja sent out a party of *brahmacārīs* to perform *kīrtana* in the villages. On Prabhupāda's request, Acyutānanda and Rāmānuja joined them, leaving before sunrise and returning at dusk. Although Prabhupāda and Śrīdhara Mahārāja usually remained at the temple, one day they got into a ricksha and accompanied the chanting party through the streets of Navadvīpa.

The festival at the Devānanda Math was a big affair. In contrast to Bhaktisāraṅga Goswami's *āśrama* in Calcutta, where only widows had attended, B. P. Keśava Mahārāja's Devānanda Math had about two hundred *brahmacārīs* and twenty *sannyāsīs*. Some of the *brahmacārīs*, however, were not full-time but were attending school outside; so the *āśrama's* atmosphere was a little like that of a social club. But when the *kīrtana* and the circumambulation of the temple began, seven hundred people took part. The impeccably dressed *sannyāsīs*—whose every piece of saffron cloth, including their cloth-wrapped *daṇḍas*, was dyed exactly the same shade—danced back and forth before the Deities. A dozen *sannyāsīs* danced in a group, their *daṇḍas* moving together, dipping and rising, forward and back, to the delight of the *brahmacārīs*.

Prabhupāda sat on a dais with other dignitaries and spoke to the festival audience. Acyutānanda, on Prabhupāda's request, spoke a few words in Bengali, bringing laughs and applause. Śrīdhara Mahārāja spoke gravely in Bengali. A *sannyāsī* from the Devānanda Math, speaking for their absent leader, B. P. Keśava Mahārāja, proclaimed in empassioned tones that although Lord Caitanya Mahāprabhu's movement had been predicted to spread throughout the world, no one had known how it could be possible. Now, thanks to the work of Bhaktivedanta Swami, it was happening.

After a large feast in the evening, Prabhupāda's party returned to Śrīdhara Mahārāja's *āśrama*. Śrīdhara Mahārāja intimated to Prabhupāda that the Devānanda Math emphasized quantity whereas his own *āśrama* emphasized quality. Curious as to what this meant, Acyutānanda wanted to ask Prabhupāda. But the time didn't seem appropriate.

After nine days in Navadvīpa Prabhupāda was ready to return to Calcutta and prepare for his trip back to the United States. He and his two disciples took rickshas to Navadvīpa and caught a morning train to Calcutta.

On the train, Acyutānanda timidly put forward the question that had been on his mind: "Swamiji, what did you and Śrīdhara Mahārāja discuss?"

"Oh, many, many things," Prabhupāda replied. "But if I were to tell you now, you would faint." After a silence Prabhupāda added, "Still, I offered him to be president of our Society. I knew he would not accept. He is keeping things within him. Anyway, this is all beyond you. Do not have any ill feelings towards any of my Godbrothers. They are all great souls. There are just some differences on preaching and spreading. Even in your mind do not feel any ill will towards them. At the same time, do not mix very thickly with them."

Acyutānanda suggested, "Maybe if these two *sannyāsīs* had each other's qualities combined . . ."

"Ah, yes," Prabhupāda said, "now you have understood me."

* * *

Śrīla Prabhupāda's intention in coming to Calcutta was simply to prepare to leave for America. He had his visitor's visa already, but he thought that if he stayed in India a little longer, in San Francisco Mukunda might be able to secure permanent American residency for him. He went to his sister's house to spend his last days in Calcutta there, but after only a few days he felt that the Rādhā-Govinda Deity—the Deity he had worshiped in his childhood—was calling him.

When Prabhupāda had been no more than an infant, his servant used to take him and his cousin Subuddhi Mullik on a perambulator, wheel them into the temple courtyard, and take them before the altar of Rādhā-Govinda. And as soon as Prabhupāda could walk, his father would hold his hand and take him before the Deity every day. Sometimes Prabhupāda would go alone and stand for hours gazing upon Rādhā and Kṛṣṇa, who appeared very beautiful to him with Their slanted eyes and fine dress and ornaments. It had been for the pleasure of Rādhā-Govinda that as a child, beginning at the age of five, he had performed his miniature Ratha-yātrā festival.

Just two weeks ago, when Prabhupāda had been staying at his sister's house, his health had prevented him from going to north Calcutta to see the Deity; so he had gone to Navadvīpa without taking Their blessings. But now, although still weak and although preoccupied with traveling to the U.S., he felt that the Deity was calling him.

For the past 150 years, the Rādhā-Govinda temple had been maintained by the aristocratic Mulliks, a branch of Prabhupāda's own family. The Mulliks had owned the entire block on Harrison Road (now Mahatma Gandhi Road), and rents from the block-long building opposite the temple had financed the opulent worship of Rādhā-Govinda. In those days the Deities had been worshiped on a gorgeous altar in the large *kīrtana* hall, and They had been dressed in silks and ornamented with gilded and bejeweled crowns and necklaces. All the pious Vaiṣṇava families of the neighborhood would visit; and on Janmāṣṭamī, Kṛṣṇa's birthday, even British gentlemen and ladies would come.

But today the Mullik family possessed only remnants of the European art and furnishings that had once filled their homes and temple—relics from an age of former grandeur. And the worship of Rādhā-Govinda had pitifully deteriorated.

Śrīla Prabhupāda was pained to see the neglect. No longer were Rādhā and Govinda the center of the Mulliks' lives. The Deity worship still continued—conducted by paid *brāhmaṇas*—but few people came to see. The main attraction now was the golden deity of the goddess Kālī on the large altar in the *kīrtana* hall. Rādhā and Govinda, "in the family" for many generations, had been relegated to a small upstairs room in the Mullik compound. Their dress was no longer elegant, Their valuable crowns and ornaments had disappeared, and there were no large *kīrtanas* as before. Only a paid *brāhmaṇa* came in the morning to rub sandalwood pulp on Their shining bodies, dress Them carefully in whatever simple clothes remained, and place jasmine garlands around Their necks while a widow or two watched the silent proceedings.

Kṛṣṇa consciousness was dying in India, dying from neglect. At least it was dying here in Calcutta. And in many other places in India, even in Vṛndāvana, the impersonal philosophy prevailed, and grand old temples had become residences for pigeons, monkeys, and dogs. Sad as it was, it only reinforced Prabhupāda's conviction of the need to return to the fertile ground in the West. Although here in India the spirit of devotion was dying, in the West it was just beginning to grow—in New York, San Francisco, Montreal, Boston.

If pure Kṛṣṇa consciousness were dying in India, then why shouldn't it be transplanted in the fertile West? There it would flourish. It would spread worldwide and even back to India again. When India, bent on following the West, saw the materially advanced Americans taking to Kṛṣṇa consciousness, she would reevaluate her own culture.

Prabhupāda saw a Kṛṣṇa conscious revolution beginning in the United States. He didn't consider himself its creator; he was the servant of Kṛṣṇa consciousness. Lord Caitanya's desire was that every Indian help to spread Kṛṣṇa consciousness worldwide. Unfortunately, the very verses in the scriptures that prophesied a worldwide Kṛṣṇa consciousness movement were a puzzle even to most of Śrīla Prabhupāda's Godbrothers. They admitted it.

But soon they would see. There was great potential in the West. Prabhupāda had shown many of his Godbrothers the newspaper articles—"Swami's Flock" chanting in Tompkins Square Park, "Ancient Trance Dance" at Stanford University—and he had brought some disciples with him. These were only beginnings. Much more had to be done.

And who would help? B. P. Keśava Mahārāja was dying. Śrīdhara Mahārāja couldn't come out. Who else? Most Indians were impersonalists, nondevotional *yogīs*, or demigod worshipers. As Śrīla Prabhupāda stood before the Rādhā-Govinda Deity, explaining to Acyutānanda and Rāmānuja how he had worshiped Them in his childhood and how They had been his first inspiration in Kṛṣṇa consciousness, he understood deeply that he must take Kṛṣṇa consciousness all over the world, even if singlehandedly. Of course, he was not alone; he had disciples. And they were opening new centers even in his absence. He would have to return to them very soon and supervise his growing movement.

The Mulliks regarded Prabhupāda more as a relative than as a spiritual leader. To them he was a hometown cousin who had done something successful in America. Narendranath Mullik, a childhood friend of Prabhupāda's, called Prabhupāda Dādā, "brother," and regularly joked with him.

The Mulliks were glad to give Prabhupāda and his two followers a large room in the temple compound for as long as they wanted to stay in Calcutta. Prabhupāda set up his usual arrangement: a mat on the floor, a low table for a desk, and beside the desk his few possessions. Here he could study and write, receive guests, or rest. Daily some local women brought Prabhupāda and his disciples simple *prasādam* in a *tiffin*.

The Kālī-pūjā celebrations drew large crowds into the main hall before the Kālī deity, and Prabhupāda gave regular lectures there from *Śrīmad-Bhāgavatam*. He also spoke in the homes of various Mullik families. The hosts, members of the dwindling Bengali aristocracy, would offer Prabhupāda and his disciples Rādhā-Govinda *prasādam:* cut fruits, water chestnuts, minced ginger, and soaked, salted mung beans.

Most of those who came to visit Prabhupāda in his room were not really interested in spiritual life, but they wanted his blessings. There was a local *brāhmaṇa* whose occupation was to go from shop to shop carrying a few flowers, a cup of water, and a brass container with sandalwood paste and *kuṅkuma* powder. Using this paraphernalia, he would offer a blessing to the shopkeepers every day and receive a few *paisā* in payment. Knowing Prabhupāda to be a Vaiṣṇava, the *brāhmaṇa* came to see him to receive a spiritual benediction. The man's forehead was decorated with both Vaiṣṇava *tilaka* (two vertical lines) and Śaivite *tilaka* (three horizontal lines). After the man left, Acyutānanda asked, "Swamiji, who was that?"

"He is a hired *brāhmaṇa*," Prabhupāda said. "When he goes to the Vaiṣṇavas he gives them blessings, and when he goes to the Śaivites he gets money. He has to make a living."

Another man came, asserting that he wanted to teach Prabhupāda's disciples Hindi. He asked Prabhupāda to help him get to America, but Prabhupāda told him, "You must take *sannyāsa*. Then I will bring you to America." After two visits, the man stopped coming.

A Mullik relation, a small, bald, bright-eyed man, came by one day carrying a book entitled *Interesting Studies*. He posed philosophical questions—simple queries about *karma*, *jñāna*, and *bhakti*—but then would interrupt Prabhupāda and answer them himself. Finally when the man asked one of his questions, Prabhupāda replied, "So what is *your* answer?" The man gave a general answer. But later, when Prabhupāda began explaining that Lord Kṛṣṇa, the speaker of *Bhagavad-gītā*, is the Supreme Personality of Godhead, the man interrupted: "You may call God 'Kṛṣṇa,' call Him 'Śiva,' call Him—"

"No," Prabhupāda said. "Kṛṣṇa is the Supreme Lord, and all others are demigods." The man became a little nervous and quoted a popular Bengali impersonalist who taught that all gods and all methods of worship are the same.

"He's an upstart," Prabhupāda said. "That is not the teaching of the *Gītā*. What is this other teaching? It is all utter confusion."

"If you go on speaking like this," the man said angrily, "I'll have to leave this place. Please don't criticize this *paramahaṁsa*."

"Why not?" Prabhupāda said. "He is a concocter." The man got up and left, calling out, "You don't know Kṛṣṇa!" as he left the room.

Prabhupāda turned to Acyutānanda and Rāmānuja and smiled: "Every time you introduce Kṛṣṇa they say, 'Why only Kṛṣṇa?' But that is what Kṛṣṇa says. *Mattaḥ parataraṁ nānyat:* 'There is no truth superior to Me.' These rascal impersonalists have ruined Bengal."

One day a man gave Prabhupāda a two-hundred-rupee donation, and Prabhupāda immediately asked the *pūjārī* for an old set of Rādhā-Govinda's clothes, gave the clothes to some of the temple ladies along with the two hundred rupees, and asked that the ladies make gold-embroidered dresses for Rādhā-Govinda. "Rādhā-Govinda are taking care of us," he said, "so we can take care of Them also."

Rāmānuja's beard was huge. Looking like an ordinary hippie, he misrepresented Śrīla Prabhupāda wherever they went. Prabhupāda told Acyutānanda, "Tell your friend to shave." Acyutānanda and Rāmānuja talked, but Rāmānuja wouldn't shave. Wanting Rāmānuja to agree on his own, Prabhupāda didn't ask him again, but when a copy of the latest *Back to Godhead* magazine arrived from the States, Prabhupāda got an idea. Two illustrations in the magazine showed Haridāsa Ṭhākura converting a prostitute. After her conversion the prostitute had shaved her head. Showing the pictures to Rāmānuja, Prabhupāda asked, "What is the difference between this picture and that picture?"

"I don't know, Swamiji," Rāmānuja replied.

"No," Prabhupāda said, pointing to the pictures. "What is the difference in this picture?"

"Oh, she's a devotee."

"Yes," Prabhupāda said, "but what else?"

"Oh, she has a shaved head."

"Yes." Prabhupāda smiled. "A devotee has a shaved head."

"Do you want me to shave my head?"

"Yes."

Rāmānuja shaved. But within a few days he began growing his beard and hair back. "From now on," Prabhupāda told Acyutānanda, "no more cheap initiations. They have to know something."

Rāmānuja hung on. Prabhupāda wanted Rāmānuja and Acyutānanda to remain in India after his departure and continue to try for the American House in Vṛndāvana. Rāmānuja wrote his own impressions to his friend Mukunda in San Francisco.

> Please be advised that we're doing all we can to get him off as soon as possible but this primitive Indian government is putting obstacles in our way.

> The man who could have given Swamiji clearance for his P-form has just drowned, so the clearance has to be made in Bombay. This is the delay. Here in Calcutta we are having lots of fun addressing different people. Swamiji makes Acyutananda and myself give a short speech. I am becoming more and more expert at this. I think that he makes us speak in order to show the audience that we American Vaisnavas are for real. And also he wants everyone to preach Krishna Consciousness. . . . It is very difficult to take care properly of Swamiji's health here. For one thing it is a big thing to serve sweets in India and it is impolite to decline. Also we get all kinds of visitors. We have not been able to go to bed before 11 o'clock and Swamiji automatically wakes at 3. In this respect the people here are very inconsiderate but if Acyutananda and I ask them to leave they will ask Swamiji if they should and Swamiji of course says no. Anyway his heart beat is a little fast and sometimes it is alarmingly fast, so I suggest that you get a good heart specialist to see him. . . . Please arrange for this doctor and above all make sure that Swamiji gets plenty of rest. You need not restrict visitors too strictly because if the company is good Swamiji seems to enjoy visitors. Please do all you can to get Swamiji's beat to normal again. His chariot needs to be fixed up so that he can remain on this earth for at least another ten years.

* * *

Knowing that Swamiji would soon be returning, the devotees in America began to increase their entreaties, each group asking him to come to their particular city. On November 4 Prabhupāda wrote Mukunda, "As you say that my absence is being felt now surely more deeply than ever, so I also feel to start immediately without waiting." And to Mukunda's wife, Jānakī, he wrote, "Every minute I think of you and as you asked me to go to San Francisco while returning from India, I am trying to fulfill my promise. I am thinking of going directly to San Francisco." At the bottom of the same letter to Mukunda and Jānakī, Acyutānanda added a health report:

> Swamiji is looking healthy and living and working regularly, but his pulse rate is generally too fast. Last night it was 95—unusually fast even for him as it generally hovers between 83 and 86.

Prabhupāda decided not to wait any longer on the chance that Mukunda might secure him permanent residency. "I want to return to your country, where there is good air and good water," he told Acyutānanda one day. "Every day we are receiving letters that the devotees want me there. I thought that in my absence they might deteriorate, and I was reluctant to even come to India. But now I see that it is growing. There is need for me to go and supervise the expansion. So I want to go back."

The only impediment now seemed to be a delayed P-form, a clearance from the Bank of India required for an Indian citizen traveling abroad.

> I am just ready for starting for America but as you know our competent government is very slow in action. The P-form was submitted almost a month ago, but still it is undergoing red tapism. The visa was granted to me within half an hour. The passage money was deposited within two days but unfortunately the Reserve Bank of India is delaying the matter unnecessarily. I expect the P-form at any moment and as soon as I get it I shall start for your country.

Just to make certain that Swamiji would come first to San Francisco, Mukunda sent a telegram to Calcutta: "SWAMIJI. BRAHMANANDA AND I AGREE YOU START IMMEDIATELY. ADVISE EXACT ARRIVAL DATE. MUKUNDA."

Prabhupāda had planned his route through Tokyo, intending to stop for a day "to probe if there is any possibility of starting a center." In Tokyo he would let Mukunda know by telephone his arrival time in San Francisco. But three weeks passed while Prabhupāda continued to wait for his P-form.

Meanwhile, he received good news from New York. The Macmillan Company's interest in *Bhagavad-gītā* was real; the contract was being drawn. Pleased with Brahmānanda, he wrote to him on November 11 explaining his visions for distributing Kṛṣṇa conscious literature.

> If publications are there we can work from one center only like New York or San Francisco for propagating our cult all over the world. Let us stick to the publication of BTG more and more nicely and publish some Vedic literatures like Srimad Bhagavatam, Chaitanya Charitamrita, etc. . . .

As Prabhupāda's mind turned more to the preaching that awaited him in America, he assessed what he had done so far, what he would do, and the process by which he would do it.

I am not in agreement with Mr. Altman that we are expanding very thinly. In my opinion, a single sincere soul can maintain a center. You know I started the center at 26 2nd Ave. alone. I took the risk of 200.00 dollars per month for Rent. At that time there were no assistants. Mukunda was at that time a friend but there was no responsibility for him for maintaining the center. Gradually Kirtanananda and Hayagriva joined but they did not take any responsibility. Still I was maintaining the establishment simply depending on Krishna and then Krishna sent me everything—men and money. Similarly, if a sincere soul goes out and opens a center in any part of the world Krishna will help him in all respects. Without being empowered by Krishna, nobody can preach Krishna Consciousness. It is not academic qualification or financial strength which helps in these matters, but it is sincerity of purpose which helps us always. Therefore I wish that you [Brahmananda] will remain in charge of New York, let Satsvarupa be in charge of Boston, Let Mukunda be in charge of San Francisco, Let Janardan be in charge of Montreal. Let Nandarani and Dayananda be in charge of Los Angeles. And let Subal das be in charge of Santa Fe. In this way you will follow my example as I did in the beginning at 26 2nd Ave. That is Preaching, cooking, writing, talking, chanting everything one man's work. I never thought about the audience. I was prepared to chant if there were no man to hear me. The principle of chanting is to glorify the Lord and not to attract a crowd. If Krishna hears nicely then he will ask some sincere devotee to gather in such place. Therefore be advised that thousands of centers my be started if we find out a sincere soul for each and every center. We donot require more men to start. If there is one sincere soul that is sufficient to start a new center.

On November 12 Śrīla Prabhupāda wrote to Kṛṣṇā-devī,

I am coming soon to San Francisco. I shall let you know the exact date some time next week. I am coming over very soon to see you when everything will be adjusted. Hope you are well.

And the health notes from Acyutānanda continued to arrive.

Please tell the devotees out there to take good care of him. It is a very hard task trying to restrain him from overworking himself, but they must be strict. He still has to take his medicines and get his massage every day.

On November 20 Prabhupāda dispatched by boat to New York more than eight hundred copies of the first three volumes of his *Śrīmad-*

Bhāgavatam. And on the next day his P-form finally cleared. Immediately he booked passage on Pan American Airlines and sent a cable informing Mukunda that he would arrive in San Francisco on November 24 at 12:45 P.M.

But again his departure was delayed—this time by a strike by the Communist Party in Calcutta. Businesses closed. Cars, buses, rickshas, and trains stopped running. Riots broke out. There were murders and assassinations. Meanwhile, Prabhupāda remained at the Rādhā-Govinda temple.

> My return to your country is already settled. But due to a petty revolution in Calcutta I am not able to leave. . . . Our San Francisco friends may be very anxious because I sent them two telegrams, one informing them of my arrival and the other canceling it. Future arrangements are pending.

Two weeks passed. While waiting in his room for the political strike to end, Prabhupāda received a letter from Umāpati, one of the devotees he had initiated at the first initiation in New York, in September of 1966. Umāpati had given up practicing Kṛṣṇa consciousness for half a year, but now he wrote to say he was back. Prabhupāda replied:

> It is my duty to deliver you the right thing in right earnestness and it is the duty of the receiver to act in the standard spiritual regulation. When you left us I simply prayed to Krishna for your return to Krishna Consciousness because that was my duty. Any good soul who approaches me once for spiritual enlightenment is supposed to be depending on my responsibility to get him back to Krishna, back to home. The disciple may misunderstand a bona fide spiritual master being obliged to do so under the pressure of Maya's influence. But a bona fide spiritual master never lets go a devotee once accepted. When a disciple misunderstands a bona fide spiritual master, the master regrets for his inability to protect the disciple and sometimes he cries with tears in the eyes. We had an experience while my Guru Maharaja was alive. One of His disciples who accepted sannyas was one day forcibly dragged by his wife. My Guru Maharaj lamented with tears in His eyes saying that He could not save the soul. We should always therefore be careful of being attacked by Maya's influence and the only means of guarantee is to chant Hare Krishna offenselessly.

When Prabhupāda received news of quarreling in the Los Angeles temple he replied to Nandarāṇī,

> I know that my presence is very urgently required. Arrangement is already completed and circumstances alone have checked my departure. Please therefore don't be worried. I am coming to your place within a fortnight.

At the end of the first week of December the strike ended, and Śrīla Prabhupāda again booked passage.

> You will be pleased to know that I have purchased my ticket for New York via Tokyo and San Francisco. I am starting tomorrow morning at nine-thirty. By evening reaching Tokyo via Bangkok and Hong Kong. I shall rest 24 hours in Tokyo and on the 14th at night, I am starting for San Francisco. By local time I am reaching San Francisco on the same day, the 14th at 12:45 p.m. by P.A.A. 846. Yesterday I have sent one telegram to this effect, and I hope I shall reach there safely as scheduled. I am so glad to learn that Satyabrata and yourself are trying to get the teachings of Lord Caitanya published. You do not know how pleased I am to hear this news. When one book is published I think I have conquered an empire. So try to publish as many books as possible and that will enhance the beauty and prestige of our society. The impersonalist mission has nothing to say substantial but because they have money and have published so many rubbish literatures they have become very cheaply popular. You can just imagine how much powerful our society will become when we have as many substantial literatures published. We should not only publish in English but also in other important languages such as French and German.

When the day for Prabhupāda's departure finally arrived he gave last instructions to Acyutānanda and Rāmānuja.

"Just pray to Lord Kṛṣṇa that I can go to America," he requested Acyutānanda.

"How can I?" Acyutānanda replied. "You'll be leaving me."

"No," Śrīla Prabhupāda replied, "we'll always remain packed up together if you remember my teachings. If you preach you will become strong, and all these teachings will be in the proper perspective. When we stop our preaching, then everything becomes stagnated, and we lose our life. Even here in India people think that they know everything, but they are wrong. There is no end to hearing about Kṛṣṇa. God is unlimited. So no one can say, 'I know everything about God.' Those who say they know everything about God do not know. So everyone will appreciate you. Do not fear."

Acyutānanda: *When I returned to the room after sending off Swamiji and paying my obeisances at the airport, I felt a void. I felt very lonely and rather weak. I returned to the room in front of Śrī Śrī Rādhā-Govinda, and chanting on my beads I started pacing back and forth. "What will I preach?" The black and white marble floor passed under me. I stepped on the cracks, in between the cracks, and on the black and white marble again and again. Then I realized I wasn't seeing Rādhā-Kṛṣṇa. So I sat down directly in front and saw the brilliant form of Rādhā-Govindajī, and my eyes filled with tears.*

* * *

Śrīla Prabhupāda spent his stopover in Tokyo mostly in going to his hotel and checking into a room, bathing, resting, eating, and returning to the airport the next day in time for his flight to San Francisco. But he did speak with a government secretary, explaining that Kṛṣṇa consciousness was a universal philosophy for reviving a person's original, eternal consciousness. And he explained the crucial need for Kṛṣṇa consciousness in human society. The secretary, however, said he felt certain that the Japanese government wouldn't be able to help a religious movement.

Prabhupāda was annoyed. This supposedly educated man was so ignorant as to mistake Kṛṣṇa consciousness for merely another sectarian religion. Prabhupāda wanted intelligent men to try to understand Kṛṣṇa consciousness and understand that the *Gītā* was actual knowledge, transcendental knowledge, beyond the inferior knowledge of the senses and the mind. But he had his plane to catch. Japan would have to wait.

The passengers and flight crew saw Prabhupāda as an elderly Indian man, dressed in saffron robes. The stewardesses weren't sure at first whether he spoke English, but when he asked them for fruits they saw that he could and that he was a kind gentleman. He was quiet, putting on his glasses and reading from an old book of Indian scripture for hours at a time, or moving his lips in prayer while fingering Indian prayer beads in a cloth pouch, or sometimes resting beneath a blanket, his eyes shut.

No one knew or bothered to inquire into what he was doing. They didn't know that anxious young hearts were awaiting him in San Francisco, or that the Macmillan Company in New York wanted to publish his English translation of *Bhagavad-gītā*, or that he had spiritual centers in two countries, with plans for expansion all over the world. Prabhupāda sat patiently, chanting often, his hand in his bead bag, depending on Kṛṣṇa as the hours passed.

After a ten-hour flight the plane landed in San Francisco. Standing with hundreds of other passengers, Prabhupāda gradually made his way to the exit. Down the long attached tunnel, even before he reached the terminal building, he could see Govinda dāsī and a few other disciples smiling and waving on the other side of a glass partition. As he entered the terminal building he moved towards the glass, and his disciples dropped to their knees, offering obeisances. As they raised their heads he smiled and continued walking down the corridor while they walked alongside, only the glass partition separating them. Then they disappeared from his view as he walked down the stairway towards immigration and customs.

The downstairs area was also glassed in, and Prabhupāda could see more than fifty devotees and friends waiting eagerly. As they again caught sight of him, they cried out as a group, "Hare Kṛṣṇa!"

Swamiji looked wonderful to them, tanned from his six months in India, younger, and more spritely. He smiled and triumphantly held up his hands in greeting. Devotees were crying in happiness.

As Prabhupāda stood in line at the customs inspection point, he could hear the devotees' *kīrtana*, the glass walls only partially masking the sound. The customs officials ignored the chanting, although the connection between the saffron-robed passenger and the joyful chanters was not hard to see.

Śrīla Prabhupāda waited in line, glancing now and then at his chanting disciples. Since he had already sent ahead the eight hundred books and several crates of musical instruments, he had only one suitcase to place on the table before the inspector. Methodically the inspector went through the contents: cotton *sārīs* for the girls, silk garlands for the Jagannātha deities, *karatālas*, saffron *dhotīs* and *kurtās*, a coconut grater, and little bottles of Āyur Vedic medicine.

"What are these?" the inspector probed. The little bottles looked strange, and he called for another inspector. A delay. Swamiji's disciples became perturbed by the petty-minded customs inspectors' poking through Swamiji's things, now opening the tightly corked bottles, sniffing and checking the contents.

The inspectors seemed satisfied. Prabhupāda tried to close his suitcase, but he couldn't work the zipper. Another delay. The devotees, still anxiously chanting, watched as Swamiji, with the help of the gentleman behind him, managed to zip his suitcase closed.

Swamiji walked towards the glass doors. The devotees began chanting madly. As he stepped through the door a devotee blew a conchshell that resounded loudly throughout the hall. Devotees garlanded him, and everyone pressed in, handing him flowers. He entered their midst as a beloved father enters and reciprocates the embrace of his loving children.

Appendixes

BOOKS by His Divine Grace A.C. Bhaktivedanta Swami Prabhupāda

Bhagavad-gītā As It Is
Śrīmad-Bhāgavatam, cantos 1–10 (30 vols.)
Śrī Caitanya-caritāmṛta (17 vols.)
Teachings of Lord Caitanya
The Nectar of Devotion
The Nectar of Instruction
Śrī Īśopaniṣad
Easy Journey to Other Planets
Kṛṣṇa Consciousness: The Topmost Yoga System
Kṛṣṇa, the Supreme Personality of Godhead (3 vols.)
Perfect Questions, Perfect Answers
Dialectical Spiritualism—A Vedic View of Western Philosophy
Teachings of Lord Kapila, the Son of Devahūti
Transcendental Teachings of Prahlād Mahārāja
Teachings of Queen Kuntī
Kṛṣṇa, the Reservoir of Pleasure
The Science of Self-Realization
The Path of Perfection
Search for Liberation
Life Comes From Life
The Perfection of Yoga
Beyond Birth and Death
On the Way to Kṛṣṇa
Geetār-gan (Bengali)
Vairāgya-vidyā (Bengali)
Buddhi-yoga (Bengali)
Bhakti-ratna-bolī (Bengali)
Rāja-vidyā: The King of Knowledge
Elevation to Kṛṣṇa Consciousness
Kṛṣṇa Consciousness: The Matchless Gift
Back to Godhead magazine (founder)

A complete catalog is available upon request.

Bhaktivedanta Book Trust
3764 Watseka Avenue
Los Angeles, California 90034

ISKCON Centers Around the World

AFRICA

Accra, Durban (Natal), S. Africa—P.O. Box 212, Cato Ridge, Natal 3680 / Cato Ridge 237; **Johannesburg, S. Africa**—Elberta Rd., Honeydew (mail: P.O. Box 5302, Weltevreden Park 1715) / 6752845; **Lagos, Nigeria**—2B Coker Rd., Ilupeju (mail: P.O. Box 8793, Lagos) / 962189; **Mauritius**—White House, Celicourt Antelme St., Quartre Bornes (mail: P.O. Box 718, Port Louis, Mauritius); **Mombasa, Kenya, E. Africa**—Madhavani House, Sauti Ya Kenya and Kisumu Rd., P.O. Box 82224 / 312248; **Nairobi, Kenya, E. Africa**—Puran Singh Close, P.O. Box 28946 / 744365; **Osu (Accra), Ghana, W. Africa**— P.O. Box 01568.

ASIA

INDIA: Ahmedabad, Gujarat—7, Kailas Society, Ashram Rd., 380 009 / 49935; **Bangkok, Thailand**—99 Soi Sahakorn 1, Ramkamhaeng Road / 3778557; **Bangalore, Mysore**—34/A, 9B Cross, West of Chord Rd., Rajajinagar 2nd Stage, 560 010; **Bhubaneswar, Orissa**—National Highway No. 5, Nayapalli (mail: c/o P.O. Box 173, 751 001) / 53125; **Bombay, Maharastra**—Hare Krishna Land, Juhu, 400 049 / 566-860; **Calcutta, W. Bengal**—3 Albert Rd., 700 017 / 44-3757; **Chandigarh**—Hare Krishna Land, Dakshin Marg, Sector 36-B, 160 036 / 26674; **Chhaygharia (Haridaspur), W. Bengal**—Thakur Haridas Sripatbari Sevashram, P.O. Chhaygharia, P.S. Bongaon, Dist. 24 Pargonas; **Gauhati, Assam**—Post Bag No. 127, 781 001; **Hyderabad, A.P.**—Hare Krishna Land, Nampally Station Rd., 500 001 / 51018; **Imphal, Manipur**—Tiddim Rd., Shangaiprou 795 001; **Madras, Tamil Nadu**—232 Kilpauk Garden Road, Madras 600 010; **Mayapur, W. Bengal**—Shree Mayapur Chandrodaya Mandir, P.O. Shree Mayapur Dham (District Nadia); **New Delhi, U.P.**—M-119 Greater Kailash 1, 110 048 / 624-590; **Surat, Gujarat**—21-A Dhawelgiri Apts., Athwa lines, 395007 / 87668; **Vrindavan, U.P.**—Krishna-Balarama Mandir, Bhaktivedanta Swami Marg, Raman Reti, Mathura / 178.

FARMS: Hyderabad, A.P.—P.O. Dabilpur Village, Medchal Taluq, Hyderabad District, 501 401; **Mayapur, W. Bengal**—(contact ISKCON Mayapur).

RESTAURANTS: Bombay—Hare Krishna Land; **Vrindavan**—Krishna-Balarama Mandir.

OTHER COUNTRIES: Colombo, Sri Lanka—188, New Chetty St., Colombo 13 / 33325; **Hong Kong**—5 Homantin St., Flat 23, Kowloon / 3-7122630; **Kathmandu, Nepal**—8/6, Battis Putali, Goshalla; **Mandaue City, Philippines**—231 Pagsabungan Rd., Basak, Cebu / 83254; **Selangor, Malaysia**—No. 18 Jalan 6/6, off Jalam Anak Gassing, Petaling Jaya / 564957; **Tehran, Iran**—Felistin Ave. (old Kakh), Shemstad St., No. 3 / 644-272; **Tokyo, Japan**—3-13-4 Kamirenjyaku, Mitaka-shi, Tokyo T181 / 0422-47-5874.

AUSTRALASIA

Adelaide, Australia—13-A Frome St., Adelaide 5000, South Australia / (08)223-2084; **Auckland, New Zealand**—Hwy. 18, Riverhead (next to Huapai Golfcourse) (mail: c/o R.D. 2, Kumeu) / 412-8075; **Bali, Indonesia**—Jalan Sagamona 17, Denpasar / 8045; **Brisbane, Australia**—56 Bellevue Terrace, St. Lucia 4067, Queensland (mail: P.O. Box 649, Toowong 4066) / 07-370-7478; **Christchurch, New Zealand**—30 Latimer Sq. / 65689; **Jakarta, Indonesia**—Jalan Rawamangun Muka Timur 80 / 4835-19; **Lautoka, Fiji**—5 Tavewa Ave. (mail: c/o P.O. Box 125) / 61-633, ext. 48; **Melbourne, Australia**—197 Danks St., Albert Park, Melbourne, Victoria 3206 (mail: c/o P.O. Box 125) / 699-5122; **Perth, Australia**—79 Armidale Crescent, Coolbinia 6050, Western Australia (mail: P.O. Box 148, North Perth WA 6006) / 444-9678; **Singapore, Malaysia**—103 Wellington Rd., Singapore 2775 / 257-4255; **Sydney, Australia**—112 Darlinghurst Rd., King's Cross 2011, N.S.W. (mail: c/o G.P.O. Box 1477) / (02)357-5162.

FARMS: Auckland, New Zealand (New Varshana)—contact ISKCON Auckland; **Colo, Australia (Bhaktivedanta Ashram)**—Upper Colo Rd., N.S.W. (mail: c/o P.O. Box 493, St. Mary's, 2760, N.S.W.) / 045-75-5284; **Murwillumbah, Australia (New Govardhana)**—'Eungella,' Tyalgum Rd. via Murwillumbah, N.S.W. 2484 (mail: c/o P.O. Box 687) / 066-72-1903.

RESTAURANTS: Adelaide—Govinda's, 13 Frome Street; **Melbourne**—Gopal's, 237 Flinders Lane / 63 1578; **Melbourne**—Gopal's, 251 Malvern Road, Prahran / 240 0202; **Parramatta**—Gopal's, 18A Darcy St. / (02)635-0638; **Sydney**—Mukunda's, 233 Victoria Street, Darlinghurst / 357 5162.

EUROPE

Amsterdam, Holland—Keizersgracht 94 / 020-249 410; **Antwerp, Belgium**—25 Katelijnevest / 031-320987; **Athens, Greece**—133 Solonos; **Bristol, England**—11 Kensington Park, Easton, Bristol 5 / 51 02 93; **Catania, Sicily**—Via Empedocle 84, 95100 / 095-522-252; **Copenhagen, Denmark**—Korfuvej 9, 2300 Copenhagen S / 972337; **Dublin, Ireland**—2 Belvedere Place, Dublin 1 / 743-767; **Gallarate, Italy**—Via A. Volta 19, Gallarate 20131 (VA) / 0331-783-268; **Glasgow, Scotland**—571 Sauchiehall St., Charing Cross, Glasgow G3 7PQ / 041-221-5999; **Göthenburg, Sweden**—Karl Gustavsgatan 19, 41125 Göthenburg / 031-110955; **Grödinge, Sweden**—Korsnäs Gard, 140 32 Grödinge / 0753-29151; **Heidelberg, W. Germany**—Kürfursten-Anlage 5, 6900 Heidelberg / 06211-15101; **Las Palmas de Gran Canaria, Canary Islands**—Néstor de la Torre. 26-5B; **London, England (city)**—10 Soho St., London W1 / 01-437-3662; **London, England (country)**—Bhaktivedanta Manor, Letchmore Heath, Watford, Hertfordshire WD2 8EP / Radlett 7244; **Madrid, Spain**—Velásquez 24 2da. dcha., Madrid 1/276-0447; **Manchester, England**—106 College Road, Whalley Range, Manchester 16 / 061-881-1947; **Munich, W. Germany**—Govinda's Club, Parzivalstrasse 3,

Munich / 089-368456; **Paris, France**—20 rue Vieille du Temple, Paris 75004 / 887-52-07; **Rome, Italy**—Salita del Poggio Laurentino 7, Rome 00144 / (06)593-075; **Septon, Belgium**—Chateau de Petit Somme, Septon 5482 / 086-322480; **Stockholm, Sweden**—Grevgatan 18, 11453 Stockholm / 08-623411; **Strasbourg, France**—A.I.C.K. 57, Ave. des Vosges, 67000 Strasbourg / (88)362409; **Vienna, Austria**—Govinda Kulturzentrum, Lerchenfelderstrasse 17, A-1070 Wien / (0222) 96 10 633; **West Berlin, W. Germany**—ISKCON bei Renate Utri, Wendehalsweg 12, 1000 W. Berlin / 030-6019471; **Worcester, England**—Chaitanya College at Croome Court, Severn Stoke, Worcester WR8 9DW / 090 567-214; **Zürich, Switzerland**—Bergstrasse 54, 8032 Zürich / (01)69-33-88.

FARMS: **Bavarian Forest (Bayrische-Wald), W. Germany (Nava-Jiyada-Nṛsiṁha-Kṣetra)**—(contact ISKCON Munich); **Brihuega, Spain (New Vraja Mandala)**—(Santa Clara) Brihuega, Guadalajara / (11) 280018; **Düdingen, Switzerland**—Im Stillen Tal, CH 3186 Dudingen (FR) / (037) 43.26.97; **Florence, Italy (Villa Vṛndāvana)**—Via Comunaledegli Scopeti, No. 108, St. Andrea in Percussina, San Casciano Val di Pesa 56030 (Firenze) / 055-820054; **Kiryat, Tivon, Israel**—Neve Hemed, Hamisrah St., Kiryat Haroshet, 36925 / (04)933672; **London, England**—(contact Bhaktivedanta Manor); **Valencay, France (New Mayapur)**—Lucay-Le-Male, 36 600 / (54) 40-23-26.

RESTAURANTS: **London**—Healthy, Wealthy, and Wise, 9–10 Soho Street / 01-437-1835; **Stockholm**—Govinda's (at ISKCON Stockholm); **Vienna**—Govinda (at ISKCON Vienna); **Zurich**—Govinda, Brandschenkestrasse 12, 8002 Zurich / (01)2029282.

LATIN AMERICA

BRAZIL: **Belem, PA**—Rua Cesario Alvim 795, Jurunas, 66.000; **Belo Horizonte, Minas Gerais**—Rua Goncalves Dias 2411, Lurdes, 30.000 / (031)335-1551; **Curitiba, Paraná**—Rua Pres Carlos Calvacante 1090, Sao Francisco, 80.000; **Fortaleza, CE**—Rua Demetrio de Menezes 4240, Apt. 15, Antonio Bexerra, 60.000; **Pindamonhangaba, SP**—Rua Dom Joao Bosco 848, Santana, 12.400; **Porto Alegre, RS**—Rua Eurico Lara 430, Menino Deus, 90.000 / (0512)237598; **Recife, Pernambuco**—Ave. 17 de Agosto 257, Parnamirim 50.000 / (081)268-1908; **Rio de Janeiro, RJ**—Estrada dos Tres Rios 654, Jacarepagua, 22.700; **Salvador, Bahia**—Rua Alvaro Adorno 17, Brotas, 40.000 / (071)240-1072; **São Paulo, SP**—Rua dos Franceses 323, Bela Vista, 01329 / (011)284-4075; **Victoria, ES**—Escadaria Santos 29, Ladeira Sao Bento, 29.000 / (027)223-1311;

FARM: **Pindamonhangaba, São Paulo (New Gokula)**—Ribeirao Grande (mail: C.P. 108, 12.400 Pindamonhangaba) / 279-7836.

MEXICO: **Guadalajara**—Morelos No. 1514 S.H. / 261278; **Mexico City**—Gob. Tiburcio Montiel 45, San Miguel Chapultepec, Mexico D.F. 18 / (905)271-0132; **Monterrey** —General Albino Espinoza, 345 Pte., Zona Centro, Monterrey, N.L. / 42 67 66; **Puebla**—Sierra Madre 9010, Colonia Maravillas, Puebla; **Vera Cruz**—Calle 3 Carabelas No. 784, Fraccionmiento Reforma.

OTHER COUNTRIES: **Antofogasta, Chile**—Calle las Gardenias No. 1326; **Bogotá, Colombia**—Carrera 3A No. 54-A-72 / 255-9842; **Cochabamba, Bolivia**—P.O. Box 3988 / 46441; **Concepción, Chile**—Nonguen, 588 / 23150; **Cuzco, Peru**—345 Calle Procuradores / 2277; **Georgetown, Guyana**—24 Uitvlugt Front, West Coast Demerara; **Guatemala City, Guatemala**—Sexta Avenida 1-89, Zona 1 / 24618; **La Paz, Bolivia**—Avenido Hermando Siles 6239 (mail: Casilla 10278 Obrajes) / 785023; **Lima, Peru**—Jiron Junín 415 / 47-18-10; **Medellín, Colombia**—Calle 10, No. 43F-48 / 466150; **Panama City, Panama**—43-58 Via España Altos, Al Lado del Cine, Bella Vista; **Puente Alto, Chile**—Casilla 44 / 283; **Quito, Ecuador**—Apdo. 2384, Calle Yasuni No. 404 (mail: P.O. Box 2384); **St. Augustine, Trinidad and Tobago**—Gordon St. at Santa Margarita Circular Rd. / 809-662-4605; **San José, Costa Rica**—100 mtrs. sureste de aptos Torre Blanca Urbanización Carmiol, Montes de Oca, Casa No. 49 (mail: P.O. Box 166, Paseo Estudiantes, Z-1002); **San Salvador, El Salvador**—67 Avenida Sur No. 115, Colonia Escalon; **Santiago, Chile**—Estudiantes, 150; **Santo Domingo, Dominican Republic**—Calle Cayatano Rodriguez No. 254 / (809)688-7242; **Valparaiso, Chile**—Colon 2706 / 7099.

FARM: **Guyana**—Seawell Village, Coventyne, East Berbice.

RESTAURANTS: **Cuzco Peru**—345 Calle Procurados; **Lima, Peru**—Azangaro 149; **San José, Costa Rica**—50 metros el este de la case amarilla, Avenida 7 No. 1325; **Santiago, Chile**—Govinda's (at ISKCON Santiago).

NORTH AMERICA

CANADA: **Calgary, Alberta**—429 Third Ave. N.E. T2E 0H7 / (403)269-1616; **Edmonton, Alberta**—8957 77th Ave., T5N 2N7 / (403)466-9037; **Montreal, Quebec**—1626 Pie IX Boulevard, H1V 2C5 / (514)527-1101; **Ottawa, Ontario**—212 Somerset St. E., K1N 6V4 / (613)233-1884; **Regina, Saskatchewan**—2817 Victoria Ave., S4T 1K6 / (306)-352-8071; **Toronto, Ontario**—243 Avenue Rd. M5R 2J6 / (416)922-5415; **Vancouver, B.C.**—5580 S.E. Marine Dr., Burnaby V5J 3G8 / (604)433-8216; **Victoria, B.C.**—4056 Rainbow St., V8X 2A9 / (604)479-0649; **Waterloo, Ontario**—51 Amos Ave., N2L 2W6 / (519)888-7321.

FARM: **Hemingford, Quebec (New Nandagram)**—315 Backbrush Rd., RR. No. 2, J0L 1H0 / (514)247-3429.

RESTAURANTS: **Ottawa**—The Back Home Buffet, 212 Somerset St. E. / (613)233-3460; **Toronto**—Govinda's, 1280 Bay St. / (416)968-1313; **Vancouver**—Govinda's, 1221 Thurlow / (604)682-8154.

U.S.A.: **Atlanta, Georgia**—1287 Ponce de Leon Ave. NE 30306 / (404)377-8680; **Baltimore, Maryland**—200 Bloomsbury Ave., Catonsville 21228 / (301)788-3883; **Baton Rouge, Louisiana**—859 Aster St., 70803; **Berkeley, California**—2334 Stuart St. 94705 / (415) 843-7874; **Boston, Massachusetts (city)**—72 Commonwealth Ave. 02116 / (617)536-1695; **Boston, Massachusetts (country)**—527 Canton St., Westwood, Mass. 02090 / (617) 329-7568; **Chicago, Illinois**—1716 West Lunt Ave. 60626 / (312)973-0900; **Cleveland, Ohio**—15720 Euclid Ave., E. Cleveland

44112 / (216)851-9367; **Columbus, Ohio**—99 East 13th Ave. 43201 / (614)294-9402; **Dallas, Texas**—5430 Gurley Ave. 75223 / (214)827-6330; **Denver, Colorado**—1400 Cherry St. 80220 / (303)333-5461; **Detroit, Michigan**—383 Lenox Ave. 48215 / (313)824-6000; **E. Lansing, Michigan**—319 Grove St. 48823 / (517)351-6603; **Gainesville, Florida**—1214 S.W. 1st Ave. 32601; **Hartford, Connecticut**—1683 Main St., East Hartford 06108 / (203)528-1600; **Honolulu, Hawaii**—51 Coelho Way 96817 / (808)595-3947; **Houston, Texas**—1111 Rosalie St. 77004 / (713)-526-9860; **Hyannis, Massachusetts**—127 Ridgewood Ave., 02601 / (617)771-4244; **Laguna Beach, California**—285 Legion St., 92651 / (714) 494-7029; **Lake Huntington, New York**—P.O. Box 388, 12752 / (914)932-8332; **Long Island, New York**—197 S. Ocean Ave., Freeport 11520 / (516)378-6184; **Los Angeles, California**—3764 Watseka Ave. 90034 / (213) 558-9016; **Miami Beach, Florida**—2445 Collins Ave. 33140 / (305)531-0331; **Newark, Delaware**—168 Elkton Rd. 19711 / (302)453-8510; **New Orleans, Louisiana**—2936 Esplanade Ave. 70119 / (504)-488-7433; **New York, New York**—846 7th Ave. 10019 / (212)246-3503; **Philadelphia, Pennsylvania**—51 West Allens Lane, 19119 / (215)247-4600; **Pittsburgh, Pennsylvania**—1112 N. Negley Ave. 15026 / (412)361-9949; **Portland, Oregon**—3828 S.E. Division St., 97202 / (503)231-5792; **Providence, Rhode Island**—39 Glendale Ave., 02906 / (401)-273-9010; **St. Louis, Missouri**—3926 Lindell Blvd. 63108 / (314)535-8085; **San Diego, California**—1030 Grand Ave., Pacific Beach 92109 / (714)483-2500; **San Francisco, California**—(Bhaktivedanta Institute and Fellowship) 1403 Willard St., 94117 / (415)664-7724; **San Juan, Puerto Rico**—1016 Ponce de Leon St., Rio Piedras, 00925 / (809)-765-4745; **Seattle, Washington**—400 18th Ave. East 98112 / (206)329-7011; **State College, Pennsylvania**—103 E. Hamilton Ave. 16801 / (814)234-1867; **Towaco, New Jersey**—100 Jacksonville Rd. 07082 / (201)299-0970; **Washington, D.C.**—10310 Oaklyn Rd., Potomac, Maryland 20854 / (301)299-2100.

FARMS: **Gainesville, Florida**—Rt. 2, Box 24, Alachua 32615 / (904)462-1143; **Gurabo, Puerto Rico (New Gandhamadana)**—Box 215 B, Route 181, Santa Rita 00658; **Hopland, California (New Mt. Kailas)**—Route 175, Box 469, 95449 / (707)744-1100; **Hotchkiss, Colorado (New Barshana)**—P.O. Box 112, 81419 / (303)527-4584; **Lynchburg, Tennessee (Murāri-sevaka)**—Rt. No. 1, Box 146-A, (Mulberry) 37359 / (615)759-7058; **Moundsville, West Virginia (New Vrindaban)**—R.D. No. 1, Box 319, Hare Krishna Ridge 26041 / (304)843-1600; **Ninole, Hawaii**—P.O. Box 26, 96773 / (808)595-3947; **Port Royal, Pennsylvania (Gitā-nāgarī)**—R.D. No. 1, 17082 / (717)527-2493.

RESTAURANTS: **Cleveland**—Simply Wonderful, 1725 Euclid Ave., 44112; **Los Angeles**—Govinda's, 9634 Venice Blvd., Culver City 90230 / (213)836-1269; **Miami Beach**—Govinda's (at ISKCON Miami Beach); **St. Louis, Missouri**—(at ISKCON St. Louis) / (341)535-8161; **San Francisco**—Jagannatha's Cart, 57 Jessie St. / (415)495-3083; **San Francisco**—The Seven Mothers, 86 Carl St., 94117 / (415)566-0663; **San Juan, Puerto Rico**—Govinda's (at ISKCON San Juan); **Santa Cruz, Ca.**—Govinda's, 2-1245 East Cliff Drive / (408)475-9833; **Washington, D.C.**—Govinda's, 515 8th St. S.E. 20003 / (202)543-9600.

Sanskrit Pronunciation Guide

Throughout the centuries, the Sanskrit language has been written in a variety of alphabets. The mode of writing most widely used throughout India, however, is called *devanāgarī*, which means, literally, the writing used in "the cities of the demigods." The *devanāgarī* alphabet consists of forty-eight characters, including thirteen vowels and thirty-five consonants. Ancient Sanskrit grammarians arranged the alphabet according to practical linguistic principles, and this order has been accepted by all Western scholars. The system of transliteration used in this book conforms to a system that scholars in the last fifty years have accepted to indicate the pronunciation of each Sanskrit sound.

The short vowel **a** is pronounced like the **u** in b**u**t, long **ā** like the **a** in f**a**r, and short **i** like the **i** in p**i**n. Long **ī** is pronounced as in p**i**que, short **u** as in p**u**ll, and long **ū** as in r**u**le. The vowel **ṛ** is pronounced like the **ri** in **ri**m. The vowel **e** is pronounced as in th**e**y, **ai** as in **ai**sle, **o** as in g**o**, and **au** as in h**ow**. The *anusvāra* (**ṁ**), which is a pure nasal, is pronounced like the **n** in the French word *bo***n**, and *visarga* (**ḥ**), which is a strong aspirate, is pronounced as a final **h** sound. Thus **aḥ** is pronounced like **aha,** and **iḥ** like **ihi.**

The guttural consonants—**k, kh, g, gh,** and **ṅ**—are pronounced from the throat in much the same manner as in English. **K** is pronounced as in **k**ite, **kh** as in Ec**kh**art, **g** as in **g**ive, **gh** as in di**g h**ard, and **ṅ** as in si**ng.** The palatal consonants—**c, ch, j, jh,** and **ñ**—are pronounced from the palate with the middle of the tongue. **C** is pronounced as in **ch**air, **ch** as in staun**ch-h**eart, **j** as in **j**oy, **jh** as in he**dgeh**og, and **ñ** as in ca**ny**on. The cerebral consonants—**ṭ, ṭh, ḍ, ḍh,** and **ṇ**—are pronounced with the tip of the tongue turned up and drawn back against the dome of the palate. **Ṭ** is pronounced as in **t**ub, **ṭh** as in ligh**t-h**eart, **ḍ** as in **d**ove, **ḍh** as in re**d-h**ot, and **ṇ** as in **n**ut. The dental consonants—**t, th, d, dh,** and **n**—are pronounced in the same manner as the cerebrals, but with the forepart of the tongue against the teeth. The labial consonants—**p, ph, b, bh,** and **m**—are pronounced with the lips. **P** is pronounced as in **p**ine, **ph** as in u**ph**ill, **b** as in **b**ird, **bh** as in ru**b-h**ard, and **m** as in **m**other. The semivowels—**y, r, l,** and **v**—are pronounced as in **y**es, **r**un, **l**ight, and **v**ine respectively. The sibilants **ś, ṣ,** and **s**—are pronounced, respectively, as in the German word *s***prechen** and the English words **sh**ine and **s**un. The letter **h** is pronounced as in **h**ome.

Glossary

A

Advaita Ācārya—the older associate of Lord Caitanya Mahāprabhu who prayed that the Lord appear on earth.

Age of Quarrel—*See:* Kali-yuga

Ārati—a ceremony for worshiping the Deity of the Lord with offerings of food, lamps, fans, flowers, and incense.

Arjuna—the intimate devotee of Lord Kṛṣṇa who heard the teachings of *Bhagavad-gītā* from Him on the battlefield of Kurukṣetra.

Āśrama—a place of shelter conducive to the practice of spiritual life.

Aurobindo—a popular teacher who misled his followers with false interpretations of the *Vedas.*

Avatāra—an appearance of the Supreme Lord within this material world.

Āyur Vedic medicine—a system of medicine based on the *Vedas.*

B

Bābāji—a renounced devotee who practices chanting Hare Kṛṣṇa in solitude.

Baladeva—the first expansion of Lord Kṛṣṇa, appearing as His elder brother.

Balarāma—*See:* Baladeva

Bhagavad-gītā—"Song of God"; the essential summary of spiritual knowledge spoken to Arjuna by the Supreme Lord, Śrī Kṛṣṇa.

Bhāgavatam—*See: Śrīmad-Bhāgavatam*

Bhāgavata-prasādam—*See: Prasādam*

Bhajanas—worship of God by the chanting of His holy names.

Bhakti—devotion to the Supreme Personality of Godhead.

Bhaktisiddhānta Sarasvatī Ṭhākura—the spiritual master of A. C. Bhaktivedanta Swami, Śrīla Prabhupāda.

Bhaktivedanta Swami—Śrīla Prabhupāda's title as a member of the renounced order of spiritual life.

Bhaktivinoda Ṭhākura—a great Kṛṣṇa conscious spiritual master in the chain of disciplic succession from Lord Caitanya.

Bhakti-yoga—devotional service as the means of linking up with the Supreme.

Brahmacārī—a celibate monk; the first of the four *āśramas*, or spiritual orders of life.

Brāhmaṇa—an intelligent man who understands the spiritual purpose of life and can instruct others; the highest Vedic social order.

Brahma-saṁhitā—a Vedic scripture describing Lord Kṛṣṇa, the Supreme Personality of Godhead.

Buddha—an incarnation of the Supreme Lord who taught nonviolence.

C

Cādar—a blanket or cloth used to cover the upper part of the body.

Caitanya-caritāmṛta—the standard biography of Lord Caitanya Mahāprabhu, written by Kṛṣṇadāsa Kavirāja.

Caitanya Mahāprabhu—the *avatāra* of Lord Kṛṣṇa in this age whose mission is to teach love of God through the chanting of His holy names.

Capātīs—whole wheat flat breads.

Chandi Chowk—a street in Old Delhi.

Chawri Bazaar—a shopping street in Old Delhi.

Chippiwada temple—a temple of Lord Kṛṣṇa in Old Delhi where Śrīla Prabhupāda maintained an office before coming to America.

Chutney—a spicy relish made of fruits, spices, and herbs.

D

Dāl—a spicy soup made from *dāl* beans.

Dāmodara—a name of Lord Kṛṣṇa.

Daṇḍa—the sacred staff carried by a person in the renounced order of life.

Daṇḍavat—prostrate obeisances.

Deity—the authorized form of the Lord worshiped in temples.

Delhi—the capital of India.

Demigods—powerful living beings who control natural forces under the direction of the Supreme Lord.

Devakī—the mother of Lord Kṛṣṇa.

Dhāma—an eternal abode of the Supreme Lord.

Dhotī—the standard garment of men in Indian society, a simple piece of cloth wrapped around the lower body.

Durgā—the demigoddess who predominates over the Lord's material energy.

E

Ekādaśī—the eleventh day of the waning or waxing moon.

G

Gāndharvikā—another name for Rādhā, Lord Kṛṣṇa's eternal consort.

Ganges—a sacred river in northern India.

Gaudiya Math—the mission established in India by Śrīla Bhaktisiddhānta Sarasvatī Ṭhākura for spreading Kṛṣṇa consciousness.

Gauḍīya Vaiṣṇava—a follower of Lord Kṛṣṇa (Viṣṇu) in the line of Lord Caitanya Mahāprabhu.

Gāyatrī—a *mantra* chanted three times daily by the *brāhmaṇas*.

Gaurakiśora dāsa Bābājī—the initiating spiritual master of Śrīla Bhaktisiddhānta Sarasvatī Ṭhākura.

Gaurāṅga—a name for Lord Caitanya.

Gaurī-Śaṅkara—a temple of Lord Śiva and his consort, Gaurī, in Old Delhi.

Ghee—clarified butter, used as oil in cooking.

Giridhāri—a name for Lord Kṛṣṇa glorifying His pastime of lifting Govardhana Hill.

Gītā—*See: Bhagavad-gītā*

Gītopaniṣad—*See: Bhagavad-gītā*

Godbrother—a fellow disciple of the same spiritual master.

Gopīs—the cowherd girls of Vṛndāvana, who are the most advanced and intimate devotees of Lord Kṛṣṇa.

Gosvāmī—one who has mastered his senses. *See also:* Six Gosvāmīs

Goudiya Vaishnava: *See:* Gauḍīya Vaiṣṇava

Gouranga—*See:* Gauraṅga

Govardhana—the sacred hill in the region of Vṛndāvana lifted by Lord Kṛṣṇa as a child.

Govinda—the Supreme Lord, Kṛṣṇa, proprietor of the senses of all living beings.

Gṛhastha—one who is practicing spiritual life while living with wife and children; the second *āśrama,* or spiritual order.

Guru—spiritual master.

Gurukula—the school of the spiritual master.

Guru Mahārāja—a form of respectful address to the *guru,* or spiritual master.

H

Haight-Ashbury—the hippie district of San Francisco in the late 1960s.

Halavā—a dessert made from toasted grains, butter, and sugar.

Hanumān—the monkey chieftain who became a great devotee of Lord Rāma.

Hare Kṛṣṇa—the holy names of the Lord. *See also: Mahā-mantra*

Hari Bol—"Chant the names of Lord Hari!"

Haṭha-yoga—the physical practice of postures and breathing exercises as a means toward controlling the senses.

I

Initiation—the formal establishing of the connection between the spiritual master and disciple.

Iṣṭa-goṣṭhī—a meeting of devotees to discuss the instructions of their spiritual master.

J

Jagannātha—"Lord of the universe"; a special Deity of Lord Kṛṣṇa, originating in Orissa on the east coast of India at Purī.

Janmāṣṭamī—the birthday of Lord Kṛṣṇa.

Japa—measured chanting of the Lord's holy names.

Jñāna—the path of knowledge.

K

Kacaurī—a fried pastry.

Kali—the being who introduces the principles of sinful life in the Age of Quarrel.

Kālī—*See:* Durgā

Kālī-pūjā—the worship of Kālī, or Durgā.

Kali-yuga—the present age of confusion and quarrel, which began five thousand years ago.

Karatālas—sacred hand-cymbals.

Karma-yoga—the process of linking up with the Supreme by selflessly offering the fruits of one's work.

Karma—fruitive action, for which there is always a reaction, good or bad.

Kārttika—a lunar month of the autumn season.

Kāśīnātha Miśra—an associate of Lord Caitanya.

Keśavajī Gaudiya Math—the temple in Mathurā where Śrīla Prabhupāda accepted the renounced order of spiritual life.

Khādī—homespun cotton.

Ki jaya—an expression of acclaim.

Kīrtana—glorification of God, especially by the chanting of His holy names.

Krishna Loka—*See:* Kṛṣṇaloka

L

Lalitā—one of the female associates of Lord Kṛṣṇa's eternal consort, Rādhārāṇī.

M

Mādhavendra Purī—the grand–spiritual-master of Lord Caitanya Mahāprabhu.

Mahā-mantra—the great chanting for deliverance:

Hare Kṛṣṇa, Hare Kṛṣṇa, Kṛṣṇa Kṛṣṇa, Hare Hare
Hare Rāma, Hare Rāma, Rāma Rāma, Hare Hare

Mantra—a sound vibration that liberates the mind.

Masālā—a standard mixture of spices, which can be of several varieties, used in Vedic cooking.

Maṭha—monastery.

Mathurā—the city where Lord Kṛṣṇa took birth, eight miles from Vṛndāvana.

Māyā—the illusory energy of the Supreme Personality of Godhead.

Māyāvāda—the impersonal philosophy of Śaṅkarācārya and his followers.

Māyāvādī—a follower of Māyāvāda philosophy.

Miṣṭi—Indian sweets.

Mleccha—meat-eater.

Mṛdaṅga—a sacred drum, made of clay, used in *kīrtana.*

N

Nāmācārya—Haridāsa Ṭhākura, the foremost teacher of the chanting of the holy names of the Lord.

Nanda Mahārāja—Kṛṣṇa's father in the village of Vṛndāvana.

Nārada Muni—the sage among the demigods, who is the son of Lord Brahmā and the spiritual master of Vyāsadeva.

Navadvīpa—the holy birthplace of Lord Caitanya Mahāprabhu, in Bengal.

Nimaka—a type of salty food.

Nityānanda—the chief associate of Lord Caitanya

Nṛsiṁha(deva)—an incarnation of Kṛṣṇa as half-man, half-lion.

O

Oṁkāra—the syllable *oṁ.*

P

Pān—an intoxicant.

Paṇḍāl—a tent.

Paṇḍita—a scholar.

Paramahaṁsa—"the topmost swanlike person"; a self-realized personality.

Paramparā—the authorized line of disciplic succession.

Prabhupāda—"the spiritual master at whose feet all others take shelter."

Prasādam—food spiritualized by first being offered to the Supreme Lord for his enjoyment.

Pūjā—worship according to authorized ceremony.

Pūjārī—priest.

Purī—the abode of Lord Jagannātha, in Orissa (on the east coast of India); also, puffy wheat bread fried in ghee.

R

Rādhā-Govinda—a Deity of Kṛṣṇa and His eternal consort, Rādhā.
Rādhā(rāṇī)—the eternal consort of Lord Kṛṣṇa and manifestation of His internal pleasure potency.
Rāma(candra)—the incarnation of the Supreme Lord as the ideal king.
Rāmānanda Rāya—one of Lord Caitanya's intimate associates.
Rāsa dance—Kṛṣṇa's pastime of dancing with the *gopīs.*
Rasagullā—a milk sweet made from curd soaked in sweet water.
Ramakrishna—a teacher of impersonalist philosophy.
Ratha-yātrā—the annual cart festival of Lord Jagannātha.
Ricksha—a cart pulled by a man.
Rūpa Gosvāmī—*See:* Six Gosvāmīs

S

Sabji—vegetables.
Sādhu—a saintly person.
Śaivite—a worshiper of the demigod Śiva.
Saffron robes—orange-colored robes worn by celibate men in the spiritual orders of life.
Samādhi—yogic trance.
Samosā—a fried pastry, stuffed with spiced vegetables.
Sanātana Gosvāmī—*See:* Six Gosvāmīs
Saṅkīrtana—congregational chanting of the holy names of the Lord, the recommended process of *yoga* for this age.
Sannyāsa—the renounced order of life; the fourth *āśrama,* or spiritual order, of Vedic society.
Sannyāsī—one in the *sannyāsa* order.
Sārī—the standard garment of women in Indian society, a single piece of cloth covering the entire body.
Sārvabhauma—an associate of Lord Caitanya.
Śāstra—scripture.
Sikh—member of a Hindu sect.
Śikhā—the tuft of hair remaining on the back of the shaven head of a Vaiṣṇava.
Six Gosvāmīs—Rūpa, Sanātana, Raghunātha dāsa, Raghunātha Bhaṭṭa, Gopāla Bhaṭṭa, and Jīva Gosvāmī; the followers of Lord Caitanya Mahāprabhu who established devotional service as a scientific process of God realization in the modern age.

Śrī—a form of respectful address indicating great beauty and opulence.

Śrīla—a form of respectful address.

Śrīmad-Bhāgavatam—the voluminous scripture composed by Śrīla Vyāsadeva to describe and explain Lord Kṛṣṇa's pastimes.

Subhadrā—the younger sister of Lord Kṛṣṇa and personification of His spiritual potency.

Śukadeva Gosvāmī—the great sage who originally spoke *Śrīmad-Bhāgavatam.*

Swami—*See:* Gosvāmī

Swamiji—familiar form of *swami.*

T

Taj Express—train running from Delhi to Agra.

Tiffin—a stacked set of metal food containers.

Tilaka—sacred clay marking the body of a devotee as a temple of God.

Tompkins Square Park—a park on Manhattan's Lower East Side.

Tulasī—the plant most sacred to Lord Viṣṇu.

V

Vaiṣṇava—a devotee of Viṣṇu (or Kṛṣṇa).

Vedas—the four original texts first spoken by the Lord Himself and their supplements, compiled by Śrīla Vyāsadeva.

Vedic—based on the *Vedas.*

Vigraha—the authorized Deity form of the Lord.

Viṣṇu—the Supreme Lord, Kṛṣṇa, appearing in His majestic four-armed form.

Vivekananda—a teacher of impersonalist philosophy.

Vraja—*See:* Vṛndāvana.

Vṛndāvana—the personal abode of Lord Kṛṣṇa, the inhabitants of which are all His intimate servants.

Vrindaban Behary—a name of Kṛṣṇa as the enjoyer of pastimes in Vṛndāvana.

Vrindaban Bihar—*See:* Vrindaban Behary

Vṛṣṇi—the family in which Lord Kṛṣṇa appeared.

Vyāsa-pūjā—the observance of the appearance day of one's spiritual master, who is worshiped as the representative of Vyāsadeva.

Vyāsāsana—the honored seat of the spiritual master.

Y

Yamunā River—sacred river flowing through Vṛndāvana.
Yaśodā—the mother of Lord Kṛṣṇa in Vṛndāvana.
Yoga—any of various spiritual disciplines meant for purification and ultimate realization of one's position as servant of God.
Yogī—a *yoga* practitioner.

Index

A

Abolafia, Louis, 127
Absolute Truth
features of, three, 96
See also: Kṛṣṇa, Lord
Acyutānanda dāsa
Bon Maharaja met by, 186–87
in Calcutta, 198–202, 208–10, 213, 215–16
Chandrashekar &, 191
in Chippiwada temple, 188, 189, 190–91, 192
in Delhi, 184, 188–92, 197
Haridāsa Mahārāja &, 200
illness of, in India, 187
in India, 184–216
letters by, 211, 213
letters to, by Prabhupāda. *See:* Prabhupāda, letters by...
in Navadvīpa, 202–4
in New York, 123, 127–28, 129, 135, 138
Prabhupāda &. *See:* Prabhupāda, Acyutānanda &
quoted
on Institute of Oriental Studies, 187
on Prabhupāda in hospital, 135
on Prabhupāda's departure from India, 216
on Prabhupāda's doctor, 129
on Prabhupāda's illness, 127–28
at Rādhā-Dāmodara temple, 184–86
in Rādhā-Govinda temple, 208–10, 213, 215–16
Śrīdhara Mahārāja &, 203
in Vṛndāvana, 184–88
Advaita Ācārya, 158
Age of Quarrel, 109
Agra University, 183, 186
Air India, Prabhupāda travels on, 173, 175, 176
Airports. *See: specific airports*
Ajāmila, story of, 82
Allen Burke (TV show), 125–26, 143
Allen Ginsberg
at Cosmic Love-In, 127
at Human Be-in, 2
kīrtana endorsed by, 13, 14, 41
as Mantra-Rock participant, 10–11, 13–14
Prabhupāda discusses chanting with, 11
Prabhupāda greeted at airport by, 2, 3
quoted on *kīrtana*, 13, 14, 41
Altman, Mr., 213
Ambassador of India, 175
American House, 182–84
Analogies
of battlefield & Haight-Ashbury, 40
of cat & death, 140
of crows & nondevotees, 48
of fresh food & disciples, 29
of grinding wheel & material world, 149
of husband & human form of life, 76
of lakes & literature about Kṛṣṇa, 48
of matchboxes & houses, 1, 5
of ocean & death, 136–37
of ripened fruit & transcendental message, 84
of swans & devotees, 48
"Ancient Trance Dance" article, 114–15, 208
Andrews, Julie, 199
Aniruddha dāsa, 163
Ārati ceremony
to Jagannātha, 99–100
to Prabhupāda, 198
Ārati defined, 101
Arjuna, 13
Atheists, 151
Atmarama & Sons, 179

C

D

E

F

G

H

I

K

L

Prabhupāda, Śrīla
letters by (*continued*)
about Vṛndāvana, 182
to Acyutānanda about serving Kṛṣṇa, 54
to American disciples, 180, 182
to Brahmānanda about *Bhagavad-gītā's* publication, 181
to Brahmānanda about *māyā*, 182
to Brahmānanda about Price affair, 61
to Brahmānanda about publishing, 53, 181, 193, 212
to Brahmānanda about Ratha-yātrā, 158
to Brahmānanda about temple management, 213
to Brahmānanda about visa, 175–76
to Gargamuni about finance, 54
to Gargamuni about Price affair, 59
to Hayagrīva, 202
to Jānakī, 211
to Janārdana, 195
to Kīrtanānanda about Price affair, 59, 125
to Krishna Pandit, 133–34, 195
to Kṛṣṇā-devī, 213
to Montreal devotees, 159, 201
to Mukunda dāsa, 211
to Nandarāṇī, 215
to New York devotees, 52, 53–54
to Price, 60, 90
to Rāya Rāma about *Back to Godhead*, 195
to Rāya Rāma about Price affair, 89–90
to Rāya Rāma about risks for Kṛṣṇa, 87
to Rūpānuga about American House, 187
to Rūpānuga about San Francisco, 54
to San Francisco devotees, 139–40
to Satsvarūpa about Harvard's invitation, 203
to Satsvarūpa about Price affair, 60, 90
to Satsvarūpa about spiritual understanding, 53–54
to Satsvarūpa about Śrīdhara Mahārāja, 203–4
to Satsvarūpa about temple opening, 194
to Satsvarūpa about typing, 53, 195

Prabhupāda, Śrīla
letters by (*continued*)
to Sumati Morarji, 159, 168–69
to Tompkins Square Park gathering, 142–44
to Umāpati about spiritual master, 214
to Umāpati about U.S. return, 202
letters to
from Price, 60
from Himalayan Academy, 61
Līlāvatī &, 70–72
Linda Katz &, 69
in London, 175–76
in Long Branch, 146–52
Los Angeles temple desired by, 168
LSD prohibited by, 5, 11
lunch program started by, 38, 39
maha ula affair &, 46–48
Mālatī &, 92
at Mantra-Rock Dance, 13–15
massage treatment for, 127–28, 132, 136, 141, 151, 154, 181
māyā &, 140, 182
Michael Blumert &, 124
at Morning Star Ranch, 117–18
on morning walk
in Golden Gate Park, 48, 49–50
on San Francisco beach, 15–16
on Stinson Beach, 154
in Moscow, 176
mṛdaṅga played by, in park, 65
Mullik family and, 206–7, 208, 209
Mukunda &
at airport, 2, 3
in San Francisco, 6–7, 17, 22–23, 47, 70, 99
at Stinson Beach, 153, 155, 160
Mukunda quoted on. *See:* Mukunda, quoted on...
Mukunda's relationship with, 22
Mukunda's telegram to, 212
Mukunda taught *mṛdaṅga* by, 22–23
Mukunda dāsī &, 190
Nandarāṇī &, 31–33, 66, 215
"Nandarāṇī" defined by, 32
Nandarāṇī quoted on, 167
in Navadvīpa, 202–5

Q

R

S

T

U

V

W

Y

The Author

Satsvarūpa dāsa Goswami was born on December 6, 1939, in New York City. He attended public schools and received a B.A. from Brooklyn College in 1961. Then followed two years as a journalist in the U.S. Navy and three years as a social worker in New York City.

In July 1966, he met His Divine Grace A. C. Bhaktivedanta Swami Prabhupāda, and he became his initiated disciple in September of that year. Satsvarūpa dāsa Goswami began contributing articles to *Back to Godhead*, the magazine of the Hare Kṛṣṇa movement, and later became its editor in chief. In August 1967 he went to Boston to establish the first ISKCON center there. Satsvarūpa dāsa Goswami was one of the original members selected by Śrīla Prabhupāda to form the Governing Body Commission of ISKCON in 1970. He remained as president of Boston ISKCON until 1971, when he moved to Dallas and became headmaster of Gurukula, the first ISKCON school for children.

In May 1972, on the appearance day of Lord Nṛsiṁhadeva, he was awarded the *sannyāsa* (renounced) order by His Divine Grace Śrīla Prabhupāda and began traveling across the United States, lecturing in colleges and universities. In January 1974 he was called by Śrīla Prabhupāda to become his personal secretary and to travel with him through India and Europe. In 1976 he published *Readings in Vedic Literature*, a concise account of the Vedic tradition. The volume is now being studied at various American universities. In 1977 Śrīla Prabhupāda ordered him to accept the duties of initiating *guru*, along with ten other senior disciples. He is presently working on a long-term literary project, preparing further volumes of the biography of His Divine Grace A. C. Bhaktivedanta Swami Prabhupāda.

The Author